PRAISE FOR OTHER BOOKS BY GUY P. HARRISON

50 Popular Beliefs That People Think Are True
(Prometheus Books, 2012)

"What would it take to create a world in which fantasy is not confused for fact and public policy is based on objective reality? I don't know for sure. But a good place to start would be for everyone on Earth to read this book."
> —Neil deGrasse Tyson, astrophysicist,
> American Museum of Natural History

"Harrison has added to the growing body of skeptical literature a contribution that will continue to move our culture toward one that openly embraces reason, science, and logic."
> —Michael Shermer, publisher of *Skeptic*,
> columnist for *Scientific American*, and
> author of *The Believing Brain*

"Being a skeptic can be hard work, but Harrison makes it a lot easier. . . . This is the book I wish I had written."
> —Phil Plait, author of *The Bad Astronomer*

"Deserves to be shelved alongside the works of such giants of the field as Randi, Shermer, Kurtz, and Nickell. . . . A valuable, not to mention very entertainingly written, addition to the literature of skepticism."
> —*Booklist*

Race and Reality: What Everyone Should Know about Our
Biological Diversity (Prometheus Books, 2010)

"This is a very important, profound, enjoyable, and enlightening book. It should go a long way in helping disprove man's most dangerous myth."
> —Robert W. Sussman, professor of anthropology,
> Washington University; editor of
> *Yearbook of Physical Anthropology*; and
> editor emeritus of *American Anthropologist*

"A tour de force that conveys the current science on racial classification in a rigorous yet readable way. A book so clearly written, so elegantly crafted, so packed with nuggets that even those who think they know it all about race and racial classification will come away changed."
—David B. Grusky, professor of sociology,
Stanford University

50 Reasons People Give for Believing in a God
(Prometheus Books, 2008)

"Deep wisdom and patient explanations fill this excellent book."
—James A. Haught, editor of the *Charleston Gazette*

"Engaging and enlightening. . . . Read this book to explore the many and diverse reasons for belief."
—Michael Shermer, publisher of *Skeptic*,
columnist for *Scientific American*, and
author of *The Believing Brain*

"Doesn't bully or condescend. Reading Harrison's book is like having an amiable chat with a wise old friend."
—Cameron M. Smith and Charles Sullivan,
authors of *The Top 10 Myths about Evolution*

Visit the author's website at www.guypharrison.com

Guy P. Harrison

simple questions for
every christian

PB Prometheus Books

59 John Glenn Drive
Amherst, New York 14228–2119

Published 2013 by Prometheus Books

Cover design by Nicole Sommer-Lecht

Inquiries should be addressed to
Prometheus Books
59 John Glenn Drive
Amherst, New York 14228–2119
VOICE: 716–691–0133 • FAX: 716–691–0137
WWW.PROMETHEUSBOOKS.COM

17 16 15 14   5 4 3 2

Library of Congress Cataloging-in-Publication Data

Harrison, Guy P.
    50 simple questions for every Christian / by Guy P. Harrison.
        p. cm.
    Includes bibliographical references and index.
    ISBN 978-1-61614-727-3 (pbk.: alk. paper)
    ISBN 978-1-61614-728-0 (ebook)
    1. Christianity—Miscellanea. 2. Apologetics—Miscellanea. I. Title.
II. Title: Fifty simple questions for every Christian.

BR121.3.H373 2013
230—dc23

2012044569

Printed in the United States of America on acid-free paper

Dedicated to the world's Christians.
May they find peace and happiness.

CONTENTS

Introduction   9

  1. Does Christianity make sense?   13
  2. What is a god?   21
  3. Is it rude to ask?   25
  4. Does Jesus answer prayers?   33
  5. Who is a Christian?   41
  6. Does Christianity make societies better?   45
  7. What is atheism?   49
  8. What are miracles?   57
  9. Does the complexity of life reveal   67
    an intelligent designer?
10. Have you read the Bible?   73
11. Why do some Christians do bad things   79
    in the sight of Jesus?
12. How can we be sure about the resurrection?   83
13. How do we know that heaven is real?   89
14. Why is God so violent?   97
15. What do prophecies prove?   103
16. How important are the Ten Commandments?   109
17. Do you know the real Ten Commandments?   117
18. Is Christianity good for women?   121
19. Is it smarter to believe or not believe?   125
20. Is the born-again experience in Christianity unique?   131
21. Is faith a good thing?   141
22. Should children be Christians?   147
23. Does Jesus heal the sick?   153
24. How do we know that the man Jesus existed?   159
25. What about all the other gods?   165
26. Are Christians happier?   171
27. Is the United States of America a Christian nation?   177
28. How can we be sure that Jesus performed miracles?   183

29. What do evil atheist dictators prove? 187
30. Is the universe fine-tuned for us? 197
31. Could we design a better world? 203
32. What has archaeology proved? 209
33. Why isn't everyone a Christian? 213
34. What is the problem with evolution? 219
35. Is it better to be safe than sorry? 227
36. Why did God sacrifice his son? 231
37. Did God drown the world? 237
38. Why do birth location and family matter so much? 245
39. Why do Christianity and science 249
    so often come into conflict?
40. Why do people go to hell? 255
41. Can atheists be trusted? 261
42. Why hasn't the Bible convinced more people? 269
43. Are angels real? 275
44. Is Christmas under attack? 281
45. Will the End Times ever end? 287
46. Does Christianity make individuals better? 295
47. Why does a good god allow so much suffering 303
    in the world?
48. Would you take Jesus's place on the cross? 309
49. Should Christians try to be good skeptics? 313
50. Will Christianity endure? 321

Notes 325

Bibliography and Recommended Reading 339

Index 345

INTRODUCTION

This book is not an attack on Christian people. While it does challenge many claims made by the Christian religion and various factions of Christians, it is not an extended argument aimed at turning every Christian in the world into an atheist. This book is far more humble and far less threatening than that. My goal is to help Christians gain a better understanding of why, after two thousand years, the majority of the world is still unconvinced by the basic claims of their religion.

The title of each chapter is not a "gotcha question" crafted to stump Christians or argue them into a corner. They are, as the book's title indicates, nothing more than "simple" questions. Each one is fair and worth considering. These are the questions non-Christians ask aloud or in the privacy of their thoughts when they think about Christianity. Many Christians will find these questions familiar because at some point in their lives they have probably wondered about them too. In most cases, however, they likely were left unanswered or perhaps were answered by a pastor, priest, or fellow Christian. But those answers were likely very different from the ones found in this book.

This book presents a skeptic's perspective, the view many Christians never hear. It is important for them to become aware of these ideas in order to expand their worldview, improve their knowledge, and come to better understand so many of their fellow humans. I know from experience that many Christians are not familiar with or misunderstand many of the ideas presented in this book. It has nothing to do with intelligence or education. This is about having the will to think vigorously and honestly within the safety of one's mind. Unfortunately, critical thinking about religion is often discouraged and sometimes forbidden in many churches and families. But no one should feel compelled to restrain their intellectual wanderings. Thinking is the greatest of all our abilities. To suppress it is to deny our humanity.

If Christianity is true—"obviously true," as many Christians say—

then why isn't everyone a Christian? Why are there billions of Muslims, Hindus, Buddhists, atheists, and other non-Christians? This book provides an answer to this important question that every Christian should be asking. Of course, many Christians already claim to know the answer; they say the existence of nonbelievers is the result of corrupt organized religion, Satan's influence on the world, or simply God's plan. But these reasons are not why non-Christians say they do not believe. They have very different explanations.

We all have to share this planet, so we should make the effort to understand one another. To that end, it is necessary for Christians to grasp why so many people think Christianity doesn't make sense. It is all too common for many Christians to dismiss atheists and other nonbelievers as immoral, rebellious, damaged, or dishonest people. Not only is this inaccurate; it does not help move us toward a safer and saner world. Making such baseless assumptions about non-Christians is destructive for all because it promotes fear, prejudice, disunity, and hate.

Those looking for a clichéd and cartoonish angry atheist attack on crazy Christians will have to keep looking, because they won't find it here. While I pull no punches in explaining many of the reasons why I and so many others remain unconvinced of Christianity's claims, I have no interest in scoring debate points or attempting to make myself feel intellectually superior to anyone. I'm smart enough to know that many Christians are smarter than I am, and I'm honest enough to admit that I don't have all the mysteries of life and the universe figured out.

I wrote this book because I genuinely think it would be better for the world if Christians were to think more deeply about their beliefs while also gaining a better understanding of what is going on in the minds of non-Christians. The best way to achieve this, I believe, is to communicate the reasons for doubt forcefully and respectfully. Undoubtedly, some Christian readers will find parts of this book disturbing. Some may even feel insulted. But I ask those readers to remember that I am approaching them as one adult to another and speaking to them as equals. I'm not arguing; I'm explaining what many skeptics, right or wrong, honestly think about Christian claims. Although books are one-way communication, my hope is that this book will feel to readers like a friendly chat with someone who wants only good things for all. My skepticism is nothing personal. I don't usually single out Christianity for special scrutiny. I have written other books that challenge many other extraordinary claims. I'm an equal-opportunity skeptic. In my opinion, everything is open to question. Skepticism is a positive and constructive force that needs to be applied to all important and unusual claims.

It is important to make one thing very clear: I understand that Christians are an extremely diverse group of people. There are many different kinds of Christians who hold many different views. By some counts, there are more than forty thousand distinct versions of Christianity, and there is significant variation within each of them. This means, of course, that one cannot always represent the beliefs of all Christians accurately and fairly in one sentence, in one chapter, or in one book. Many millions of Christians say the Bible is the inerrant word of God, and many millions say it is not. Many Christians say the world is less than ten thousand years old, while many others agree with the overwhelming scientific evidence that says our planet is more than 4.5 billion years old. Clearly, I can't provide skeptical analysis of popular Christian claims that fit perfectly with every Christian's point of view in every case. I hope readers will notice that I have tried to be careful with my words. I do not project all Christian beliefs onto all Christians. This is why I often use qualifiers such as *many*, *most*, or *some* when referring to Christians.

Veteran skeptics will find much that is familiar in this book. However, they are also likely to learn new and useful ways of engaging Christians in thoughtful discussions. I offer fresh perspectives that will inspire nonbelievers to think in different ways about this religion and the people who adhere to it. I have had many encounters with many Christians in many countries, some casual and some in formal interviews. One of the things I have learned to do well over the years is to interact with Christians in a way that inspires them to think more deeply about their beliefs without annoying or angering them. It might be simple questions I inject into the conversation here and there, a bit of background information on some aspect of science or history, or it could be nothing more than the passing mention of one tiny idea that does it. I'm proud to say that I walked away on friendly terms every time. I hope this book keeps that streak alive.

—Guy P. Harrison

WASHED IN THE BLOOD. A woman prays inside Jerusalem's Church of the Holy Sepulchre at an altar on the exact spot many Christians believe Jesus was executed more than two thousand years ago. *Photo by the author.*

DOES CHRISTIANITY MAKE SENSE?

These may be the most simple and important questions of all: Does this religion make sense? It is true? Am I sufficiently convinced about this to honestly call myself a Christian? While these may seem like fair questions to an unsure skeptic, those within Christianity might consider it impolite, unnecessary, and even idiotic to ask such things. *Of course it's true. Of course it makes sense.* Given the high stakes of this religion's global influence and possible afterlife repercussions, however, shouldn't everyone—Christians included—be asking these questions?

Does it make sense? This simple question goes far beyond nitpicking contradictions in the Bible or citing problems with popular claims about the benefits of Christianity and the reliability of prayer. It is about the basic concept, the core claim that distinguishes this religion from others. It is, of course, impossible to summarize it in a way that satisfies all Christians, but it goes something like this: *God sent his son, Jesus, into the world so that he could die for us. His sacrifice was a pardon for our sins that allows us to be saved from death and enjoy eternal life in heaven. Without Jesus, we would all be doomed because of our inherently sinful nature. In this great act of mercy, God saved us from ourselves. And all we have to do in return to accept this gift is to repent our sins and embrace Jesus as our only lord and savior.*

This is about as concise as one can describe Christianity without veering off into endless doctrinal conflicts. Short and simple as it is, there will still be some, I suspect, who would feel the need to subtract or add, but I hope most would agree that it's an accurate and fair synopsis. So let's analyze it line for line and see what happens.

GOD SENT HIS SON, JESUS, INTO THE WORLD
SO THAT HE COULD DIE FOR US.

We are immediately confronted with a huge problem. God is Jesus and Jesus is God. How can we say that God sent his son and sacrificed him for us when they are the same being? I understand that many Christians don't spend much time thinking about it, but according to the doctrine of the Holy Trinity, God the father and Jesus the son are the same being. (The Holy Spirit, or Holy Ghost, completes the Holy Trinity.) This is no trivial matter, and it's not some minor point that weasel doubters use to annoy Christians. Sincere skeptics recognize a fundamental problem with this story.

The Holy Trinity has long been considered one of the most important claims in Christianity. It can't reasonably be ignored in any serious discussion about Christianity because, if true, it means that God sent himself to Earth, sacrificed himself to himself, and then returned to be with himself. The skeptic can only ask how any of this makes sense. It's not rude or unfair to attempt to reconcile the "great sacrifice of Jesus's life" with the concept of the Holy Trinity. It's an obvious and necessary question, isn't it? Christians often juxtapose the horror of Jesus's crucifixion with the love God shows us by allowing his son to suffer and die. Christians have asked me to imagine how difficult it would be to sacrifice my own son. But it's not the same thing. Temporary pain aside, if Jesus was God and knew that he would return to heaven after his death, where is the big sacrifice? What did Jesus/God give up? These are the things skeptics wonder about while trying to understand Christianity. It's not about being argumentative or stubborn. It's a basic comprehension issue. There seems to be a very serious problem with the claim that God sent his son to Earth as a sacrifice for us because God and Jesus are supposed to be the same being.

HIS SACRIFICE WAS A PARDON FOR OUR SINS
THAT ALLOWS US TO BE SAVED FROM DEATH
AND ENJOY ETERNAL LIFE IN HEAVEN.

The traditional telling of Jesus's execution presents it as a gruesome and terrible event that rivals most horror movies. In fact, director Mel Gibson did depict it in a way some describe as a contemporary horror film. Released in 2004, *The Passion of the Christ* shocked moviegoers with bone-crunching sounds and flesh-ripping images. If the crucifixion of Jesus did happen and was even fractionally as inhumane and cruel as Christians claim, then the obvious question that comes to the skeptic's mind is "why?" Why did Jesus or anyone else, god or human, have to suffer and die? Human sacrifice? Really? If this did happen, as Christians say it did and for the reasons they say it did, there needs to be some better reasoning, some rational explanation for why it was necessary. Why would a god need to rely on such a disgusting and primitive act to forgive us and save us from his judgment?

Most societies on Earth realized centuries ago that ritual human sacrifice is as barbaric as it is unproductive. Tossing virgins into a volcano or carving out some guy's heart atop a temple once might have seemed like sensible investments for better times ahead, but eventually it dawned on most that such practices were cruel, stupid, and unnecessary. As an act of punishment and/or religious rite, it is beneath us. We are better than that. So why would God need such an act to offer humankind an escape clause? Surely he could think of a better way to save us from death and eternal damnation. But wait, isn't God in charge of everything? Why would he have to *do* anything to provide us with a route to salvation and heaven? Couldn't he simply have skipped the whole slow, agonizing death of Jesus and just forgiven us? Is he bound by some laws that even he must follow? What is going on?

I have asked this sincere and simple question of many preachers and devout Christians over the years. To date, none have come up with a good answer—at least, no answer that would satisfy a typical skeptic. The best they offer is: "We can't understand God's ways." Or they simply repeat the alleged point of the act: "Jesus had to take on our sins so that we could be saved." But *why*? This is the central most important event that Christianity is based on, and it seems completely unnecessary to many non-Christians. Why did Jesus have to absorb our sins in a manner that involved whipping, punching, stabbing, hammers, and nails? It sounds very much like a story that ancient mortals would tell, believe, and admire, rather than the real-life actions of a god who runs the universe.

WITHOUT JESUS, WE WOULD ALL BE DOOMED BECAUSE OF OUR INHERENTLY SINFUL NATURE. GOD SAVED US FROM OURSELVES.

Original sin is such an old concept that it has come to be viewed as far less bizarre than it really is. But thoughtful Christians who pause to think about this idea for a moment are likely to recognize that something doesn't add up. We are inherently guilty? Condemned before we even learn to walk and talk? What sort of justice is that? To skeptics of Christianity, it seems crazy to view newborn babies as defective and doomed forever without spiritual intervention. Of course all people are imperfect, but hopelessly flawed at birth and deserving of endless agony in hell? Really?

Let's not dwell on the charge that we are all members of a corrupt and "fallen" species by birth. Rather, we should ask why it is we need saving in the first place. What is it we need saving from? The answer is God. He and his rules are the threat that we imperfect humans are up against. Therefore, God, in the form of Jesus, has offered to save us from *himself*. This is odd, to say the least, yet billions of Christians, generation after generation, say they are profoundly grateful to God for his gift of salvation. I do not mean this in a disrespectful way, but God in this context seems very much like a gangster who promises to make sure your business doesn't meet with unfortunate circumstances and happen to burn down—so long as you give him whatever he asks for. If you don't pay up, of course, he is the one who sets fire to your business. No matter what he says, however, the reality is that the gangster is protecting you from the gangster.

The Christian salvation story might make more sense if God was equally matched or somehow the underdog to Satan and was saving us from him. But this is not the case; it is supposed to be God who is totally dominant and runs the world. It is God who judges and condemns us (according to most versions of Christianity). If God wants to save us from hell, why not simply stop sending people to hell? If he wants to forgive us for being imperfect, then why not just forgive us? I have for-given people in my life many times without requiring an oath of eternal loyalty and love from them. I just forgave them because it seemed like the right thing to do. If a firefighter intentionally sets a house on fire and then rescues half of the family inside while the other half burns to death, is he or she really a hero? This is coming from the perspective of an outsider to Christianity, so it might seem harsh to some Christians, but it's not meant to be argumentative. If anything, many skeptics tend to feel frustrated by their inability to make sense of something that so many millions of Christians insist makes perfect sense. We simply acknowledge openly what seems obvious to us: that there is no reason to heap praise on anyone, a person or a god, who saves people from a particular harm that exists only because of that person or god.

AND ALL WE HAVE TO DO IS EMBRACE JESUS AS OUR ONLY LORD AND SAVIOR.

This directive sounds so simple, but it is by no means easy for those skeptics who value truth and honesty. One cannot sincerely embrace Jesus without first becoming convinced that he is a real god. Christians often fail to acknowledge this primary obstacle for non-Christians. All the details about Jesus's life, words, and offer of salvation matter very little to a person who doubts he exists. It is easy to repeat the ancient man's quotes found in the Bible. Anyone can tell the basic story of the Messiah who died for our sins. Describing heaven and hell is effortless. It's a lot more difficult, however, to prove that there is a god named Jesus in our presence right now.

Some Christians tell me that all one has to do is believe first and then the belief will become real. Start going to church and reading the Bible, they say, and I will find Jesus. I know they mean that Jesus will be revealed to me if I show faith in him, but it sounds a lot like trying to voluntarily induce a delusion. If I try my absolute best to believe in Zeus, would he become real too? If I attend ceremonies at a Hindu temple and pray to Hindu gods for a few years, might they become real to me too? No self-respecting skeptic is going to pretend to know that any gods exist without proof or very good evidence. Sure, some people can and do fake it. One can adopt the practices and play the role of a Christian while still unconvinced, but how can that be right? Anyone can show up at church, sing a few hymns and call it a day, but is this what God would want? Wouldn't an omniscient god know if a prayer is spoken with empty words and no confidence? Isn't there a chance that doing such a thing would insult or anger him? Shouldn't we think before we believe, if for no other reason than to show respect for this potentially real god?

Non-Christians who have been encultured and raised by loving parents to believe in the god or gods of a rival religion have a tough challenge before them if they are to end up following the "correct" religion and worshipping correctly. Not only must they "find" Jesus but they also have to jettison their original beliefs. Not easy for most. Those who are in the most difficult spot, however, are skeptics, people who are compelled to put in the hard work of thinking about a claim before climbing aboard. A good skeptic doesn't accept or reject an unusual claim because it feels right to do so or because of what the majority says. Any extraordinary and important claim has to run a gauntlet of critical thinking and, if appropriate, survive the scientific process. The same reasoning process that so easily pokes gaping holes in astrology, psychics, and ghosts also works for supernatural claims made by all religions. The idea of gods is certainly unusual and important, so doesn't it deserve thoughtful analysis too?

Skeptics begin with the same basic questions: Does the quantity and quality of the evidence balance the importance or unusual nature of the claim? The bigger the claim, the more evidence required. Are more reasonable alternate explanations more likely to be true? Is there too much reliance on authority and tradition with too little attention paid to good evidence and reason? We don't know what the future holds, but so far the supernatural claims of Christianity, like all other religions, have not been validated by the scientific process. If Christianity, or at least some aspects of it, had been confirmed in this way, then it would have crushed all other religions and would likely be the only one left standing today.

Where does this leave the open-minded skeptic who is willing to believe but not without good reason? Out in the cold, it seems. Faith, trust, tradition, and confirmation bias may lead many people to the gods, but critical thinking rarely does so. This is one of Christianity's primary flaws, according to many nonbelievers. Why in the world should thinking *hinder* one's belief in a real god? Shouldn't clear thinking be encouraged? Shouldn't the courage to accept reality as it is and not as we would prefer it to be an admirable quality? Why aren't skeptics the first to find God? Wouldn't those who make an honest effort to sort out sense from nonsense be the first people to discover a real god if he is there?

Why would any god who wished to share himself and his message with the world make himself invisible and silent to billions? If Christianity made sense to anyone who analyzed it, if it were obviously true to all sensible people, then it would attract and retain more sincere believers than other religions that only relied on faith and tradition. It would be so easy to set up Christianity for rapid global acceptance. And wouldn't that have been the goal of a loving god who wanted the best for his creations? How could he not foresee that there would be doubts and mass rejection of an unproven story about God sending himself to Earth so that he could be killed horribly—for us—before returning to heaven to be with himself? And that this human sacrifice was necessary because we are all guilty of a crime we did not commit. (Adam tasted the forbidden fruit, remember, not I and not you.) Furthermore, where is the *proof* that the important events of Jesus's life really happened two thousand years ago? How can we trust the account of his death and what it means for us? How can we be sure that the death of Jesus was not entirely a human event with no supernatural component to it? These are the obstacles that keep many nonbelievers from becoming believers.

Have I succeeded in destroying Christianity in this chapter? Of course not. Have I disproved the existence of God? I didn't even try. Have I made a compelling case for Christians to abandon Jesus? That was never my intent. The aim of this chapter was merely to show why so many people are able to hear Christianity's basic claim and walk away unconvinced. I understand how mysterious this must be for many Christians who see a divine Jesus and the Bible as obviously real and true. Some Christians were raised to believe and have never known anything else. They experienced the external case for Christ and accepted it. Some Christians experienced profound internal events and became convinced that Jesus is a real god. But the fact remains that there are aspects of the basic story here that just don't add up for many people who respect Christians enough to give Christianity a fair hearing. It would be better for everyone if more Christians understood and accepted this rather than entertaining nonsense notions such as that all nonbelievers reject Christianity because they want to sin, are angry, or are simply too arrogant to submit to God. For virtually all skeptics, it's about nothing more than the absence of evidence that makes believing in Jesus so difficult. And for the majority of the world's non-Christians, the barrier that stands between them and Christianity is another belief system. They likely are followers of another religion for no other reason than they trusted their society, friends, and family to tell them the truth, a situation every Christian ought to understand very well.

ULTIMATE JOURNEY. It has been a universal constant for humans to seek ways to escape death. Virtually all cultures throughout history have attempted various creative ways to tunnel or climb their way toward an afterlife. Is Christianity's effort substantially different from all the others? Or is it just one more pyramid reaching for a heaven we can't see? *Photo by the author.*

WHAT IS A GOD?

For all the talk about gods today and throughout history, few people seem to spend much time thinking about what these gods are supposed to be. We have many names for them and many religions designed to praise, appease, control, or tolerate them, but how do we define *gods* in the first place? What are they? The question could hardly be any simpler, but the answer is strangely elusive. Do you know? I'm not sure I do. People have been so enthralled with gods and religions for so long, many willing to kill and die for them, that this question ought to be considered among the most important of all, yet most people sail right by it and instead obsess over secondary issues such as which gods exist, how we should worship, which book gets it right, and how the gods mean for us to behave.

I think it is not only reasonable but necessary for all of us to slow down and confront this primary question. Set aside for the moment the challenge of whether or not this god or that god is real. Let's consider what makes a god. Are they all supernatural? Are they all immortal? Can all of them fly, or only some? Can they walk through walls? Can they read our thoughts? Do they know the future? Can a god have mental and physical frailties? Can a human become a god? Can a god become a human? What is it that makes someone or something a god in our eyes? *What is a god?*

Most Christians perform terribly when asked to define *god*. But they shouldn't feel singled out or picked on, because few others do any better. In my experience, most non-Christian religious people and atheists stumble when defining *gods*. This is probably why so many simply skip the issue completely. "Let's not bother being clear about what we are talking about, let's just talk about it" is standard protocol. When asked to define *god* (lowercase *g*), Christians tend to list various attributes, personality traits, and biographical details about *their* specific god. But this is not helpful. We have an idea of who that particular god is supposed to be from ancient texts and traditional beliefs, but he is just one of many millions of gods claimed to be real by sincere and sane people. This is why I and other skeptics often ask, "Which god?" when religious people bring up their beliefs. When discussing Jesus, for example, it needs to be made clear that we're talking about one specific god out of many.

Simply describing your god is not a reasonable definition for *gods*. It just doesn't work. A sensible definition of *police officer*, for example, can't be "Joe Johnson, middle-aged, slightly overweight, veteran officer with eighteen years in the field, earned two special citations for bravery on duty, and winner of the 2014 South Philly Inter-Police League Darts Championship." That is not a definition of *police officer*. It's a description of one particular policeman out of millions of active and former policemen and policewomen. In the same way, the biography of Yahweh/Jesus/Allah is not the definition of *god*.

Although dictionaries try, there is no satisfactory definition of *god* currently in mainstream use. Because religion is the way it is, there is little or no meaning to be found in the god label. Religions tend to be based *not* on solid, verifiable evidence but on things like personal divine revelations and "supernaturally inspired" writings that cannot be verified to everyone's satisfaction. This obviously leaves a lot of room for interpretation, debate, judgment, opinion, and disagreement. It's like the Wild West of the human mind. Anything goes. The best definitions I've seen are intentionally weak and vague, describing a being who is special and perhaps outside the bounds of the natural universe we inhabit. But even these definitions are flawed because we have to decide who gets to judge what "special" and "outside the bounds of the natural universe" mean.

Alexander the Great was a man who changed the world by conquering the Persian Empire and spreading Greek culture deep into Asia. He was also a god—at least that's what many people said at the time. Most religious people today probably reject that god designation and consider Alexander to have been nothing more than a human who was feared and revered in ancient times. Of course, Alexander was probably just a flesh-and-blood man, but how can we know for sure more than two thousand years after his reign? Maybe he was a god. Perhaps those who lived then know better than us. Christians who want to push Alexander off his god pedestal have to consider how they feel when people do the same to Jesus for similar reasons. I'm not arguing that Alexander the Great was a supernatural being who had magical powers, but I am willing to argue that he should be considered a god if only because people once believed he was. If ancient Macedonians and Greeks said he was a god, then who are we to say otherwise? By what right do we correct their beliefs all these years later?

Those who try hard to impose a more precise and dense definition of *gods* inevitably fall into the trap of unintentional prejudice. It's very easy to assume that one's culture and time period are the best and most important. "My god is real and best because he's my god" seems to be a near-universal instinct among religious people. They cite traits commonly attributed to one or some gods while excluding all the gods without those traits. For example, it is common for a clumsy definition of a god to include terms like *creator* and/or *immortal*. But there have been many gods, according to their believers, who did not create the universe, the Earth, or life and who were quite capable of dying. Again, who are we to say they were not gods if believers said they were?

Keep in mind that existence is an entirely different issue. This is about defining gods, real or not. An atheist may not be convinced that Allah exists, for example, but she won't deny that Allah qualifies as a god in human culture. The definition of *god* must be far more encompassing than we are accustomed to if it is to be fair, consistent, and logical. For example, it is unfair, inconsistent, and illogical to deny god status to the queens and pharaohs who once ruled ancient Egypt. After his death, Roman general and dictator Julius Caesar was officially declared a god in 42 BCE. Any definition of *god* must accommodate Caesar. Preacher David Koresh died in the fiery climax of the Waco, Texas, standoff in 1993, and there are people today who still say that he is a god.[1]

For many Christians, I'm sure it might seem absurd to think of King Tut, Julius Caesar, and David Koresh as gods, but on what grounds can they be dismissed? Just as no atheist has ever disproved the existence of the God of Abraham, no Christian has ever proved the nonexistence of the millions of gods various other religious people have believed in throughout history. No one has disproved the claims that Tut, Caesar, and Koresh are gods of some kind. Such things are difficult, if not impossible, to disprove no matter how worthy of doubt they may be. We have to keep in mind that most religions are not based on proof, good evidence, and scientifically verifiable claims. They are based instead on shared stories, personal experiences, claims of divine revelation, and the words of authority figures. Because of this, it is impossible to fairly reject the right of anyone else to claim that their god is worthy of being called a god.

For better or worse, the concept of gods has had a profound impact on world history and continues to influence events today. I think it would be helpful for Christians to give more thought to the definition of *god*. For if gods matter—and they do—then we all would be better off thinking more clearly about them. What are they? It's a simple but important question that should nag all of us. We have loved, hated, divided, united, and even defined ourselves through our gods. They inspire us to greatness and supreme goodness. Sometimes they fuel the best in us, other times the worst. Gods have lifted us to greatness and lured us down into our darkest, most depraved episodes. Perhaps one day in the future, gods will be the end of us all via some nuclear holocaust sparked by warring religious tribes. Yet in light of all this, few of us give much time to thinking about who and what these gods are. Perhaps if more people—especially the religious—made more of an effort to define, analyze, compare, and *prove* whether or not these gods exist, religion might become less of a problem for the world. More reason and reflection can only help, I suspect.

Vanilla may be the most popular ice cream flavor, but we cannot assume to know very much about ice cream without knowing something about some other flavors and having at least a general definition for *ice cream* in our heads. And that definition can't omit 99 percent of the flavors. In the same way, it seems to me that there is but one workable definition of *god*: *A god is that which someone calls a god*. That may not be much of a definition, but, unlike all the others, it's fair and it works.

3

IS IT RUDE TO ASK?

Many think it is impolite to talk about religion in any meaningful way in most settings. Strangely, this unwritten prohibition is promoted most vigorously by people who talk about religion in virtually every setting. From football games to the Grammy Awards to presidential speeches, religious belief is brought up constantly by religious people. But the moment someone asks a relevant question or makes the slightest challenge to it, no matter how fair, protests of rudeness and perhaps even charges of intolerance are sure to be made. Is religion a private affair or not? Is it appropriate to bring up the subject and talk about it or not? Currently, the topic is mostly a one-way street; only believers are permitted to carry the conversation in most settings. This is bad for both skeptics and religious people alike.

Consider how religion is normally handled in American politics. Imagine if a reporter followed up a president's mention of scripture by asking about his specific views on the Bible. Is it entirely and literally true? If not, then which parts are true and which parts are not, in the president's judgment? And how might this distinction influence White House policy decisions? If a president says he "believes the Bible" or quotes from it regularly, then why can't someone ask if he really expects the apocalypse to occur as described in Revelation? Does he believe we are in the "End Times"? If so, does this influence the president's attitude toward environmental policy or the use of nuclear weapons?

Any journalist who asked these kinds of questions at a White House press conference would probably be ignored by the president, scolded by peers, condemned by pundits, and never heard from again. It wouldn't matter if the president had just finished quoting the Bible or making some statement about how important his or her faith is. There is little doubt that the reporter would be run over and left for dead on the one-way street of religion. Why? Why can't we just get it all out in the open and talk about religion? Especially since religious people already bring their religions out in the open every day. Christianity is hardly a secret society. Many Christians are so confident and excited about their belief that they can't seem to stop talking about it—but only within a protective cocoon that allows no challenges and no straying from the script. It is important to stress that I'm not referring to mocking, ridiculing, or even arguing about religion here. All that may have its time and place, but as far as simply *discussing* religion and *asking honest questions* about it, there should be no inappropriate time, no inappropriate place.

I once covered a faith-healing ceremony for a newspaper I worked for at the time. One of the highlights of the evening was an elderly woman who said she had been healed of a terminal illness by the visiting evangelist. I carefully took notes about what was said and what happened. I also took a photo at the key moment of contact when the faith healer's hands touched the sick woman. It was a spectacular moment, full of drama and emotion. Many in attendance shrieked, cried, and prayed. Virtually everyone around me, including the evangelist and the elderly woman, declared the illness defeated. She was saved, in this life and the next! But was she?

A couple of weeks later I found out that she died not long after that event. I proposed doing a follow-up story about it. I could try to get a few comments from the evangelist and some of the people there that night. Maybe I could also interview a prominent skeptic such as James Randi, Michael Shermer, Joe Nickell, or Ben Bradford and present an alternate view of what might really have occurred at the ceremony. Maybe it wasn't a front-page blockbuster, but it seemed worthy of at least a small report somewhere in the paper. After all, we had published a report that quoted people saying the woman was healed by a miracle.

But the second story never happened. I was shut down immediately, told it would be rude to pursue it. It wasn't a big deal to me at the time. I wasn't angry or upset over it. But I do remember thinking that this was an example of how it is that so many con artists who dress up in the cloak of a religion are able to fleece the gullible year after year, decade after decade, and century after century. Religion is so often off-limits to relevant questions and fair challenges that it's a free zone for abuse and deceit. This is one of the reasons I believe it is in the best interest of Christians to encourage rather than discourage more open talk about religion in all forums.

The reluctance of so many religious people to field questions about religion can be very confusing to the skeptic. Religion is among the most powerful forces in global human culture. It shapes societies, ignites wars, and inspires peace—but it's too fragile to withstand the wicked onslaught of a few questions? Seriously? What are we skeptics supposed to think? That religious people are not strong enough to listen to other ideas and ponder obvious questions about the things they say are most important? Perhaps some are not up to it, but I believe the vast majority of Christians today are fully capable of hearing another view and considering it without feeling insulted and oppressed. So what is the roadblock in so many situations? Perhaps the problem is that too many of them have been misled into believing that a skeptic's curiosity and doubt are the equivalent of ridicule and rage. But this is wrong. For example, when I ask a Christian how he or she can be so sure that Jesus rose from a tomb in Palestine and went to heaven, I'm not trying to stump them or make them feel bad. I'm genuinely curious. I think a story about something so extraordinary occurring more than two thousand years ago is unlikely to be true, but I ask because my mind is open and I'm always willing to learn something new.

Returning to the example of American politics, how can politicians publicly declare that God is their source of strength, that American government and culture rest on Christian principles, that Jesus is their inspiration, that prayer works, that faith is everything to them, and so on, but then bristle if anyone so much as hints at trying to figure out what their words really mean? During most local, state, and national campaigns, religion is constantly brought up by the candidates, but rarely if ever are their religious comments explored or analyzed in any meaningful way by the reporters covering the races or the public following them. In recent years, the following politicians said publicly that God told them to run for office: Michele Bachman, Rick Perry, Rick Santorum, Herman Cain, Sarah Palin, Mike Huckabee, and George W. Bush.[1] But these amazing and seemingly contradictory claims were never probed to any significant degree by the news media because "personal faith" is out of bounds, no matter if politicians themselves drag it onto the playing field virtually every time they open their mouths. Just imagine the very different level of scrutiny that a candidate would face for saying that she received a message from an extraterrestrial who instructed her to run for office. Or what if a candidate was a follower of a much less popular religion such as Scientology or Wicca, for example? If that person claimed to have received special instructions from outer space or an inner spirit, would he or she be exempted from meaningful questions too? I doubt it. Asking people about their religion is not rude when they are the ones who made a big deal about it. It's not only appropriate to explore such extraordinary claims by candidates; in a democracy, it's a responsibility.

During the 2012 presidential campaign between President Barack Obama and Mitt Romney, it was left to atheists and comedians—"the rude people" in American society—to ask all the obvious and basic questions about Romney's religious beliefs. Of course, none of them were in any position to expect an answer, but the questions were fair: Does he believe that temple garments (underwear) provide literal or merely symbolic protection for the Mormons who wear them? What about the planet/star Kolob described in Mormon scripture? Does he think it exists out in space somewhere, and is the throne of God located there? Does he really believe God waited until 1978 to tell the Mormon prophet to allow black people into church leadership positions? Many more questions like this should have been asked, not to mock Romney's religion or make him look bad, but simply to gain a better picture of a man who repeatedly stressed how profoundly important his specific religious beliefs are to him. Such questions matter because they speak to the way Romney's reasoning works and how analytical he is, surely important abilities for someone who might lead a large nation. The issue of blatantly racist rules in a church of which he was an enthusiastic member at the time raises possible character issues.

Since Obama often brings up God, the Bible, and faith, he should have been asked similar questions about his beliefs during the last campaign and now. Does he think the Bible is wrong in declaring that gay men should be put to death (Leviticus 20:13)? Does he agree with the Bible that people who say there is no God are fools? Does he think that Christianity is the only path to heaven, as the Bible clearly declares? How does he reconcile sending troops to war when Jesus instructed us to love not only our neighbors but our enemies as well? How do drone attacks that often kill noncombatants fit with the concept of "turn the other cheek"? Is there a conflict between American-style capitalism and Jesus's Sermon on the Mount? How exactly does President Obama determine which parts of the Bible to obey and which parts to ignore?

It's fine if politicians feel the need to repeatedly mention their religious beliefs when campaigning. That's their choice. But why does it have to be all fluff and platitudes that no one queries? If a candidate hints that he or she might raise taxes or tinker with immigration laws, then a news blitzkrieg is immediately launched and journalists go into overdrive with their questions. But if a candidate mentions that they are an agent of God destined by divine mandate to rule America, deafening silence is sure to follow. Why can't we add some substance to the topic? Shouldn't we, after all? I'm curious why more religious voters don't feel insulted when so many politicians sprinkle "God" throughout their speeches in what seems suspiciously like nothing more than an attempt to appease the yokels and create the popular image of a person with high moral character. I would think that thoughtful Christians who are sincere about their beliefs would be with me on this. Christians, rather than skeptics of religions, ought to be the first and the loudest in demanding more transparency and intelligent discussion about their religion from the public leaders who so often display it like a cheap tin trophy.

THE RUDE SKEPTIC

Clearly, some nonbelievers are rude to Christians and other religious people. No denying that. But rudeness exists in every form of human interaction. Football fans are often rude to one another. People can go far beyond being impolite to one another based on political leanings. There is rudeness in schools and in the workplace, and it can probably be found in a church or two as well. However, much of what is labeled offensive and mean-spirited by religious people is actually no such thing. I know this personally because there have been occasions when I have written soft words and said gentle things that were not received well by all religious people. Although I do very well at staying on friendly terms with the majority of religious people I encounter, at times I have ruffled a few feathers, unfortunately.

But most of the things that I and most other skeptics say about religion cannot reasonably and fairly be viewed as hitting below the belt. For example, questioning the existence of a god should not be seen as a capital offense or even rude in the slightest. It is a sensible and fair question to ask in light of two key facts. First, no gods have ever been scientifically verified to exist. Good and unambiguous evidence is totally absent for any of them. This alone justifies the simple question of whether or not any gods are real. Second, *everybody*—including every religious person—questions the existence of most gods. Nobody thinks *every* god is real. Hindus doubt the existence of traditional African gods, Muslims reject Hindu gods, Christians challenge the reality of ancient Roman gods, and so on. Does this mean everyone is rude when it comes to religion? Is a Christian vulgar and boorish for merely expressing her doubts about the veracity of the Koran or the existence of Ganesha?

Another common misconception is that fairness for all religions is unfair. Somehow tolerance for all religions and no religions is intolerant to one religion. For example, the US government is constitutionally bound to avoid favoring and promoting one religion over all others. But some Christians incorrectly view this neutrality in practice as a bias against their religion. I encourage Christians to listen carefully to what virtually all the world's atheists and skeptics actually say in regard to religion. They call for freedom of thought, the right to believe or not believe as one chooses, not a ban on religions. They seek more positive discussion and debate, not imposed silence and censorship. It is my hunch that most nonbelievers could not care less if the bulk of humanity remained religious or not. What they care about is that religious people are not so swept up in their faith that they lose sight of all reason or fairness and compassion for others. They don't want religious people oppressing women and children in the name of gods. They don't want one group of people's belief in a god slowing or halting scientific and social progress. They don't want a religion dictating laws for all of us. This is something Christians tend to agree with passionately, by the way, when it is some other religion trying to impose laws.

Many skeptics and atheists may hope for a new age of enlightenment in which all religion fades, yes, but only by free choice. It is amusing when I hear religious people describe well-known atheists such as Richard Dawkins or the late Christopher Hitchens as "militant atheists." Militant? Are you serious? Words are not bullets. Reason and logic do not make a gulag, no matter how vigorously they are championed. A lecture is not a terrorist attack. Piercing questions about God delivered to the faithful are not assault and battery. Skepticism threatens only that which is not true. A joke here and there is not the end of the world. I would never condemn a Christian for using thoughts and words in an attempt to convince me that Jesus is a real god. I cannot imagine fearing or hating a Christian because he attacked atheism with humor or highlighted the errors of atheists. I save my condemnation for those who genuinely deserve it, and so should Christians.

THE POLITE SKEPTIC

I believe that in most cases skeptics should strive to be exceedingly polite about the way in which the existence of a god is questioned. I'm not saying it should be given a pass, of course. I'm not suggesting that anyone should hold back from asking the tough questions or delivering the hard truth. But we have to consider the emotional investment many people have in their god belief, so I make it a point to be as respectful of them as possible. Skeptics must keep in mind that for most people religion can't be argued like two robots playing a game of chess. It's too personal. There is too much tradition, too much emotion, and too many years invested. Tone of voice matters. Facial expression counts. Carefully chosen words delivered calmly with a smile usually go a lot farther than name calling and ridicule.

There is a significant difference between respecting a person and respecting that person's specific claims about a religion. Some religious people disagree, but I think the two can be thought of as separate. I may have no respect for the claim that mediums carry on conversations with dead people, for example, but that doesn't mean I have no respect for the people who believe they do. My inability to accept the claims of astrology does not prevent me from liking and respecting all the good-hearted people who faithfully read their horoscopes every day. In fact, I not only respect such people; I care about them. That's why I spend so much of my time promoting science and reason. It bothers me to see people wasting their time and money on bogus ideas. Over the years, I am sure many religious people wrongly assumed that I am only interested in trying to beat up their ideas and belittle their beliefs. But the truth is that I have only ever wanted to help make the world a little more rational, more sensible, and safer for all. My ideas and suggestions, every one of them on this topic, are offered with only kindness and optimism in mind. And I am hardly unique among skeptics. Virtually every one of us wants a better world for *everyone*.

Religion is too important for us to continue avoiding meaningful conversations about it. It impacts our world, for better and for worse, every moment of every day. We have to talk about it. I am convinced that one of the reasons there is so much madness, violence, and dysfunction linked to religions around the world is that, for all the noise about gods and faith, there is very little straight talk. The world needs skeptics, if only to help dial down the religious fervor that so often runs off the rails. A little doubt here and there is one of the easier ways in which we might achieve a more peaceful planet.

Every meeting between believer and nonbeliever need not be a tense confrontation. A little courtesy does wonders, I have discovered. Many Christians do not take any offense from a politely worded skeptical challenge of their beliefs. Sadly, however, too many do. Such hypersensitivity is not only unnecessary; it is a drag on all of us, including Christians. Very few challenges are ever solved without first talking about them, and religion clearly presents key problems for the world that are screaming for solutions. Perhaps it would be helpful for believers to keep in mind that their religion is but one of many and that religious beliefs have been with us from our earliest days, probably reaching very far back into prehistory. Religion is tough, to say the least. Christianity specifically has not only endured for two thousand years but today thrives as the world's most popular religion with more than two billion followers. Surely it should be strong enough and sufficiently mature by now to face up to the words and ideas of a few well-meaning skeptics. If not, then Christians ought to wonder why.

4

DOES JESUS ANSWER PRAYERS?

Ithis simple question by merely listing a
few scientific studies that fail to show prayer works.[1] But there is
another way to address this important question, one I hope will make
a greater impression on Christians. It's a simple way of looking at the
issue that cuts right to the heart of the matter. It doesn't rely on double-
blind tests, doesn't hinge on researchers' credentials, doesn't require
reading a dense and demanding article in some journal, and definitely
doesn't require any finessed or tortured interpretation to make the
point.

THE GREATEST TEST OF ALL

Suppose we could identify the most important and deserving prayer
request of all and then measure its effectiveness objectively. Would that
say something meaningful about the claim that God/Jesus answers
prayers? I think so. Consider the prayer of a mother, spoken aloud or
thought in silence, as she embraces her suffering and dying baby: "I
beg you, God, save my baby. *Please*, God, don't let her die." This is a
prayer for a young child, easily the most innocent and worthy of rescue
of anyone. It's about as sincere and unselfish as any prayer could be.
I think this is the prayer that provides us with an ideal way to judge
whether or not God answers prayers.

During travels across six continents, I took notice of how prominent belief in a god or gods is among the poorest of the poor. Based on
my observations, the poor tend to pray hard and pray often. Extreme
poverty and religious belief seem matched in some weird joust between
hope and despair. As we shall see shortly, credible data back up this
conclusion. As a longtime advocate for awareness about global poverty,

I always pay close attention to the condition of the poor wherever I go. The primary purpose of a visit may have been to experience the stunning beauty of the Taj Mahal or to photograph African wildlife, but habit always led me to conversations with the poor. I ask them about their lives, their struggles, and their hopes. Heart-wrenching though it can be, I am often uplifted by their energy and optimism. I met an old man in Nepal who apparently lived in a street gutter—literally in the gutter. Despite such severe conditions, he flashed perhaps the most infectious smile I have ever seen on a human being anywhere. I met a young mother in India who begged strangers in order to feed herself and her baby. Beneath the hunger and dirt was an astonishingly beautiful woman. Dealt a different hand, she might have been a supermodel. I saw a child in India with a body so mangled by polio that he seemed to defy several laws of physics when he crawled. In East Africa my heart was broken a hundred times in a single day. The street beggars, hustlers, and hardworking people I have encountered tend not to be the pathetic losers some people in more fortunate circumstances might imagine. There is often a surprising brightness in their eyes and a determination to not simply exist but to live well. There may be no glory in their poverty alone, but it has been my experience that these people carry within them as much of humanity's strength and goodness as any of us, if not more. This helps me to remember that they are no less alive and valuable than anyone else. The statistics of suffering and death that shadow the developing world are more than numbers. They are people.

THE MOTHER'S PRAYER

Religious belief is important to the world's poorest people, just as it is to most of the rest of the world, perhaps more so. Whenever I ask about religion, the poor eagerly describe how important one or more gods are in their lives. And they often stress the confirming power of prayer. If I ask, for example, how it is they are sure that their religious beliefs are accurate and true, prayer is a likely answer. It is for this reason that I included the topic of prayer in my book *50 Reasons People Give for Believing in a God* (Prometheus Books, 2008). "Answered prayers" is easily one of the most common justifications for belief that I hear from believers around the world, regardless of whatever particular religion they adhere to. It is this intersection of the world's poorest people and the popular claim that gods answer prayers that offers us a very revealing real-world test of prayer's effectiveness.

If the world's poorest societies tend to be the most intensely religious (they are), and if most religious people pray often (impossible to accurately measure but a reasonable assumption), then how does the world play out? If prayer works, then we should see the most religious societies on Earth—the places with the most praying going on—as the most "blessed," secure, and safest places to live. Meanwhile, the least religious societies ought to be more distressed, because there is much less praying for positive divine intervention. Is this the world we see? Not even close.

Contradicting the claim that gods answer prayers, the most religious societies tend to be the most hellish of all places to live. And the least religious societies tend to be the best places to live. An objective ranking of countries—based on key measures such as security, health, literacy, human rights, corruption, and so on—reveals a world in which prayer doesn't seem to matter very much, if at all. The real world looks just like it might look if prayer didn't work and no gods existed. For example, Save the Children, a charity organization that focuses on the world's poorest children, produced the Mothers' Index. This ranking of nations reveals the best and worst places to be a mother. The best countries, in order, are Norway, Australia, Iceland, Sweden, Denmark, New Zealand, Finland, Belgium, Netherlands, and France. These countries have some of the lowest rates of religious belief and church attendance in the world. They also rank highest in levels of atheism. At the bottom end of the Mothers' Index, we find that the worst places on Earth to be a mother with a baby are also among the most intensely religious countries.[2] The number and intensity of prayers seem to have no impact on the constant suffering and dying of babies in extreme poverty.

It's important for readers to understand that I am not claiming that Christianity, Islam, Hinduism, or any other religion directly causes babies to die. Nor am I suggesting that any of this conclusively disproves prayer's effectiveness or the existence of gods. The important point here is that religious belief and prayer *do not save the lives of babies or ease their suffering in any detectable way*. But this is precisely what many religious people claim. God answers prayers? No, he doesn't, it seems, even if you are a religious and loving mother begging for her dying child's life. Please understand that malnutrition, malaria, and other parasitic diseases are horrible ways to die in the poorest of societies. These are not quick and painless deaths. In virtually every case, these children suffer long and die slowly. Despite all the relatively high levels of praying taking place in these places, babies die at the highest rates in all the world—especially as compared with babies in the least religious societies. An objective observer can't help but notice that it's as if no gods exist or that, if one or more do exist, they choose not to answer the most sincere, important, and just prayers in all the world. Either way, prayer advocates have plenty of reasons to reconsider their conclusions.

Some Christians have told me that Jesus does answer every prayer, but sometimes the answer is "no." This is a clever response, but it doesn't line up very well with the promise found in the Bible: "And all things, whatsoever ye shall ask in prayer, believing, ye shall receive" (Matthew 21:22). Nor does it fit well with the tears and pleadings of all those mothers holding near-dead babies in their arms right now at this very moment. A god who ignores those prayers has no business answering any others.

One obvious explanation for this problem of unanswered prayers is that some combination of human failure and environmental conditions are responsible. Babies die in poor places mostly because there isn't adequate healthcare, safe water, and food. But this is the secular explanation. How can Christians argue that the power and compassion of Jesus is bound by the shortcomings of human infrastructure? Why would Jesus be at all concerned with the quantity and quality of local healthcare personnel, medicine inventories, and facilities when he decides whether or not to act on a mother's desperate prayer? If he exists, is all-powerful, and does answer prayers, then such details would be irrelevant.

MUSLIM PRAYERS VERSUS CHRISTIAN PRAYERS

Another problem with the idea that the Christian god answers prayers is the seemingly endless list of other religions making the exact same claim. A little awareness goes a long way on this issue. If we are going to think seriously about prayers, then we have to think about *all prayers* and not just those of one religion. This might not be important to many Christians, but it matters to skeptics. We just can't ignore the obvious contradiction in claims of answered prayers made by Christians, Muslims, Hindus, and others. The concept of communing with a god, communicating with a god, and requesting something of a god is not exclusive to Christianity, of course. All Christians know this. They know that Muslims pray too. But how many Christians pause to think about all the non-Christians who tell dramatic and sincere stories of answered prayers and use it to "prove" that their religion is accurate and their gods are real, just like Christians do?

If prayer works as advertised and proves that a god is real, then by what logic does a Christian dismiss the prayer claims of today's non-Christians and all the non-Christians throughout history and prehistory who also prayed and reported favorable results? Why are their claims less credible and less important? I have spoken with Muslims and Hindus, for example, who explained to me that they "know" their religion is accurate and true because some of their important prayers have been answered. These prayers must have been fulfilled by their god or gods, they assured me, because the circumstances were too unusual and could not have been anything other than divine intervention.

So what are we to make of these stories? I certainly don't think billions of Muslims and Hindus across multiple generations are all crazy or lying. No, a more likely explanation is that they are failing to think critically about prayer and the events of their lives related to specific prayers. It is easy for people to misinterpret unexpected or unlikely events as necessarily supernatural when they aren't. Also, something called confirmation bias probably misleads many people to remember "answered prayers" and forget the much higher number of unanswered prayers. Better record keeping would likely show a pattern of nothing more than the random success one would expect from a long list of wishes.

Confirmation bias, by the way, is something we all have to contend with. If you are not aware of it, you will tend to remember the hits and forget the misses in a way that confirms your previously held beliefs. So watch out for it. Resist it or be led astray many, many times throughout your life. Confirmation bias leads to faulty conclusions about everything from how mean your neighbor is and how fair your boss is to politics and prayer. Christians are human too, so they are no safer from this bias than the rest of us. I wonder what a typical Christian thinks about "answered prayers" within other religions. Surely they don't think billions of non-Christians who pray and claim positive results are all either lying or mentally ill. The only sensible conclusion is that these people are sincere but mistaken. And, in fact, that is precisely what I usually hear when I ask Christians about this. But this presents a problem. It opens a door to the possibility that Christians are sincere but mistaken about prayer in the same way. If non-Christian believers are wrong about their prayers, then whatever psychological pothole trips them up might be doing the same to Christians who claim to have had their prayers answered. It's easy to forget, or never realize, that we are all the same species. The languages, dress, food, music, politics, and gods can make it seem at times that we are from different planets. But no, beneath all that self-inflicted variation we are just people with pretty much the same batch of strengths and weaknesses.

Christians might also want to keep in mind that these prayers do not occur in a vacuum. Many prayers are requests for real things in the real world, and people don't always sit idly by hoping a god makes the wish comes true. Some believers do things toward making it happen. *God helps those who help themselves.* For example, what if a man prays to Jesus to overcome obesity, then changes his eating habits and begins walking for an hour every day. If he then loses a substantial amount of weight, can we really credit Jesus for answering his prayer? Isn't it more likely that the real explanation is that he consumed fewer calories than he burned? His belief in Jesus and prayers may have helped to motivate him to get off the couch and to eat better, but no supernatural forces or real god is necessarily required in such a scenario. Many Christians have told me stories about how prayer delivered a miracle that cured them or a family member of a serious illness. Usually until I bring it up, however, no mention is made of the doctors, nurses, and medicine or operation that might have had something to do with it. If you don't control your confirmation bias, it will control you.

THE ATHEIST'S PRAYER

It may surprise some readers to learn that I do not condemn prayer as meaningless nonsense. I suspect that it may indeed serve a useful function for many people. Although I am unconvinced that supernatural beings are tuned in to anyone's prayers and responding to them, I do accept that it's probably very healthy to consciously contemplate challenges, imagine optimal solutions, articulate your concern for the well-being of people you know, as well as for strangers or for all humanity. Talking to yourself about hope and solutions is productive. Prayer can also be a form of meditation that is well known to calm people and improve health. Prayer may not be the communication link to real gods that believers say it is, but I believe Christians when they tell me that they get a lot out of the practice.

I recall the four days I spent voluntarily roughing it alone on a small deserted island in the Caribbean. I often talked to myself, both silently and aloud, while trying to figure out challenges and reassure myself that I would be okay. I mumbled things such as "I hope drug smugglers don't show up in the middle of the night and find me," "I'm sure I brought enough water. I'll be fine," and "I really hope the rat that invaded my tent and nibbled on my toe last night doesn't have rabies" (he didn't). Although I wasn't talking to a god, I suspect that this solitary chatting, the atheist's prayer, served some positive psychological purpose for me.

In the end I believe we can all be honest and mature enough to confront what is most likely the truth about prayer. Either no gods are there to listen, or, if there are, the gods do not respond to us in the way many religious people claim they do. If Jesus really is listening and really does fulfill the wishes of Christians, then wouldn't the entire world have noticed by now? If Christian prayer requests to Jesus were successfully answered for two thousand years at a rate high enough to discount chance and faulty interpretation, don't you think at least a majority of the world's population would want in? Don't you think all rival religions, with their prayers wasted on false gods, would have faded away centuries ago? The reality, however, is that the *majority* of the world's religious people pray to gods other than Jesus and seem to claim about the same rate of success. I suppose it is possible that they are all deluded and that only Christians are right. Still, if I were a Christian, I would be troubled by the confidence we see in prayer across the borders of so many belief systems, because the claims of the non-Christian seem no different in substance or credibility than those of the Christian.

ENDLESS LOVE. For many centuries, millions of Christians have made pilgrimages to make a physical connection with what is believed to be the tomb of Jesus. This Coptic priest greets visitors in an altar at the back of the tomb that is located inside the Church of the Holy Sepulchre. *Photo by the author.*

WHO IS A CHRISTIAN?

After a week in Greece spent exploring spectacular ancient sites and imagining my feet stepping into the exact footsteps of Pericles, Socrates, Themistocles, and King Leonidas, it was time to seek the modern and the living. I found a beautiful Christian church and decided to enter and observe a service. The church was old, very old, but the stone walls were still strong. It seemed as if the Apostle Paul himself might have once worshipped there. He may well have, or at least on the same spot. The first hint I got that something was very different from churches I was familiar with were the paintings of Jesus on the walls. They were old and there were many of them. But as I watched Christians file in through the door, I saw something new to me. They all paused in front of each painting and kissed it. Some kissed their hands and then touched the image of Jesus. Most of the worshippers kissed the paintings directly, lip to canvas. This was bizarre behavior, at least to my eyes. I had never seen this in any of the Protestant churches I had attended during childhood in America. Sitting there for half an hour or so watching the constant stream of people coming in to kiss their Messiah drove home to me how different Christianity can be for many people around the world.

The same thought struck me again some years later during a Church of Christ revival meeting in the Caribbean. Jamaicans, mostly middle-aged women, reeled with joy as they sang and prayed the night away at full volume. It was vaguely similar to some of the Baptist services I'd attended in Florida, but a little louder and a lot more emotional. It certainly was very different from what I'd experienced in American Episcopal churches. But while these superficial differences between churches may have impressed me, such traits are not the usual reason for dissension among a religion. The breakups that have been a standard component of Christianity since shortly after its conception are most often due to doctrinal disputes, disagreements over interpretations of the Bible, cultural drift, and plain old human power struggles. The end result is that Christianity today is splintered beyond belief. There are, at the moment, an estimated 41,000 different denominations![1]

This is one of the key reasons why many people are skeptical of Christianity. There are a maddening number of versions of it, and this adds to the confusion and doubt. When someone tells you that they have the revealed truth from Jesus and it is just one version of thousands, there is a problem. How can any Christian blame skeptics for not embracing Christianity when the world's Christians can't even agree on precisely who Jesus is, what he wants us to do, how we are supposed to worship him, and how we get to heaven? Some denominations project live-and-let-live attitudes. Others, however, openly state that they are right and everyone else is wrong—and will pay a severe price on Judgment Day. We can get you into heaven, they say, but that other church is a one-way ticket to hell. If I were a Christian, I would lose a lot of sleep worrying if I'd chosen the right version out of so many.

How did Christianity end up with thousands of variations, anyway? The short answer is it didn't waste any time. Christianity was only a single unified religion for a few brief years after Jesus's execution. It had not even established itself as a major religion before it began breaking up in the first century. Three of the earliest branches were Gnostic Christianity, Pauline Christianity, and the version practiced by Jews who believed Jesus was God. During the first millennium, Rome became the center of power for Christianity, but in 1054 a massive split occurred when what would come to be known as the Roman Catholic Church and the Eastern Orthodox Church broke apart. Then, in 1517, a German priest named Martin Luther nailed his ninety-five theses to the door of a church to launch the Protestant Reformation. This led to the eventual creation of many more versions of Christianity. Another significant breakup occurred in the 1500s when England's King Henry VIII cut ties with the Roman Catholic Church, primarily so that he could remarry without needing papal approval. In 1830, American Joseph Smith created yet another version of Christianity. Smith said he was visited by an angel and found golden tablets that he was able to translate into the Book of Mormon by looking through "seer stones" in his hat. And, of course, it didn't stop there. Nor is the continual fracturing of Christianity likely to stop anytime soon.

In fairness to the world's most popular religion, maybe it's just not possible to corral nearly two and a half billion people into one church.

From a skeptic's perspective, however, I suspect that the primary reason for all this disunity is the basic nature of religion itself. If one has a club, organization, or world religion that is based on claims of divine revelation—something anyone can claim—then it's pretty hard to win an argument about who is right and who is wrong. There is no hard evidence to rely on, no undeniable proof that transcends the words of men and women. Compare that to science, which is based on evidence and things anyone can prove. It's the reason there are not 41,000 versions of the theory of evolution or 41,000 different scientific explanations for how the Sun produces energy.

As for the simple question "Who is a Christian?" the only answer, the only fair and logical answer, is that those who say they are Christian are Christian. But I have had friendly debates about this with many Christians who disagree. They consistently feel that they know best what is required for one to qualify as a Christian. It seems to be a consistent urge or need for Christians to define or establish eligibility requirements themselves. I disagree, however. I think it is the outsider who is in the best position to determine what makes one a Christian, for only an outsider is truly unbiased.

A Seventh-Day Adventist once explained to me in great detail how a person who does not observe the Sabbath on Saturday cannot accurately call themselves a Christian. I asked her how a person who does not accept papal authority can accurately consider himself a Christian. She then told me that the pope is not a real Christian. On the other hand, a few Catholics have told me with great confidence that theirs is the "true church" and that Baptists, Pentecostals, and the rest are doing it all wrong. I once interviewed a Catholic priest who told me off the record that many Protestant churches encourage a lot of "jumping around" but that it doesn't mean much. I have had several discussions with Protestants who told me that Pope John Paul II was the Antichrist. Since he is dead now, I assume they were wrong. Being a nonbeliever can be very enlightening because many Christians say things to me that they probably would never say to their fellow Christians across denominational lines.

Some Christians maintain that nothing matters apart from a few basic tenets centered on Jesus. That's a nice, concise, and inclusive thought, I suppose, but I don't see how it can be true. If it were true, wouldn't there just be one big unified group of Christians with only a few offshoots at most? In this case, actions speak much louder than words. Something does matter in addition to believing that Jesus is God, and it must matter a great deal because wars have been fought, people tortured, and families torn apart over disagreements within Christianity. The unresolved nature of the world's most popular religion is so profound that it leads one to wonder if it should even be thought of as one religion. The figures may sound impressive: there are more than two billion Christians worldwide, approximately 30 percent of the population.[2] But don't those numbers imply a unity that is not really there?

As the skeptical outsider, I choose to define a Christian as an anthropologist likely would: One who believes in and worships a god named Jesus—full stop. Anything beyond that is debatable, contentious, and a matter of opinion. So I'm fine with lumping all Christians together. But I shouldn't do that, according to many Christians themselves. Many of them exclude Mormons and do not consider them to be "real Christians," for example. Does that mean we should shave off about fourteen million from that global total of Christians? If Catholics don't qualify, as some Protestants say, does that mean we should reduce it by a billion?

I'm not sure how this question of who is a Christian can ever be resolved to everyone's satisfaction. What I do know is that Christianity's extraordinary diversity makes it a very interesting religion and one that is able to accommodate many different worldviews. For example, there are Christians who support gay rights, Christians who strongly condemn homosexuality, and then there are Christians who have no interest in other people's sexuality. There are Christians who say Jesus wants them to amass extravagant wealth as quickly as possible, and others who say that Jesus wants them to give it all away. Some Christians fight in wars, and some are pacifists who won't go near one. I am sure this astounding flexibility has a lot to do with the religion's popularity. But in the minds of many skeptics, it raises questions about the credibility of Christianity's claims, questions that every Christian might want to think about as well. If the Bible was inspired by God and was meant to instruct humankind, then why can't Christians at least, if not the entire world, agree on it? If Jesus really does make himself known to many of his followers by voice, sight, or feeling as is often claimed, then why is there so much conflict within Christianity about true revelations versus false revelations, true prophets versus false prophets, and scriptural meaning? To the skeptic, the last two thousand years of Christian history look suspiciously like the work of people exclusively and not of a god. The disunity that characterizes Christianity cannot be blamed on human nature alone. It also must be seen as inevitable when such big claims are supported by so little evidence.

DOES CHRISTIANITY MAKE SOCIETIES BETTER?

After growing up in Florida and then living twenty years of my adult life in the very Christian Cayman Islands, I am well aware of how common and strong the belief is that Christianity is not just good for a society but absolutely necessary. Without Christianity, I have heard repeatedly from many Christians, a country and its people are doomed to immorality, violence, corruption, and failure. A country that is committed to Jesus, however, will be blessed and is sure to prosper in every way that matters. When stated, this belief is usually followed closely by calls to strengthen Christianity, to make it more prominent in schools and government, to better fund and promote it, and to push back against rival religions, atheism, and even science. This all makes sense to many Christians, of course, because in their minds Christianity is associated with everything good. Why wouldn't we want more of it? The prejudice, hate, and violence that are sometimes tied to Christianity are seen as aberrations or problems stemming from counterfeit versions and churches that are corrupt or have lost their way. These mean nothing to a society's crucial need for "real Christianity." While it is certainly understandable why so many Christians accept and push this theme of Christianity improving societies, it is important to ask one very simple question: Is it true?

Christians should be aware that this belief about religion being the key to good societies is not unique to Christianity. Muslims in Egypt, Jordan, and Syria said the same thing to me. The only difference is that they substituted Islam for Christianity. Hindus in New Delhi and Mumbai explained to me that Hinduism is necessary for society to work well. Based on this, there are really two claims we should explore. One is whether or not Christianity specifically is the key to social success, and the second is whether religion of any kind makes societies better.

The most reliable way to assess the claim that Christianity or other religions make societies better is to simply look at the world and see if it does. If this is a real phenomenon, then we should find a pattern of social success in countries that have more Christians in their populations compared with countries that have fewer Christians. We can do the same for the more general claim that more religious belief is better for a country than less religious belief. Interestingly, the world shows us precisely the opposite of the popular claims.

The United Nations Development Program's annual Human Development Index is a ranking of the world's nations based on key factors such as health, education, living standards, literacy, and life expectancy at birth. It's an important list that clearly reveals the best and worst, the functional and dysfunctional societies of the world. Regarding Christianity and religious belief in general, the report shows a strong pattern that less Christianity and less religion of any kind is associated with overall better societies. More religion is not the answer.

UNITED NATIONS HUMAN DEVELOPMENT INDEX

Top ten	Bottom ten
1. Norway	178. Guinea
2. Australia	179. Central African Republic
3. Netherlands	180. Sierra Leone
4. United States	181. Burkina Faso
5. New Zealand	182. Liberia
6. Canada	183. Chad
7. Ireland	184. Mozambique
8. Liechtenstein	185. Burundi
9. Germany	186. Niger
10. Sweden	187. Democratic Republic of the Congo[1]

It is clear that secular governments and less religious societies can function well. The most successful countries today are certainly not Christian theocracies. Norway, the top-rated country, is populated mostly by atheists and nonreligious doubters, for example.[2] Sweden, Denmark, and the Netherlands also have some of the highest ratios of nonreligious citizens in the world. Conversely, countries struggling at the bottom of the rankings are strongly religious, mostly Christian, and have virtually no atheist citizens identified in their populations.

None of this proves that religion is necessarily a fatal toxin that always spoils societies. The United States is the most highly religious compared with other industrial nations and ranks an impressive fourth. The only reasonable conclusion is that there are many complex factors that help or hinder societies. What is clear, however, is that the current state of the world's countries strongly refutes the popular claim that Christianity is a good and necessary ingredient. Phil Zuckerman, professor of sociology at Pitzer College in California, has studied this.

> While it is certainly true that Christianity has and can contribute many benefits to society, from building hospitals to motivating the Civil Rights Movement, the fact still remains that when we look at societies today, the world over, we see that most of the least religious nations on Earth are faring the best—places like Japan, Sweden, etc.— while most of the most religious countries are faring the worst—places like Zambia, Uganda, El Salvador, etc. Extensive sociological research is clear on this front: Christian beliefs do not correlate with positive societal outcomes. Even the most Christian states in the USA—like Mississippi, Louisiana, and Arkansas—are faring much worse than the less religious states, such as Vermont, New Hampshire, or Oregon. I don't think that such problem-ridden states or nations are having a hard time because they are Christian. It is just that being Christian doesn't seem to help much. Is Christianity bad for society? I wouldn't go that far. Is it good for society? Perhaps yes, in some instances. Maybe not in others. But is it necessary? No way.[3]

As Zuckerman points out, American Christians do not even have to look beyond their own borders to discover that Christianity doesn't guarantee a superior society. Just like the world overall, the United States shows a pattern of less religion associated with fewer problems, and more religion associated with more problems. For example, a 2012 Gallup® study found that Mississippi was the most religious state in America and Vermont the least religious.[4] But Mississippi's religious intensity doesn't save it from having much more severe social problems than Vermont, which is one of the best states in the United States by several key measures.

AMERICA'S MOST RELIGIOUS STATES	AMERICA'S LEAST RELIGIOUS STATES
1. Mississippi	1. Vermont
2. Utah	2. New Hampshire
3. Alabama	3. Maine
4. Louisiana	4. Massachusetts
5. Arkansas	5. Alaska[5]

Specifically, Mississippi's fervor for Christianity and high church attendance does little for the welfare of its babies. The state has the highest infant mortality rate in the country at 10.6 (deaths under one year old, per thousand live births). This is bad by international standards, not just in America. For comparison: Botswana's rate is 10.49; Bahrain, 10.20; Sri Lanka, 9.47; Qatar, 6.81; and Cuba, 4.83.[6] In the United States, least-religious Vermont has the forty-second–lowest infant mortality rate at 5.5.[7] A 2012 CNBC report ranked the fifty states by overall quality of life, and Vermont placed third. New Hampshire, the second-least-religious state, was first in quality of life, and Maine, the third-least-religious state, was fourth in quality of life. At the other end of the list were Alabama (third-most-religious state) ranked forty-seventh for quality of life, and Louisiana (fourth-most-religious state) ranked fiftieth for quality of life.[8]

A 2012 ranking of the most and least peaceful states in America showed the same pattern. States with the lowest violent crime are 1. Maine, 2. Vermont, and 3. New Hampshire, the three least-religious states in America. The most dangerous state in America, with the highest murder and incarceration rates, is also the fourth-most-religious state, Louisiana.[9]

Statistics and rankings do not prove that Christianity caused or exacerbates the challenges faced by the most religious states in America, of course. What is clear, however, is that Christianity has not solved its most serious problems, despite repeated assurances from Christians that it can and does. The nonbelievers' perspective seems reasonable in light of the way in which our world appears today: human problems require human solutions.

WHAT IS ATHEISM?

The majority of Christians, like most religious people worldwide, do not seem to have a very good understanding of what atheism is and what it means to be an atheist. It's easy to see why. Atheism is rarely discussed in schools or at family dinner tables. It's just one of those things that most people assume they know all about but really don't. Unfortunately, this common lack of awareness leads to unnecessary prejudice and problems. The negative image of atheists that exists in the minds of many Christians is as frustrating as it is disturbing. Studies have revealed that most Americans, for example, are less likely to vote for an atheist candidate, are less likely to want their sons and daughters to marry atheists, and are more likely to categorize atheists with criminals, including rapists, than they would other groups of Americans.[1] Rapists!

The reason for this harsh view of nonbelievers, I suspect, is because the feelings of most people are rooted in misinformation and fear of the unknown. Fortunately, these are two things that can be addressed rather easily. This is a fixable problem. But before we get to that, let's define *atheism*. Atheism is the absence of belief in a god or gods. That's it; there is nothing more to it. If you do not think that at least one god is real, then you are an atheist. It has nothing to do with political or economic philosophies. It is not a "rejection" of God or gods, nor is it a rebellion against them. To be an atheist is not to hate a god or gods. How could it be? If one doesn't think any gods are real, then one can't reject them, rebel against them, or hate them. Sure, one can reject, rebel against, or hate a religion or organization, but that is an entirely different matter. No atheist has doubts about the existence of religions.

COMMON GROUND

A key point for Christians to recognize is that atheism is not the bizarre and outlandish concept they may have been led to believe it is. Not even close. As many skeptics point out over and over, *everyone* is an atheist. It's just a matter of degree. Nobody thinks *every* god is real. No sensible person could make such a claim because there are millions of gods, too many to even list and remember, much less believe in. Many of the gods are too contradictory for coexistence to even be logically possible. A typical Christian is a skeptical nonbeliever just like every atheist when it comes to most gods. So when a Christian asks an atheist why she doesn't believe Jesus is a real god, her answer might be "Probably for the very same reasons you don't believe [insert preferred god's name here] is a real god." Depending on the tone in which it is delivered, this fairly standard reply can be perceived by the Christian as being either rude or revelatory—or both. The point of it, however, shouldn't be lost, no matter what. Christians too often fail to think about all the gods they dismiss and why it is that they view them as fictional creations. Simply recognizing this skepticism toward religion that they already wield with great force can have a great impact.

Christians and atheists share many ideas about other religions. Both camps are unconvinced that ancient Greek and Roman gods exist because the evidence is lacking and no one has ever managed to prove they are real. Christians and atheists share the same basic skepticism when they hear claims that the Koran is the flawless transcript of a god's words. Atheists don't think that Ganesha, Vishnu, and all the other Hindu gods are real—just like Christians. Christians are not impressed by claims that the African creator god Ngai made us—neither are atheists. Atheists don't fear the Islamic hell—and neither do Christians. Whether or not they realize it, Christians and atheists have much in common. Out of millions of gods and trillions of sacred words written on stone, clay, and paper, the Christian and the atheist part ways only on one specific god and one particular book. Seeing this common ground can help Christians gain a better understanding of atheism and atheists. Whether or not they remain Christian, it can only help to humanize atheists in their eyes. Then, perhaps, the levels of prejudice and irrational fear might be reduced.

THE DEVIL MADE ME DOUBT

Explaining what atheism is not is another way to explain what atheism is. First, let's address what is probably the most absurd charge of all, that atheists are Satan worshippers. Variations of this are that atheists are somehow working for Satan or are possessed by one of his demons. I trust most Christians do not believe this, but enough do to warrant its mention. I have heard the charge repeated many times. Based on personal experience, it seems to be particularly common in the Caribbean and in the American South. The truth is, however, atheists are not and cannot be Satan worshippers. Remember, by definition, atheists don't think any gods are real, and Satan is just another god, or close enough, in the view of most atheists. If you find an atheist who thinks that Satan is real, then you probably haven't found an atheist. Some say that atheists are "in the grip of Satan" whether they know it or not. Maybe so, but this nonsensical claim is not worth much time or thought because it can't be proved or disproved. Could you disprove a charge that you are the brainwashed member of an al-Qaeda sleeper cell with no conscious knowledge or memory of your training and mission? Maybe you are. One could just as easily make the counterclaim that all Catholics, or all Protestants, or all Mormons are under the spell of Satan and just don't know it. In fact, some Christians do hurl that very accusation at rival Christians. But I'm not sure it gains much traction with them. Do any Christians lose sleep when Muslims say they have been tricked into worshipping Jesus by Satan or some devious *jinn*? Probably not, I suspect, because it's a hollow charge without proof.

ATHEISTS ARE COMMUNISTS

This is a strange but surprisingly common association many American Christians make. Decades past the Cold War, the link between communism and official state atheism as seen in the former Soviet Union is still alive and well in the minds of many Christians, whether or not it makes any sense. Remember the complete and comprehensive definition of atheism: *No gods*. That's it. There is nothing inherent within atheism that has anything to do with politics and economics. There are intensely conservative patriotic American capitalists who are atheists. Atheists can be liberals, fascists, anarchists, neocons, slackers, nerds, geeks, yuppies, hippies, NRA members, whatever. The only requirement to wear the label is that they don't think any gods are real. Therefore, the idea that all atheists are communists, that all communists are atheists, or that atheism inevitably leads to communism is absurd. After hearing about "godless communists" all my life, I was somewhat amused to find so many devoted Catholics in Cuba when I visited there. People can believe anything, religious or political, because the human mind is an infinitely flexible thing.

A HAVEN FOR SCOUNDRELS?

Another common belief among many Christians is that atheists, at least deep down, know God is real but choose to turn their back on him in order to be free of his demands. They want to use drugs, have lots of sex with many people, lie, cheat, steal, be selfish, and mistreat others, so they "pretend" there is no God. Atheists don't want to be fenced in by God's strict moral guidelines, so the answer is to dismiss God as a fairy tale. It has nothing to do with evidence, logic, science, and skepticism. It's really all about nothing more than a bunch of weak-willed rats wanting the freedom to run wild.

I'm not entirely sure what to say about this bizarre claim other than to point out the obvious: one doesn't need to pretend to be an atheist to "run wild" or do things that are illegal and indecent. Just check the daily news. Christians pretty much do it all. Every day, many Christians abuse alcohol and drugs, have sex outside of marriage, kill, lie, cheat, and steal. They even have a cute phrase to explain all this behavior: "Christians aren't perfect, just forgiven."

Are the Christians who make this claim suggesting that their religion is the only reason they don't murder, rape, and rob people? Are they saying they wouldn't care about the safety and well-being of others if not for Jesus? If so, that's scary. I had always assumed that nice Christians were nice people, regardless of whether or not they attended church and read the Bible. It is profoundly disturbing to think that the only thing holding them back from a life of crime and destructive decadence is belief in a god. Fortunately, it's almost certainly not true. One reason to doubt it is the example of atheists and non-Christian religious people. They don't believe in Jesus, and yet most of them conduct themselves just fine in everyday life. Whether or not they agree, I'm confident that most Christians would be good people without their religion.

Regarding the claim that atheists know God is real but pretend he's not, I can't imagine who would be that stupid. If I believed in Jesus but really, really wanted to do meth and burglarize homes, for example, then I certainly wouldn't add to my problems by lying and denying his existence. Why compound my guilt? I would just do what so many Christians do. I would make some bad choices in life, ask Jesus for forgiveness, and try to do better tomorrow. If I sincerely thought God was real, calling myself an atheist would not hide me from his gaze, nor would it free me from his judgment. It's silly and a waste of time for Christians to mislead themselves into thinking that atheists are not being truthful when they say they are not convinced that gods exist.

ATHEISTS ARE ARROGANT

This one fascinates me because it is precisely backward. Why would any Christian think atheists are smug know-it-alls who lack humility? I think this common view may come from the fact that atheists in recent years have become more outspoken and more likely to publicly challenge religious claims. Many who feel religion is beyond reproach and off-limits to rigorous challenge see this as a massive breach of etiquette, nothing less than barbarians at the gate. Yes, some atheists do play rough one-on-one. However, given the prominence and power of religion in human culture, it's ridiculous to suggest that they are the bullies picking on the religious. More to the point, I see this accusation of atheist arrogance as inaccurate. Ask a typical Christian how the universe began, and he or she is likely to give you a confident answer without hesitation. Ask me how the universe began, however, and I'll tell you a bit about the big bang theory followed by a long list of exciting mysteries and questions not yet answered by science. A Christian "knows" how life began on earth. I do not. I am up to speed on *Homo erectus*, *Australopithecus afarensis*, and many other details of human evolution. But I'm nowhere near as confident as many Christians are about the specifics of the origin story found in the Bible. A Christian "knows" what happens to us when we die. I do not. A Christian "knows" how and why the world will end one day. Some even "know" when. I don't know any of that. Even regarding the question of God's existence, most Christians say they are certain he is real. I, however, don't know either way. Maybe one or more gods are real. I can't say for sure that no gods exist. All I know is that the evidence is lacking and no one has ever proved the existence of one. Now who is the know-it-all?

As far as atheists being arrogant, I can't speak for all nonbelievers, but I certainly don't have that problem. Thanks to atheism, I have no divine blessings, no god watching over me, no place in heaven waiting for me, no angels who know my name, no predetermined mission set for me before my birth. I am not the greatest creation of the greatest creator in the cosmos. I'm just a fortunate collection of atoms, a speck of organic matter, trying to make it through another day without being mean to anyone or doing anything too stupid. I'm here for a flash and then I'll be gone. I'm adrift in an incomprehensibly vast universe filled with places, events, and wonders that I will never know. Now who is the humble one?

ATHEISTS CAN'T DISPROVE GOD

Another common error that Christians make when thinking about nonbelievers is that they believe atheism is a declaration that no gods exist. It is not. Again, remember atheism is no belief in gods. That's all. The absence of belief is not the same as knowledge about the nonexistence of gods. I don't think gods are real. My best guess is that they are the creations of imaginative people who were coping with deep fears, hopes, and curiosity about life and the universe, but I certainly don't claim to know this for certain. How could I know such a thing? The universe is a big place. A few gods might be hiding somewhere over in the next galaxy. Yet Christians wrongly think atheists have failed to make their case because they haven't disproved God's existence. There are three problems with this. First, the burden of proof rests on the shoulders of the person making the claim and no one else. If, for example, someone says to me, "Fairies are real and you should believe in them," it's not my responsibility to prove that fairies don't exist. It's the believer's job to make the case for fairies. If, however, an atheist says that she or he *knows* no gods exist, then a believer could justifiably demand proof for such a bold claim. Second, what do Christians have to say about all the gods they have failed to disprove? Does their inability to disprove the existence of the ram-faced god Daksha mean that he must be real so they should worship him? Of course not, but this is the same logic some try to impose on nonbelievers. Finally, exactly how would one go about disproving the existence of all gods anyway? Most of them, according to those who believe in them, are magical, otherworldly beings capable of flight, invisibility, and many other superpowers. How could a mere human with all our limitations ever rule out the possibility that at least some gods exist somewhere? It can't be done. That's why sensible atheists who have thought about this readily admit that, unlikely though it may be, gods *could* be real in one form or another, somewhere in this universe or another.

I DON'T BELIEVE IN AGNOSTICS

A frequent point of confusion and occasional contention among both the religious and nonreligious is the concept of agnosticism. Loosely defined as the "I don't know" position, agnosticism has the look and feel of a reasonable stance on religious belief. Perhaps some people embrace the label because it is commonly viewed as the cozy and polite middle ground between belief and atheism. But it's not. The common assumption among religious people is that atheists claim to know that gods aren't real and agnostics admit they don't know whether or not gods are real. Many Christians view atheists as angry militants who adhere to a negative godless religion and agnostics as people who are merely confused souls nearer to the truth.

Regardless of what you may have been led to believe, *agnostic* is a largely useless and meaningless term. For example, it does not even answer the basic and important question of whether or not one believes in gods. There are only two valid answers to this question. They are "Yes, I believe" or "No, I do not believe." An answer of "I don't know" is not a valid option because it merely describes a state of one's knowledge about gods. It says nothing about whether or not one believes or thinks gods are real. As I explained previously, most atheists freely admit that they don't really know whether or not any gods are real. So doesn't that make all these atheists agnostic? And if not knowing means one can't be a believer, then wouldn't that mean all agnostics are atheists?

Another problem with using the agnostic label is that it seems to suggest that we are somehow able to know that gods are unknowable. How can anyone possibly be sure of that? Maybe we missed something in the archaeological record that would prove the ancient Greek gods are real. Maybe they are knowable, but we just haven't recognized it yet. We also don't know what the future holds. It's possible that Kingu, Jesus, or Odin will walk onto the set of *The Today Show* tomorrow morning and proceed to let all of us know that at least one god definitely exists. Therefore, it's just not reasonable to assume something like a god is unknowable in any meaningful and lasting sense. Agnosticism seems to be nothing more than a flimsy opinion about gods that is external to the question of belief or nonbelief. Therefore, it's not worth our time.

ATHEISTS ARE PEOPLE TOO

Hopefully more Christians will open their minds and hearts to atheists and attempt to understand what atheism really is. It can only help to keep in mind our shared ground of skepticism toward all other gods and religions. Christians might also try to remember that the atheist does not hate your god. She or he is simply unconvinced that a god is really there. It's nothing personal. Finally, Christians must recognize that atheists are not the enemy. For most people, an atheist or two can be found among family members, friends, colleagues, and neighbors. Many of them may keep their nonbelief private because they fear rejection or abuse, but they are there. Please don't be one of the people who stoke the flames of fear and prejudice. Be nice and be tolerant to atheists where you find them. You never know, one day, the atheist might even be you.

WHAT ARE MIRACLES?

He does great things too marvelous to understand.
He performs countless miracles.

—Job 9:10

Miracles do happen. Or maybe they don't. It seems to depend on who is defining what a miracle is and how sensibly the alleged miracle is assessed. Within the context of Christianity, a miracle is usually seen as any special occurrence performed by God, Jesus, the Holy Spirit, saints, or angels that does not conform to the normal workings of the natural world. Not all miracles must violate the laws of nature, however. Some are thought to be natural events that are too meaningful to have occurred by chance, such as when a person unintentionally misses a plane that later crashes. Missing a plane is not miraculous. But missing a doomed plane is. An important aspect of miracles is that they are often used to justify and reinforce belief in Jesus. Claims that Jesus performed miracles two thousand years ago and still does today are very important to many Christians. They believe that miracles occurring in modern times are powerful evidence, if not conclusive proof, that Jesus is a real god who is active in our daily lives.

Miracles certainly are popular in the United States. According to a 2009 survey by the Harris Poll®, 76 percent of adult Americans believe in miracles, and 95 percent of born-again Christians do.[1] But problems hover ominously over belief in miracles, one of which is the issue of interpretation. Different people can experience the same "miracle" and come away with very different conclusions about what actually happened. Prior belief seems to have a lot to do with who witnesses or experiences miracles and who doesn't. The people who see miracles are almost always people who already believed in them, much like ghost believers are far more likely to think they have encountered ghosts than are people who do not believe in them. Another problem for miracles is the common tendency of people everywhere to mistake the absence of a natural explanation for evidence of a supernatural cause. Sometimes the answer is just not available. Sometimes an answer is available, but it is not satisfying or convenient, so some choose to ignore or reject it. Then there are all the problems associated with not understanding mathematical probabilities and not being aware of how common miracle claims are in religions other than Christianity.

INTERPRETATION

Several years ago, I became very ill while on a poor man's safari in Kenya. I was deep in the bush with a tiny tent and way too much anxiety. My fever was high and I was scared. I knew I was in bad shape, but I didn't know if I had malaria, food poisoning, or just the flu. The nearest hospital was many miles from my campsite, so I had no choice but to ride it out and hope for the best.

I had been sick before, of course, but this was different. I was so far away from the world I knew. No friends, no family nearby. No phone to dial 911 if things got really bad. No ambulance would rush to my rescue if I took a turn for the worse. All I could do was keep cooking inside and hope that my immune system would win the war before it killed me. To make a strange evening even more so, some nearby lions began roaring extremely loudly. They didn't sound anything like the Hollywood lion roars I was raised on. Their repeated full-throated, low-frequency blasts made my feverish evening even weirder. I looked out of my tent but couldn't see them because of the trees and darkness. The lions were in different locations, perhaps clashing over territory or arranging a date. They seemed close, but I guessed that they were probably half a mile or more away. Too tired to be afraid, I returned to the tent to lie down and resume my suffering.

During the night, I needed to urinate, so I got up and walked several yards from my tent. The cool night air felt good, and, for reasons I'll never know, I kept walking. At some point during my foolish midnight trek, I collapsed. I don't know how long I slept in the tall grass, but when I woke up, I felt surprisingly good. My fever seemed to be gone. "Hey," I thought, "things are looking up." And then I saw him.

Standing close to me was one of the most unexpected and intimi-dating sights I've ever seen. A Massai man, wearing a tunic and holding a wicked-looking spear, stood less than five feet away. A lion would have scared me less. From my prone position, he looked fifteen feet tall. In that pose, spear in hand and illuminated by the moonlight, he looked capable of singlehandedly dispatching Xerxes's army. It was a strikingly beautiful scene—in retrospect. At that moment, however, it was terrifying. It was night, I was weak, disoriented, alone, and unsure if this guy intended to rob me, kill me, or just say "jambo" and offer me a friendly slug of cow's blood.

I spoke to him, but the expressionless Massai didn't respond. "Uh-oh, this might not go well," I thought. Realizing that I probably didn't look very impressive sprawled on the ground, I summoned up a bit of courage and strength for what might be my last stand. I rose to my feet slowly, keeping my eyes on him the whole time. Standing as upright as I could manage, I inflated my chest and tried to transmit through my posture a universal man-to-man message: "If we are going to do this, of course you and your spear are going to win—but I won't go down easy." Still hoping for the best, I smiled and spoke again, but he was unresponsive, so I slowly backed away and made it back to my campsite safely.

The next morning I felt great. A little stiff, but no fever and no dizziness. I told my guide how sick I had been. I may have also mentioned something about how I singlehandedly defended the camp from a midnight attack by Massai warriors. Then, unexpectedly, the man from last night came striding into camp. I couldn't believe it. He still had the spear, too. The man spoke with my guide, who then filled in the missing pieces for me about my late-night adventure. It turns out that the lions I had heard earlier in the evening were very close after all and the passing Massai either heard me fall in the grass or simply found me by chance. He believed that I had been in serious danger from the lions so he stood guard over me *for a few hours*. I was moved by his kindness, to say the least and thanked him repeatedly.

Looking back, I think it unlikely that the lions would have been interested in eating my pathetic, half-dead carcass, but who knows? My Massai friend may well have saved my life that night. Doesn't it seem very strange that a good-hearted man—armed with a spear, no less—would just happen to find me in the dark and decide to protect me from lions for half the night? But it did happen. So was it a miracle? Did heaven send me an angel in the form of an African tribesman to watch over me and keep me safe? It all depends on interpretation.

My conclusion about that night comes down to my prior attitude toward miracles. It is expected that unexpected things will happen over the course of a lifetime. There is little doubt, however, that if I were a Christian who believed in angels and miracles, I would have confidently concluded that my Massai encounter was proof that Jesus is real, that he cares about me, and that I had been in the presence of a miraculous guardian angel. I probably would go to my grave never doubting that a miracle had saved me that night. But because I'm a skeptic who tries to think like a good scientist would, I didn't see the event that way at all. It was dramatic, weird, and wonderful, yes, but supernatural? There is no evidence for that. Given the total absence of direct evidence for supernatural intervention, the only reasonable conclusion is that I benefited from a fortunate coincidence. I crossed paths with someone who was kind enough to care about a stranger's safety. Maybe it wasn't even such an unlikely coincidence. Maybe there are factors I don't know about. Maybe that man habitually wanders that area looking for dumb tourists to help. Maybe in a delirious state I screamed for help just before crash-landing. And, don't overlook the fact that, had I been a devout, miracle-believing Muslim, Hindu, or animist, I surely would have viewed it as a miracle, but with a key difference. The miracle would be credited to my particular god or gods and would have nothing to do with Jesus.

WHO BELIEVES IN MIRACLES?

American Adults	76%
Born-Again Christians	95%
Protestants	87%
Catholics	81%
Jews	63%[2]

IGNORANCE DOES NOT A MIRACLE MAKE

It's okay to admit it when we don't know things. Really, it's fine. In fact, pretending to know something we don't is dishonest. For example, I am not convinced that extraterrestrial spaceships have visited the Earth. I have looked at claims of ancient alien visitors and of modern-day UFOs buzzing our planet, and I have found no good evidence for them. However, just because I have the mind of a UFO skeptic doesn't mean I can't have the heart of a UFO believer. I want there to be something out there. My educated hunch is that there probably is. It's difficult to imagine that we are alone, given all the space, time, and opportunities for life beyond Earth. I would love for aliens to visit Earth—so long as they don't intend to eat or enslave us, of course. But I'm not so intellectually dishonest that I'm willing to suspend my thinking and pretend to know that extraterrestrials exist up in our skies or anywhere else in the universe. Until science confirms it, I can't know it. Shouldn't the same logic apply to miracles? If something happens that is highly unusual, and no explanation is readily available, isn't "I don't know" the only appropriate response? How can we justify leaping to the extraordinary conclusion that an unexplained event is the work of a god? Unknown means *unknown*.

I have traveled in more than twenty countries on five continents, and I have noticed that the less people know about basic science and the normal workings of the world, the more often they seem to see miracles. Even with significant formal education in other areas, people seem predisposed toward miracle belief if they have a weak science education. For example, I've seen firsthand that people who don't know much about medical science frequently call it a miracle when they or someone they know is treated and then recovers from an illness in a way that is considered routine in other societies. Religions may be the foundation of belief in miracles, but it is ignorance that often fuels it. To avoid unnecessarily offending anyone, it is important to point out that ignorance only means a lack of knowledge about something. If I say that someone claimed a miracle occurred because of ignorance, I'm not suggesting that the person is necessarily stupid or uneducated. The most brilliant person in a typical Iron Age village, for example, probably would have seen an eclipse as a miracle in large part because of her or his ignorance about basic astronomy.

Even many people today who lean toward skepticism might find themselves grasping for supernatural answers if they were sufficiently stumped intellectually and overwhelmed emotionally. Imagine encountering a time-traveling visitor from the far future or a highly advanced alien. Their technology might so thoroughly shock and baffle our twenty-first-century minds that magic would seem to be the only possible explanation. But we do not have everything figured out about nature and the universe, so it is foolish for anyone to presume to know where the natural ends and the supernatural begins, or to even assume such a border exists.

Having no available explanation in a given moment is never an excuse to make one up, which is what most miracle claimants do. Such claims are made-up responses to questions people can't answer. If a sick girl unexpectedly recovers from a serious illness and her doctor is at a loss to explain how, the default answer should not be "Jesus did it," unless someone can show evidence that Jesus really did do it. Ignorance proves nothing.

THE NUMBERS GAME

Christians are no different from the rest of the population when it comes to understanding probability. They are very bad at it too. Accurately estimating the likelihood of occurrences is not something we naturally excel at. Given the way our brains work, assessing odds and making calculations involving large sample sizes doesn't come easily to us. We are far more likely to be influenced by a good story we hear or by how we react emotionally to an event. If you don't believe me, go to Las Vegas and look at all the very expensive hotels and casinos that were paid for with money extracted from people who failed to recognize their own mathematical limitations.

More than two thousand years ago, Aristotle wrote that unlikely events are likely to happen. Before and after he wrote that, unexpected things that we could have expected have happened again and again, and countless millions of people have misinterpreted them as miracles. "What are the odds? It must be a miracle!" is the incessant chant of believers around the world when confronted with an event that seems to them impossibly unlikely. But this is only because they don't gauge probabilities well. For example, if something is said to have one-in-a-million odds, then it must be extremely rare, right? Maybe, but if you look at the big picture, it could be a different story. If only one person per million experiences some strange thing each day, then that means this "rare" event would occur seven thousand times per day and 2,555,000 times per year! This is because there are seven billion people on Earth. Even a one-in-a-billion event would still happen seven times a day and 2,555 times per year! To an individual Christian, however, experiencing one of these events may seem so fantastic and unexpected that only God could explain it. But once the relevant numbers are considered, it might not seem so special.

I have known several Christians, including a few friends and family members, who told me they have had dreams that were some kind of message from God/Jesus. Those I questioned about this extraordinary claim explained that the dream accurately predicted something that happened later and therefore could not have been "just a dream." This is a common claim, and the explanation is simple. How many dreams does a typical person have over the course of a lifetime? Probably many thousands, so, given all these dreams, isn't it likely that many people would have a few that just by chance seem to accurately predict future events?

Then we have to consider all the people in the world. With some seven billion people dreaming, don't you think it's likely that some significant number of people, maybe in the millions, will have dreams that just happen to accurately anticipate future events? It would be weird if no one ever had a dream that didn't foreshadow tomorrow or next year. There is also the problem of human memory. Try your best not to forget that it can't be trusted. Trying to accurately remember a dream is even more unreliable than trying to remember real-world events. Confirmation bias is also at work here, no doubt. A person can go his entire life having dreams that mean little or nothing and are soon forgotten, but the instant a single dream seems to have correctly predicted the future, it is hailed as "proof" that dreams are communications from God/Jesus. We should all try to keep in mind that remembering the hits and forgetting the misses is sloppy reasoning and can steer us offtrack from reality. We also have to consider the possibility of self-fulfilling prophecies. People can make predictions come true, which proves nothing about the source of the prediction. For example, someone might dream about dating her perfect mate and then, perhaps motivated consciously or subconsciously by the dream, ask the target of her desires out on a date and get a positive response. Nothing supernatural about it.

Consider how lotteries exploit our natural mental frailties. Every day, despite horrible odds, vast herds of people buy lottery tickets. They are seemingly unaware of what an outrageous long shot winning is. Truth is, each player is probably more likely to get struck by lightning than become an instant millionaire. But among the few who do win, there will be those who are tempted to think that their winning was divine intervention, a miracle arranged by Jesus. How could it not be a miracle, they might ask, given how unlikely it is to win a multi-million-dollar jackpot? The fact is, however, somebody does win those things, week after week, because that is how lotteries are designed. Just because the perspective of a winner is different from that of all the losers is no reason to conclude that Jesus picks winning numbers.

WHAT ABOUT ALL THE NON-CHRISTIAN MIRACLES?

From the perspective of an outsider, something is obviously wrong when Christians point to miracles as confirmation of Christianity's claims, because followers of virtually all other religions make the same claims with the same conviction and sincerity. For millennia, diverse believers have cited "miraculous" visions, healings, and events. They claim these miracles are proof that their belief system is right and all the other religions are wrong. Perhaps Christians don't realize it, but that list of "other religions" is extensive. It includes Muslims, Hindus, Sikhs, Buddhists, animists, Jews, New Agers, members of numerous ancient religions now out of favor, and so on. Perhaps attempting to prove one god is real over all the others by citing miracles works well if one is tucked safely inside the bubble of his own religion and is unaware that believers belonging to contradictory religions have been doing the same for thousands of years. The gods may change, but the game remains the same. Given the many logical conflicts, believers of so many religions cannot all be correct about miracles, and this simple truth casts doubt over all such claims.

How does the Christian who claims a weeping statue of Mary is a miracle explain the milk-drinking statues of the Hindu god Ganesha? How does the Christian who says a healing miracle proves the existence of Jesus feel about millions of claims of divine healings by Muslims and Hindus? What are we to make of the countless women and men throughout history and prehistory who saw miracles all around them and credited gods ignored today or long forgotten? It is difficult to understand how a Christian reasonably expects one to accept her miracles while ignoring or rejecting so many more outside of Christianity. Come to think of it, why don't Christians believe all those miracle claims that come from non-Christians? I suppose they are just too skeptical.

WE ARE ALL TOO EASY TO FOOL

A common justification for believing that Jesus is a god is that he performed miracles during his life. Setting aside for the moment that there are good reasons to doubt the accuracy of biblical reports about events that were supposed to have occurred two thousand years ago, one should not be too quick to accept the stories of miracles performed by Jesus because they may have been misinterpreted by observers. Even if such events were accurately reported by people who saw them, we cannot possibly know if they were actually supernatural feats or nothing more than well-executed illusions. It is important to keep in mind the time period during which Jesus was supposed to have lived. It would not have been difficult to amaze and baffle most people back then. For example, any mediocre magician today could easily have his or her way with an Iron Age audience. They wouldn't know what hit them. Soon after the first bunny rabbit was pulled out of a top hat, the audience would be on their knees. I am not suggesting that ancient people were necessarily dim thinkers, only that they were less aware of what magicians can do than we are today. Neither am I accusing Jesus of being a fraud. Maybe he was sincere in everything he said and did but his flair and confidence led observers to "see" things that did not happen. Do not underestimate how easy it for people to be misled.

We can see it today in rural India, where a plague of con men, known as "godmen" and "gurus," travel from village to village performing mostly mediocre tricks in order to spook unsophisticated locals and separate them from their money. Imagine if Harry Houdini, David Copperfield, James Randi, or David Blaine were to walk the Earth two thousand years ago. Do you think any of them would have any difficulty convincing virtually everyone they performed for that they were sorcerers or maybe even gods?

WHY NOT MIRACLES FOR ALL?

Many Christians see miracles as signs from Jesus to grab the attention of believers and strengthen their belief. Maybe, but doesn't this seem like a misdirected effort? Why do Jesus and other gods almost always perform their miracles exclusively for people who are already convinced? If miracles are important signs, then why aren't they unambiguous and why don't they occur in front of people who are skeptical and have good critical-thinking skills? If one of the purposes of miracles is to inspire belief, then who needs miracles more than skeptics and atheists?

Given what we know about how common miracle claims are throughout the religious world, both now and in the past, it should be clear that most miracles can be explained as exaggerations, lies, or mis-interpretations of coincidences and natural occurrences. Even a claim that might defy explanation should not automatically become certified as a supernatural event based on nothing more than not knowing how it occurred. Common sense should tell us that our ignorance proves nothing, least of all the existence of gods.

DOES THE COMPLEXITY OF LIFE
REVEAL AN INTELLIGENT DESIGNER?

Several years ago, I was on a talk show promoting science and skepticism when the topic of religious belief came up. I politely shared a few basic reasons why the existence of a god or gods is uncertain. The host or a caller, I can't remember, responded with that popular line from the believer's playbook: "But just look outside," he said. "Look at all the life. Look at a single leaf. It's so complex and mysterious, but it works and it had to come from somewhere, right? What more evidence for God do you need?"

Pointing at life's complexity is an immensely popular "commonsense" justification for belief in the Christian god (and other gods, as well). One can easily see why this works for so many people. Life and the things life can do really are astonishingly complex. The abilities of our own brain and body to coordinate and perform simple tasks such as picking up a piece of paper are remarkable. Even with all our considerable achievements in engineering and computing power, we are unable to build a self-contained machine that comes close to matching the human body movement for movement, much less thought for thought. And we are just one small piece of the puzzle. We share this world with a staggering number of species. According to one recent estimate, for every person alive today, there are ten million trillion microbes on the seafloor alone.[1] From blue whales to bacteria, life saturates virtually all the Earth's surface zone. Within this vast brew of life, there are orchestras of genes at play that produce an endless stream of unique individual creatures. Plants, fungi, tiny arthropods, and microbes live in strange parallel worlds all around us. Mostly beyond our notice, they exploit, influence, help, and sometimes harm us.

Life is so abundant, complex, and widespread that we don't even know how many species exist today. There are just too many species in too many habitats for us to count. We know relatively little about the microbes on and inside our own bodies. Yes, it's the twenty-first century, and we probably have a better understanding of the Moon than we do the microbial ecosystem that is every human being. For both the scientist and the layperson, thinking about the amount of life and how physically and behaviorally diverse it all is can seem incomprehensible and feel overwhelming. It is certainly understandable why many people would want to throw their hands up in the air and conclude that it can only be the work of a god. It seems like a reasonable hunch that it couldn't have "just happened all by itself." Life *is* complex, and, in many ways, life *is* beyond our comprehension today. But a hunch—no matter how comfortable and satisfying it may feel—is not necessarily the correct answer to an important question. Sometimes important questions have maddeningly complex or inconvenient answers that neither satisfy nor soothe. Sometimes we just have to accept that there are no available answers, at least for the time being.

Contrary to what some science advocates say, the problems with creationism and intelligent design are not obvious. If they were, people wouldn't keep relying on it, generation after generation. It's also too easy to write it off as science illiteracy. If people just understood a little modern biology, says the frustrated professor, they wouldn't think this way. It's not that simple, however. I have encountered people who know more than a little modern biology and even accept evolution as the process by which life changes over time. But they still think it makes perfect sense to default to their god as the answer to science's unanswered questions about the origin of life and other remaining mysteries, for example. They point to a big, fat blank in our scientific knowledge about how it all started and fill in "God." They are correct about there being a gap in our knowledge. Scientists today have very respectable ideas on the matter but no conclusive answer at this time. Let's be fair, however. It's tough to scientifically pin down the details of an event that happened more than three or four billion years ago at least. The key point some Christians miss is that scientific ignorance about the beginning of life, or any of life's processes, is not evidence of a god. Sometimes we need to be brave enough and patient enough to leave a question unanswered for the time being. Keep working the problem, sure, but don't cheat by inserting a solution we haven't earned through effort.

HOW DID GOD DO IT?

An effective way to help people see for themselves that there is a problem with this idea of biological complexity and scientific unknowns proving that a god created life is to turn it around and launch it right back at them. If my inability to provide a comprehensive, detailed, evidence-based explanation for life's origin and every complex biological function means a god is real, then believers are obligated to answer the following question: *How* did God create all this life and *how* does he control or guide it? No believers, of any religion, can answer that. They don't even try. There are many creation stories in many religions, of course. They may mention the gods' names and some creation ingredients such as dirt, dust, mud, bones, water, spit, semen, and so on, but they are silent on *how*. It's just some undefined and unexplained magical act. "Who" does not answer "how?" There is no formula offered, no theory of biochemical creation involving the interaction of supernatural energy with natural atoms as an explanation. There is nothing remotely like what science has produced with its evidence-based ideas about life's origin and evolution.

So what does this inability to explain how the Christian god created life say about his existence? By the same logic of the "look at a leaf" argument, it means God is not real and did not create life. Saying, "A natural origin of life is complex and you can't explain it in complete detail so *God* must have done it" is no better than a biologist saying, "A divine origin of life is complex and you can't explain it in complete detail so *nature* must have done it." Of course I don't think that the inability of Christians to describe every step of divine creation proves that God didn't create life. I'm only pointing out that a gap in knowledge is just that and nothing more. It's a mistake to base an extraordinary claim on ignorance, which is precisely what the intelligent-design idea does. Annoying unanswered questions don't have to be seen as negative reasons to surrender anyway. They can be great motivation to keep searching and continue working on problems. But they prove nothing other than the fact that we don't know everything.

THE IRREDUCIBLE COMPLEXITY OF A BAD IDEA

Anyone who honestly investigates intelligent design is likely to notice fairly quickly that it's not substantially different from old-school creationism. It's been dressed up and adorned with science-y language. It's also generally not burdened with the overtly nonsensical claim of a six-thousand-year-old Earth. But it's still faith-based creationism. And, just like traditional creationists, intelligent-design proponents fight for their claim in all the wrong places. They call it science but seem to have little interest in doing science. One would think that anyone who has a respectable theory would want to carve out a place for it in the science community the way it's normally done. Their theory would show up in credible science journals so that scientists anywhere in the world could look it over, double-check the data, and replicate experiments in order to either confirm or disprove its conclusions.

Intelligent-design advocates ought to be arguing for acceptance in the places were science ideas win acceptance. But they don't. Their battlegrounds always seem to be popular media, courtrooms, political campaigns, and school-board meetings. Thoughtful Christians might want to think long and hard about this. If intelligent design is real science, then the real scientific process will confirm it. In other words, if intelligent design is what its proponents say it is, all the action should be taking place in laboratories where experiments are conducted and out in the field where fossils are found and specimens collected. The reality is far different, however, and suggests that the leaders of the intelligent-design movement know they can't win with evidence or the merits of their argument, so they have resigned themselves to a public-relations campaign instead.

To understand how inappropriate the marketing of intelligent design is, imagine if Moon-landing-hoax proponents filed lawsuits, launched petition drives, raised funds, and pressured school boards to teach their unproven claim as absolute fact in elementary, middle, and high schools. Or what if psychic/medium James Van Praagh spearheaded a well-funded lobbying effort to have the course Science of Communicating with the Dead taught in high school and university psychology classes? What would be the difference? They would have the same amount of scientific evidence for their position as intelligent-design advocates have for theirs—none.

No one, Christian or non-Christian, should allow themselves to be hoodwinked by intelligent design's central concept of "irreducible complexity." With a little bit of thought, it's easy to recognize why it's unworthy of our time. The claim of irreducible complexity says there comes a point in our current scientific analysis of life when no more explanations are available. We can explain many things about a living cell, for example, but not everything. There is an inevitable wall one reaches where the answers stop coming. This is the "leaf argument" all over again, only this time believers are saying, "Look at this *cell*. It's so complex and mysterious, but it works and it had to come from somewhere, right? What more evidence for God do you need?" Just as it was with the leaf challenge, our current ignorance about every detail associated with the workings and origins of a cell do not prove the existence or involvement of a god. First of all, give science a chance. We haven't been serious about doing science for very long. Considering the funding and resources we devote to it compared to other things, one can argue that we haven't started taking it seriously yet. We tend to forget, but our species was focused on little more than scrounging up berries and avoiding being eaten by large cats a relatively brief moment ago. I think we need to work on the problems a while longer before anyone throws in the towel and declares that some things are unknowable to science and therefore can only be the work of gods.

HAVE YOU READ THE BIBLE?

People who come to be religious skeptics and nonbelievers through a thoughtful process of research and discussion are inevitably surprised to discover an odd thing about Christians. Few seem to have actually read the Bible in its entirety! And those who have don't seem to retain many of the key points and stories contained in it. What's going on? Do the majority of Christians, including biblical literalists, really go no further than reading a few select passages here and there? Are preachers and popular culture, rather than the Bible, the primary source of Christian education among Christians? If so, this is a bizarre situation, to say the least. The Bible is widely believed to be history's number-one bestseller. It's supposed to be packed with amazing stories of supernatural events, details about God, and God's preference for how we should conduct our lives. To varying degrees, Christians believe that the Bible is the most important book of all time—and yet very few of them take the time to read it from cover to cover.

This weird phenomenon of Bible believers not bothering to read the Bible is not based on some personal hunch of which I am accusing Christians unfairly. In 2013 a Protestant preacher told me that he estimates no more than 15 to 20 percent of his parishioners read the Bible on a regular basis. Many Christians do read the Bible, of course. Some read it on a regular basis, even daily, but *how* are they reading it? Are they working their way through it, page by page and line by line? Or are they merely leapfrogging from familiar sentences to comforting stories? One can spend a lifetime bouncing back and forth between popular passages without ever reading the more challenging and disturbing parts of the Bible.

I have consistently found this to be the case during discussions and interviews with Christians all around the world. As most religious skeptics know, it's common for Christians to react with surprise or to express outright denial when asked about some of the more awkward, bizarre, and disturbing passages found in the Bible. Many Christians are surprised to hear about the murder of babies, the God-approved kidnapping and rape of female virgins in pillaged cities, the tips on how to be a good slave and an even better slave owner, the graphic description of extraordinarily well-endowed men and their spectacular ejaculations, the cooking and eating of dung, the executions of homosexuals, and so on. Many times Christians have confidently declared to me that such things could not possibly be in the Bible. "No way. Impossible," they say—until I show it to them. There may be reasonable arguments to be made for many of these excerpts regarding context or interpretation, but the fact remains that they are there and Christians should not be oblivious to them. Anytime one hears a Christian announcing that Bibles should be issued to children in all schools, it's a dead giveaway that this person has not read the entire Bible. The truth is, one might get arrested for reading aloud some parts of it to an elementary-school class.

It's not that Christians are insincere about their belief in Jesus or that they don't care what the Bible says. They just don't seem sufficiently motivated to do the actual hard work of reading it and retaining the information. Perhaps they feel it's not necessary because they already know all the important stuff, having picked it up from church sermons, parents, friends, and family. Maybe they tried to read it but gave up after getting bogged down in the dense genealogy data of the Old Testament. It could be that the language is too awkward for them. The text of the King James Version reads like a foreign language to many modern-day English speakers. Or, maybe the parts about God's violence, jealousy, and punishments make readers feel uneasy because such things conflict so starkly with the popular image of a forgiving and loving god.

Whatever the reason, most Christians don't read the Bible with the same commitment and enthusiasm that they might bring to one of those Left Behind novels about the rapture or even a John Grisham crime thriller. This is not my opinion. It's a fact revealed by multiple studies and is a source of much concern among some Christians. For example, George Barna, the Christian founder of the Barna Group, views the level of Bible readership in the United States as an embarrassment and a crisis for his religion. His marketing company specializes in gathering data about Christians and Christianity, so he knows this issue well. "American Christians are biblically illiterate," Barna says. "Although most of them contend that the Bible contains truth and is worth knowing, and most of them argue that they know all of the relevant truths and principles, our research shows otherwise. And the trend line is frightening: the younger a person is, the less they understand about the Christian faith. By and large, people parrot what their parents taught them. Sadly, with fewer and fewer parents teaching their kids much of anything related to matters of faith, young people's belief system is the product of the mass media."[1]

THE BIBLE BY THE NUMBERS

- 93 percent of Americans say they own a Bible.
- 41 percent of Americans own a King James Version of the Bible.
- Only 13 percent know that the KJV is paraphrased from earlier English versions.
- 41 percent say that they rarely or never read the Bible.
- 61 percent say the Bible should be easier to read.
- 49 percent of adult Americans think the Bible is the "actual word of God."
- 30 percent of adult Americans think the Bible is the "inspired word of God but not everything in it should be taken literally."
- 17 percent of adult Americans think the Bible is an "ancient book of fables, legends, history, and moral precepts recorded by man."
- 29 percent think the Bible is difficult to read out of necessity because it "must convey the loftiness of God's word."
- 14 percent of Americans report that they are currently in a Bible study group.
- Women are much more likely than men to read the Bible at least weekly. About 43 percent of women say they read the Bible either weekly or daily, compared to 29 percent of men.[2]

It may surprise some people, but 44 percent of American Catholics "rarely or never" read the Bible.[3] David R. Carlin, Catholic author of *The Decline and Fall of the Catholic Church in America*, blames his church for the fact that so many Catholic Americans aren't curious enough about what's in the Bible to open it: "The leadership of the Church in the United States has been guilty of many failures in recent times—the sex-abuse scandal, a failure to resist the sexual revolution, a failure to mobilize Catholics effectively as an anti-abortion cultural force. Add to these failures the failure to persuade Catholics to become a Bible-reading people."[4]

Stephen Prothero, a professor at Boston University's Religion Department, was so disturbed by the astounding levels of ignorance about Christianity among Christians that he wrote a book about it: *Religious Literacy: What Every American Needs to Know—and Doesn't.* The book contains many fascinating items: Only 10 percent of American teenagers can name five major world religions, and 15 percent can't name any of them. Only half of American adults can name at least one of the four Gospels (Matthew, Mark, Luke, John). A majority of Americans can't identity the first book of the Bible (Genesis). Prothero is blunt about America's strange relationship with religion: "Here faith is almost entirely devoid of content. One of the most religious countries on earth is also a nation of religious illiterates."[5]

A secondary but no less serious problem is that Bible illiteracy adds to the issue of ignorance about religion in general. It's no surprise, of course, that those Christians who can't find the motivation to read their own sacred book aren't likely to get around to reading anyone else's either. Tragically, ignorance about the various world religions fuels the fear and prejudice that can lead to hate and violence. It's not that all these religious people are dumb; they just aren't making the effort to read what is supposed to be "God's word" and the crucial guidebook for life.

The inevitable result of so many people failing to read and absorb the Bible is that most Christians today are unfamiliar with or don't understand the tenets of their own religion. This is not about being able to pass Bible trivia quizzes or achieving consistency between the Bible and the behavior of believers. It's about a lack of basic awareness of what is in the Bible, which is supposed to be the basis for Christianity. Like all religions, Christianity is flexible and today offers many versions for its adherents. For a Christian to be a Christian, one is not obligated to believe every claim or follow every rule found in the Bible. But it seems strange that Christians would not want to be informed for themselves beyond what they hear in movies or are exposed to in highly selective sermons and sound bites. If a Christian rejects the claim of the Holy Trinity, for example, that's his or her choice. But shouldn't that Christian at least understand something about the concept of the Holy Trinity and be aware that it is mentioned in the Bible before passing on it?

I'm sure that Christians do not want to say things and hold positions that blatantly contradict some of the more important points made in the Bible and then say with their next breath that they think that everything in the Bible should be believed and followed to the letter. But many do exactly that every day. I respect Christians enough to assume that they want to be well informed and intellectually consistent about their religious beliefs. I also am sure that Christians would not want to be misled or manipulated by those preachers and politicians who would take advantage of biblical illiteracy among believers. This is why Christians need to read their book—all of it—including the parts that may be disturbing, boring, and perhaps even threatening to their personal beliefs.

NONHUMAN MORALITY? Some say our moral instincts could only have come from the Christian god. Therefore, our ability to recognize some acts as good and others as evil is itself proof of that god's existence. However, some nonhuman animals, such as bonobos, exhibit what most people would describe as moral behavior. This suggests that our morality may have a natural origin too. *Photo by the author.*

WHY DO SOME CHRISTIANS DO BAD THINGS IN THE SIGHT OF JESUS?

The eyes of the Lord are in every place, keeping watch on the evil and the good.
—Proverbs 15:3

I have no interest in trying to tally up bad deeds by people who happen to be Christian. That kind of scorekeeping is only useful as a counterargument against those who make the spurious claim that Christianity ensures good behavior and atheism leads to bad. The truth is, crimes and mischief committed by Christians don't prove anything one way or the other about central claims that Jesus is a god, that the Bible is the inspired word of God, that heaven and hell exist, and so on. But there is an important question to be considered here: How is it that so many Christians are able to do bad things when they supposedly believe that a judgmental god is close to them at all times and sees everything they do? From the perspective of an outsider like me, this doesn't add up. Are misbehaving Christians so impulsive that they just can't stop themselves—even though they know God is present and staring right at them? Or could it be that they are less confident in the existence of an omniscient and omnipresent god than they let on?

It is important for readers not to confuse this question about Christian behavior with an attack on Christians for falling short of perfection. Of course some Christians do very bad things, just as some non-Christians do very bad things. Many Christians lead remarkably ethical lives, and some are despicable beyond belief. Most, however, fall somewhere in between, very much like the other five billion on Earth. The specific question being addressed here is how so many Christians are able to cheat, lie, and even commit very serious crimes while professing to know that their god is always near them.

This makes no sense to an atheist. If my mother were to stand no more than three feet away from me every second of my waking life, I would find it nearly impossible to even utter a mild curse word, much less commit a crime. And yet my mother can't send me to hell forever. She is nothing more than a mere mortal woman whom I respect and love and wouldn't want to upset. If I knew for certain that an all-powerful god who would one day decide my eternal fate was always within arm's reach, I can't imagine allowing myself to lie, steal, rape, murder, or swipe candy out of my children's trick-or-treat bag when they aren't looking. Yet people who say they believe in Jesus and call themselves Christian do this stuff every day. Prisons in America are stuffed full with people who did bad things—even though they believe God exists and is always watching. This doesn't make any sense. Shouldn't it be atheists, believing they are not being watched, who commit virtually all the crimes and fill up all the prisons, while people who believe in an omnipresent god lead spotless lives out of either respect or fear? But this is far from the world we see.

Consider the examples of the Catholic Church and the Pennsylvania State University child-sex scandals. Precise numbers are impossible to come by, but it appears that thousands of Catholic priests have molested and raped stunningly large numbers of children in recent decades. The Church leadership's reaction in many cases was to cover it up and allow predator priests to continue harming children, a course of action arguably as evil as the original crimes. In 2012, a former Penn State football coach, Jerry Sandusky, was found guilty of sexually assaulting ten young boys and is suspected of abusing many more. Sandusky is a Christian. He attended St. Paul's Methodist Church in the town of State College, Pennsylvania, for thirty years.[1] It is reasonable to assume that he believed Jesus pays close attention to the activities of Christians. One can understand the power of some impulses, the lust, greed, anger within that can make some of us do things that might later be regretted, but to repeatedly rape children over many years? To coldly calculate and plan ways to be alone with children for the purpose of abusing them? And every rape in the sight and presence of God? How? How did Sandusky and all those priests commit these horrible crimes against children with Jesus standing right next to them in the room? He may have been invisible, but he was there, according to millions of Christians. I hate to keep bringing my mother into this, but I cannot imagine so much as harming a kitten if she were watching me. The idea of harming a child, with my mother or God watching, is incomprehensible.

To be fair, it is necessary to exclude from this scenario Christians who have done terrible things that they believed God wanted them to do. So we probably can't consider cases of mothers killing their children because they thought it would send them to heaven, Crusaders butchering defenseless women and children, popes having people burned alive, or David Koresh shooting at federal agents. If they sincerely believed they were doing God's will—and how we can we know for sure that they didn't?—they get a pass here. Some behavior, however, is difficult, if not impossible, to shield with divine sanction. For example, it's pretty hard to imagine priests defending child rape as something Jesus approved of. But it's not only the extreme cases that call into question the widespread claim that Jesus sees all. What about relatively minor acts of dishonesty and cruelty? How many Christians cheat on their tax returns, cheat on tests in high school and college, lie to spouses, backstab colleagues, mistreat animals, or verbally abuse children? How do they manage to do these things when God is supposed to be observing them all the time? It just doesn't make sense. The "Christians aren't perfect" defense doesn't hold up because nobody is suggesting that Christians are perfect, only that most Christians should be smart enough and have enough self-control to resist criminal acts, bad behavior, and blatant dishonesty if, as they say, the most important eyewitness of all is watching them.

ARE BAD CHRISTIANS REAL CHRISTIANS?

It is necessary to address a response that often comes up whenever the issue of terrible deeds by Christians is raised. Some claim that no real Christian can murder or rape children, for example, because the moralizing force of Christianity would make such behavior impossible. "He wasn't really a Christian" may sound like a great escape from the awkward reality of bad Christians, but it doesn't work. Behavior does not define a Christian, only the professed belief in Jesus as a god does that. The only fair, sensible, practical way to sort out who adheres to religious belief is to do it from outside of the belief because people within a religion never agree on anything. Furthermore, if behavior defined who is a "real" Christian, then there were would be no Christians in the world because all versions of Christianity are rejected by one rival Christian group or another. Even specific behaviors are too subjective to judge and can't be used. Some say real Christians can't get divorced, listen to rock music, or work on Sundays (or Saturdays), while others say none of that matters. Some say a Christian must to go to church; others say it's not necessary.

Adherents of all versions of Christianity may claim they are doing what God wants and reject all others as genuine Christians. This cross-fire gets us nowhere, of course, which is why a basic secular description of who is a Christian is necessary: If one believes in Jesus and worships or follows him in some manner, then she or he is a Christian. It's as simple as that. Sure, some public Christians might be private atheists, but one can't pretend to know something like that just because their behavior is objectionable. I don't like the way Joseph Stalin conducted his life, but I certainly won't pretend to know that he wasn't a "real" atheist because of it. If he didn't believe in any gods, then he was an atheist. His behavior is irrelevant to that designation. Simple as that.

I can't read minds, so this is only speculation, but I suspect many Christians do not really believe with great confidence that a god is literally present at all times. If two billion Christians actually thought this was true, wouldn't our world be much different? Wouldn't the crime rate be dramatically lower in societies with strong Christian majorities such as the United States, Mexico, Jamaica, and Brazil? It is easy for people to say they "know" Jesus is always watching, but actions speak louder than words.

HOW CAN WE BE SURE ABOUT THE RESURRECTION?

The brutality, horror, and repulsiveness of Jesus's death, according to Christians, is outweighed by the wonder, beauty, and allure of his resurrection. It is *the* most glorious and important event in all of history. It is also the key to Christianity's superiority over other religions, they say. Other miracles pale in comparison to the moment Jesus ascended to heaven. More preachers and lay Christians have declared to me, "The tomb was empty!" than I can remember. For two thousand years, Christians have been telling the story of how Jesus rose from the dead. But did it happen? It's a key challenge, one that has to be true if Christianity is true. No less than Paul, probably the most influential architect of the Christian religion, wrote, "If Christ be not raised, your faith is vain" (1 Corinthians 15:17).

The simple question that every skeptic asks is, How do we know that Jesus wasn't just a man who died like every other person has or will? Where's the proof for this extraordinary claim that he did not remain dead? Plenty of "proof" is offered, of course, but none of it proves anything to the typical nonbeliever. For very honest and respectable reasons, skeptics are unconvinced. Keep in mind that identifying problems with the story of Jesus's resurrection is not the same as claiming to have disproved it. The burden of proof lies with the Christians who make the claim. There is no burden on the nonbeliever's shoulders to disprove. Rather than get frustrated or assume that every skeptic has a closed mind, Christians should try to understand the reasons so many people have doubts. For their part, skeptics should strive to target their passion and energy toward the claims rather than the person making them. Doing so can often reduce the tensions in both camps that so often lead nowhere.

I don't take the resurrection story lightly. I understand how important it is and has been for billions of people spread across two thousand years of history. I am aware of the loyalty many people have for it, and I respect the good people who have embraced it as factual. But like any good skeptic, my respect for others and my appreciation of their emotional investments do not mean I have to keep silent when simple questions need to be asked. Whenever I discuss the resurrection of Jesus with Christians, I don't approach it like a debate. I don't feel a need to make them agree with me just for the sake of agreeing with me. I want Christians to think for themselves, think more deeply about extraordinary claims such as that empty tomb, and draw their own conclusions rather than simply accept an ancient story they were told about or read in a book. I explain to Christians that I'm not committed to a negative position. If it really did happen, then I sincerely want them to convince me so I can be better aligned with reality. Like most skeptics, I'm open-minded. I don't think I can disprove that Jesus supernaturally vanished from his tomb, so I don't bother trying. I ask Christians how they can be sure that Jesus rose to heaven and then I listen. To date, however, I have not heard a convincing case for the resurrection.

The following is a brief rundown of some reasons many Christians say they "know" that the resurrection of Jesus really happened. Very basic skeptical responses follow. This is by no means a complete list, but it does show where the conflicts arise.

People died for Jesus. Why would anyone die for Jesus if he wasn't who the Bible says he was? Christians point to the apostles who were martyred and the early Christians who were tortured and executed for their religion, and they ask, who would do that for a lie or a hoax? Most people wouldn't voluntarily die for a lie or a hoax, but many would. It's not hard to imagine a con artist getting caught in a web of lies but deciding to stick to his story all the way to the grave. Maybe it's a case of pride or the hope that projecting confidence will somehow win out in the end. More likely, however, early Christians stuck to their beliefs in the face of death because they sincerely believed.

It's not rare for people to believe something that is certainly or probably not true and be willing to die for it. Christians are pretty sure that Islam is an inaccurate belief system, but some Muslims trust it enough to fly planes into buildings and strap bombs to their bodies. During World War II, Japanese kamikaze pilots flew suicide missions, in part at least, for their "divine" emperor. Most Christians probably think David Koresh was not Christianity's final prophet, but he and some others apparently believed it enough to die in a violent confrontation with federal agents. Human passion and commitment are not evidence of a god or supernatural event. Passionate belief, even to the point of sacrificing one's life for it, is only evidence of belief itself.

Paul's conversion. The apostle Paul did more to spread Christianity in its early days than anyone. Without him, Christianity might not have endured long enough to gain a foothold and thrive. Remarkably, Paul had been persecuting Christians until he "saw" the resurrected Jesus on his way from Jerusalem to Damascus. Something caused a radical change in his way of thinking, no doubt. But skeptics see no proof or good evidence of a resurrected god in this story. People say they see amazing things all the time. Unusual stories are not unusual. Furthermore, many people make 180-degree turns in their lives without necessarily citing a god as the reason.

We know that eyewitness accounts of natural events are unreliable, so how can we trust eyewitness accounts of supernatural events? It's fine to trust Paul's word that he believed he saw Jesus that night, but we can't be sure that he did not hallucinate, misperceive, or misremember events. It's nothing personal against him. If he was human, with human eyes and a human brain, then some sort of down-to-earth psychological explanation is much more plausible than an actual encounter with a supernatural being.

The tomb was empty. Says who? Many Christians think this is a tough one for skeptics to deal with because no one can prove that one specific tomb in Jerusalem wasn't empty two thousand years ago. The best one can do is tell people who make this claim that the limited collection of sources that say Jesus's tomb was empty are the same limited collection of sources that say he was resurrected. These are hardly objective sources. It's not like we have corroborating Roman military reports that also mention the missing body of a certain Jewish messiah.

Even if we allow ourselves to accept the Bible's account of what happened to Jesus's body as accurate reporting of what people really said at the time, the empty-tomb claim is still based on hearsay about eyewitness accounts. How can we accept that? It's too important to accept on the word of fallible human beings alone. They could have lied or been honestly mistaken.

Five hundred witnesses. Much is made by some Christians about the number of people who Paul says saw the resurrected Jesus after his death. But no one knows who these five hundred people were or where they saw Jesus. Hundreds of witnesses may sound impressive until you consider that many more people than that have "seen" UFOs and Bigfoot. Anonymous witnesses from ancient times, no matter how many, are just not sufficient to confirm something so important. This is one of the first things skeptics think about when they hear this argument for the resurrection. Remember, for good skeptics the quality and quantity of evidence needs to at least balance the weight of the claim.

Paul wrote that he, too, saw the resurrected Jesus. Maybe he made up or exaggerated the number of other witnesses in order to support his story of a personal encounter. No one knows, but it's certainly possible. Or maybe his claim of five hundred sincere witnesses was accurate, but even then, it would still not be enough to prove that Jesus rose from the dead after his execution. We know that hundreds out of many thousands can experience similar dreams or hallucinations. People can also lie. They do it all the time. How many people say they see ghosts each year? Thousands? Millions, perhaps? These may be sincere, sane, and intelligent people, but because of what we know about the fallibility of our vision and memory, ghosts rightly remain an unproven claim. It may be tempting to think that numbers are proof, but they are not when it comes to supernatural events, paranormal phenomena, and, yes, resurrected gods. Something more than a list or number of witnesses is required. Besides, Christians probably don't want to play the game of adding up eyewitness accounts to determine if a god is real and a religious claim is true because they will lose. Many other religions can point to their own witnesses who say they saw non-Christian gods and spirits. How can we discount all these claims but not those of Paul and his five hundred?

Roman guards don't sleep on duty. A surprisingly popular and enduring justification for belief in the empty-tomb claim is that Roman guards were supposed to have been right outside guarding it. Only a resurrection could explain the missing body because Roman guards of the day knew they would be punished severely, maybe killed, if their negligence enabled someone to steal the body. If they slept on the job or accepted a few coins to look the other way, it could have been the end of them. This is not a sound argument. Are we to believe that no soldier in the history of the Roman Empire ever stole a quick nap on duty, were corruptible, or were incompetent? That's far-fetched. Many people in many different cultures and time periods have defied threats of severe punishment to engage in activities that put them at risk.

THE BIBLE PROVES IT HAPPENED

Finally, there is always the option of diving into the Bible and ferreting out details that either support or oppose the resurrection. Compile enough tiny bits, a word here and a quote there, and maybe you can prove Jesus did or did not rise from the tomb. This is where theologians and preachers head off to fight their battles against that breed of skeptics who love nitpicking the Bible. But some skeptics, like me, prefer to stick to the big picture. We see it as largely a waste of time to argue over discrepancies between resurrection stories. I don't really care if Mark says three women came to the tomb and Matthew says it was only two. I couldn't care less if it was daytime (Mark 16:2) or nighttime (John 20:1). For a big claim, I need big proof, so even if the Bible did get the number of women correct and the time of day right, I would still ask for more, a lot more.

Before I spend time bickering over the small stuff, I need Christians to explain why anyone should trust ancient texts written by anonymous authors in the first place. Skeptics are always wary of circular arguments, so trying to use the Bible to prove the most important claim in the Bible will never work. Christians must understand that skeptics are not convinced that the Bible is a reliable, much less inerrant, source of information about events that may or may not have happened thousands of years ago. So how can they trust it to make the case about a claim so important and unusual as a man-god's body vanishing from a tomb and rising to heaven? It's just not going to work. The Bible is an important collection of ancient texts and has had a profound impact on the world, no doubt about that, but the stories it contains are just not enough by themselves to prove that the resurrection occurred.

THE RELIABILITY OF ANCIENT JOURNALISM

One of the reasons I cringe when Christians try to make their stand on the resurrection by pointing to reports of it found in the Bible is that I know a little something about the reporting of events. After more than twenty years of experience in television and print news media, I can say with absolute certainty that you can't trust everything you see on TV or read in print. From up close and in the trenches I have seen facts mangled, truth twisted, and reality revised in ways that would shock and horrify trusting news consumers—and that's just in the sports section! It's worse in hard news.

When I founded a small charity, began writing books, and did other minor newsworthy things, I suddenly found myself on the other side of the news game, and it was eye-opening. Instead of asking the questions, I was the one being asked. Instead of writing someone else's story, someone wrote mine. Most of the time, the experience was positive. Several times, however, I would read stories about myself that included errors and misleading information. I would be dumbfounded as to how such incorrect information crept in to what was a pretty straightforward and routine report. Even a simple announcement about a lecture or book-signing event might name the wrong venue or include a butchered quote that made it seem as if I didn't know how to speak English. I found these cases to be so strange because straight news reporting is usually relatively easy. You ask good questions, find out the important information, and then write it up as plainly and directly as possible. But the reality is that mistakes happen and sometimes the reporting is done by incompetent people.

I remember misspelling the name of a man I interviewed in a story. It was years ago, and it still bothers me. As was my habit during in-person interviews, I asked him to spell his name and then showed it to him in my handwritten notes to confirm that I had spelled it correctly. Back at the office an hour later, however, I still managed to misspell it. Honest mistakes are made all the time. Some journalists are just chronically sloppy and others are hopelessly lazy. I've known several who were both sloppy and lazy. I knew one journalist who made up quotes. When it comes to consuming news, all I can say is, be careful. All journalists, no matter how good, make errors. Sometimes things go wrong and it's not even their fault. More than once, page-layout people have put the wrong headline above one of my stories and other times have placed the wrong story under the right headline. It's the twenty-first century, and human beings have not yet perfected the task of reporting events accurately. So, if professional journalists at the *New York Times*, BBC, and *Yomiuri Shimbun* can't get it right 100 percent of the time when reporting on events that happened yesterday or last week, the obvious question is, How can we trust reports by anonymous amateurs about something that happened two thousand years ago?

Maybe Jesus was a god. Maybe he did magically vanish from inside that tomb. I don't know. But what I do know is that Christians have not proved that he did. And until they do, those of us who are unwilling to suspend their critical thinking and skepticism will not accept this claim. It's simply a case of too much claim and too little evidence.

HOW DO WE KNOW THAT HEAVEN IS REAL?

For God so loved the world, that he gave his only Son, that
whoever believes in him should not perish but have eternal life.
—John 3:16

Heaven is the most appealing promise Christianity makes. It is central to the religion, the reason Jesus came to Earth and died for us. His gory blood sacrifice gave us the opportunity to defeat death and live forever in a better place. Undoubtedly, this post-death paradise is the primary motivation for many people to become or remain Christian. But slow down! Why would anyone think this place really exists in the first place? It's one of the most amazing and spectacular claims ever made. How can we trust it? Where is the proof? Some think heaven is real because they trust the Bible and the Bible says it is. But that's not good enough for people who are also skeptical of the Bible's accuracy. More than written words, they need compelling evidence, if not conclusive proof, in order to take seriously a claim this big. Keep in mind, heaven is supposed to be a perfect place where one dwells with God for eternity after dying. Few claims in the history of humankind are larger than this one. How can we be expected to just believe that it exists without some very good reasons to? Skeptics might agree with Christians that a heaven in some form or another is worth hoping for, but that's very different from "knowing" that it really exists.

Many Christians say they have that proof. They point to near-death experiences and out-of-body experiences that involve a person "dying," perhaps even visiting heaven, and then returning to Earth alive. Across cultures a few key descriptions of this experience have been reported. People feel a profound sense of peace and calm. Many see a tunnel and a bright light. They feel a sense of detachment from their bodies. Some see dead friends, family members, or religious figures such as angels, Jesus, or Mohammed. Interestingly, it seems that virtually all those who have the latter experience see only prominent figures who are associated with their religion. Hindus do not report seeing Zeus, Christians do not report meeting Mohammed, and Muslims never seem to encounter Joseph Smith. And no one ever gets greeted by a long-forgotten god from an extinct prehistoric religion. Despite some contradictory details, the argument often made is that so many people in so many different places cannot all be wrong about this similar experience. Heaven, therefore, must be real. As we shall see, however, there are reasonable explanations for all these things that require neither an afterlife nor the existence of heaven.

Near-death experiences are fascinating and well worth investigating, no doubt, but do they qualify as proof that an afterlife and heaven are real? I've read about many cases and interviewed two people who say they left their bodies for a brief period after dying. One says she visited heaven. A preacher named Don Piper "died" on January 18, 1989, and wrote about his afterlife experience in the bestselling book *90 Minutes in Heaven*. I read it and found nothing that comes close to qualifying as serious evidence for his claim. He describes the "pearlescent" gates of heaven, seeing a close friend who had died in a traffic accident years before, and hearing glorious music before being whisked back to Earth to live again.

Modern brain biology and psychology can provide reasonable and likely explanations for all these things, however. Maybe Piper went to heaven, but isn't it more likely that he and others in similar circumstances remember images and feelings that were created by their oxygen-deprived and severely stressed brains? Piper seems uninterested in doubting the accuracy of his recollections—even though it is well known that our brains can fool us into believing sights, sounds, and even complex experiences that do not match with reality. "I have no intention of trying to solve this debate," he writes. "I can only relate what happened to me. No matter what researchers may or may not try to tell me, I *know* I went to heaven."[1]

Many people say they *know* they were experimented on by aliens, too. Many people also say they *know* a horoscope accurately foretold their future. Many people *know* they saw a ghost. Clearly an individual's confidence is not enough. If it is, then we would have to believe every story ever told with conviction as if no human can be honestly mistaken or innocently deluded. Claims of seeing heaven may be true, but without evidence they are all just stories.

FINAL VOYAGE

I interviewed a man who told me about the day his soul left his body. He was dying of septic shock. His heart rate was down to four to six beats per minute. Devastated by infection, full of drugs, and empty of hope, he began to slip away. He drifted from his body and found himself looking down at the room from somewhere near the ceiling. He remembers seeing his doctor praying for him at his bedside. It was weird but all very real, he said. But he didn't die. After regaining consciousness, he told the doctor that he saw him praying. The doctor, he said, was shocked. He was stunned that his patient "saw" him praying despite being dead or near dead. This out-of-body experience, though dramatic, was brief and did not include a visit to heaven. Loretta Blasingame, however, went all the way.

An "anointed evangelist," Blasingame has traveled the world, telling people the news about Jesus's promise of the afterlife. She also loves to share the story of her amazing visit to heaven. I met Blasingame in the Cayman Islands, where she performed a faith-healing service. That night, she claimed to "dissolve tumors" and heal a wide variety of serious illnesses.[2] Nothing topped the story of heaven that she told me, however.

Blasingame said she "died" of a heart attack and then rose out of her body. She saw her physical body lying beneath her as she hovered above. Then she found herself at the literal gates of heaven. The gates were bedazzled with blinding pearls and diamonds, and the streets were paved with gold, she said. She saw angels teaching newcomers how to properly worship God. People ate fruit, and when they were finished, another piece would magically appear. No one goes hungry in heaven, she explained. And then she saw him. Jesus approached Blasingame and took her hand. She said he had beautiful wavy hair and "the most beautiful crystal blue eyes." Jesus "anointed" her and sent her back to Earth so that she could tell people about him and heal people in his name.[3]

STORIES ARE NOT PROOF

This was easily one of the best stories I have ever had the privilege to hear. I watched her closely as she spoke. I saw her lip tremble, the tears build in her eyes before streaking her cheeks. Skeptical though I may be, if I had to guess, I would say that she was telling me the truth that night. Maybe she fooled me, but I think she was sincere. No, I'm not convinced that she actually went to the place we know as heaven. Maybe she did, but I doubt it. However, I do think she probably went there in her mind. She felt it, experienced it, and now she remembers it, probably more clearly, in greater detail, and with more confidence than I remember some of the real places I have actually been to. I think this explanation is more likely to be accurate because I know enough about the human brain to know that it can take us to places that do not exist and leave us with unshakeable memories of having really been there. The fact that we know the brain can do this means we need to have much more than a story to be sure.

While researching alien abduction claims for another book, I was surprised to find out how common sleep paralysis is. This likely explanation for stories of extraterrestrials invading bedrooms and molesting people involves the brain's failure to fully awaken from a dream state coupled with false memories. At least 20 percent of the population is thought to have had at least one episode of sleep paralysis with hallucinations.[4] I was amazed to discover that I had friends and family members who experienced sleep paralysis. The tacking on of elaborately constructed memories of alien mischief is less common, of course, but apparently it does happen to many people. Science has revealed much about the brain's ability to fool us into thinking we have physically experienced things that never really happened. This knowledge must not be forgotten or diminished when people tell extraordinary stories without supporting evidence.

This knowledge should fuel our skepticism when we hear extraordinary stories, such as the one Blasingame told me. The good skeptic, even if he likes the person and is impressed with her story, recognizes that, without proof, it's only a story. Don't forget, we have stories of just about everything imaginable. There are stories out there about people being kidnapped by Bigfoot, time traveling, talking to ghosts, and so on. But they all have one thing in common—no proof. How can we sensibly decide which ones are true and which ones are probably not true? This is where the scientific process comes in. If we really want to get to the bottom of things, all we have to do is feed the story into the machinery of science. If it survives to emerge from the other end somewhat intact, then we might have something to be excited about.

But without submitting to the scientific process, extraordinary stories wither and die, or at least they should. They still could be true, but how can we know? A story may stir us emotionally and may appeal to us in ways that make us want it to be true. It might even be believed enthusiastically by most of the people we know. But without evidence and testing, it's just a story and nothing more.

Heaven is an irresistible hope for most people. Why wouldn't it be? Our extraordinarily intelligent brains burden us with an awareness of our ultimate fate. Unless the singularitarians and transhumanists turn out to be right, we all will die. It's the big finish, the ultimate end. The ever-present shadow of that realization is probably one reason most people seem so determined to keep themselves busy with either productive work or nonsense distractions. Sit still too long, and you might actually contemplate your own existence—and eventual nonexistence. One doesn't need to be Freud to suspect that the extraordinary appeal of heaven is tied to a universal concern with death and our desire to avoid it. Many religions offer an answer that is very soothing to this concern. Christians should understand that skeptics are not necessarily opposed to an afterlife. We would love to get some more time on the clock (although eternity seems a bit much and leaving most of humankind behind would feel very wrong). We can hope too. Who wouldn't want to be reunited with loved ones and exist in a place without want or suffering? The difference is that skeptics aren't willing to pretend to know something that we don't. The skeptics' problem with heaven is not that we wouldn't be willing to jump through the appropriate theological hoops to get there. Within reason, most of us probably would. The problem is that we are unconvinced. Stories about heaven, whether they are found in the written words of anonymous authors from thousands of years ago or in the spoken words of people who claim to have been there, fall short.

Michael Shermer, founding publisher of *Skeptic*, says that the absence of proof leaves us with no choice but to withhold belief in heaven at this time: "Here is the reality. It has been estimated that in the last fifty thousand years about 107 billion humans were born. Of the hundred billion people born before the seven billion living today, every one of them has died and not one has returned to confirm for us beyond a reasonable doubt that there is life after death. This data set does not bode well for promises of immortality and claims for an afterlife."[5]

The first thing nonbelievers wonder about regarding dramatic stories of near-death and out-of-body experiences is whether or not there are natural explanations that might explain them. If there are no afterlife and no heaven, then what is going on? It seems unlikely that all these people are lying. Once again, science comes to the rescue and leads us to possible answers that are far more likely to be true because they rely on testable human biology and psychology rather than on gods and supernatural forces that are so elusive to testing and confirmation. Not all is understood, of course, but enough is to make it clear that the dying or oxygen-deprived brain is probably behind these events. For example, the tunnel of light that many dying or distressed people have reported seeing is likely nothing more than the tunnel vision that occurs when the eyes don't get enough blood and oxygen. Researchers have also found that some drugs can trigger hallucinations and out-of-body experiences.[6] Other researchers have induced the same sensation in people by stimulating specific parts of the brain with mild electrical currents. Let's think about this: we are not gods. We do not send people to heaven. Yet we are able to induce the near-death and out-of-body experience. None of this disproves heaven, of course. But it does strongly suggest that there is a physical, biological cause and not necessarily a supernatural one.[7]

A key factor in many of these experiences is likely the influence of prior beliefs. Those who deeply believe that death is the gateway to heaven may already be halfway there. Psychologists know very well that expectations can color perceptions of reality. If one thinks Jesus is real and frequently prays to Jesus, then it is not surprising that an image of Jesus may be conjured up by the brain during one of these near-death events. The person doesn't even necessarily have to be religious. Simply being exposed to religious beliefs in his or her culture might trigger one's brain to place or interpret the psychological experience into a religious context. For example, I am not religious, but if I had one of these near-death psychological events and "saw" a religious figure in my mind, it would most likely be Jesus or "God the Father." This is because I have lived among so many Christians and been exposed to Christianity for so many years. The Christian god likely would be first in the queue for such an experience. It is much less likely that I would encounter Khepri, an ancient Egyptian god, for example.

Being skeptical of heaven does not necessarily diminish its importance. Just as fears of death have haunted us, dreams of heaven and other escapes have driven us in profound ways. Philosopher Stephen Cave believes a deep wanting to avoid death is behind much of what we do: "All living things seek to perpetuate themselves into the future, but humans seek to perpetuate themselves forever. This seeking—this will to immortality—is the foundation of human achievement; it is the wellspring of religion, the muse of philosophy, the architect of our cities and the impulse behind the arts. It is embedded in our very nature, and its results are what we know as civilization."[8]

As a skeptic of heaven, I tell people to consider both the absence of evidence and the very reasonable scientific explanations for the dramatic near-death-experience stories about it. I tell no one, however, that they should not hope for an afterlife and a heaven. Hope, if you wish, so long as doing so does not reduce your passion for this life or diminish your desire to make it the best it can be. I see nothing wrong with hoping, so long as we do not confuse it with knowing.

THE SOURCE. Jesus was Jewish, and it was Judaism that gave rise to Christianity. However, most Jews two thousand years ago were unconvinced that Jesus was a god, just as today most Jews remain unconvinced. *Photo by the author.*

14

WHY IS GOD SO VIOLENT?

God is love. It's a popular sentiment among Christians. However, skeptics of Christianity who have taken the time to read the Bible find it to be a very strange claim indeed. After all, killing is talked about a lot more than love in the Bible. God is responsible for the worst mass killings in history. His death toll, as reported in the Bible, is astonishing. I'm not stating this to be provocative, certainly not to irritate or anger Christians. But given the consistency with which so many Christians speak of their god as being the very definition of pure love, the simple question has to be asked: Why is God so violent? If he is so loving, then why does he kill so many people? To be clear, this chapter is not designed to argue with Christians about their beliefs. The only purpose is to share with Christians why it is that so many skeptics do not understand this popular claim that says "God is love."

I am aware that some Christians attempt to push all this aside as old news. They acknowledge the violence and hate but dismiss it as behavior limited to "the god of the Old Testament" as if that stuff occurred in a galaxy far, far away and has no connection to our world. They feel that the Old Testament horror and bloodshed is primarily historical, great for referencing but definitely in the past. Those were brutal times when men were barbaric, so God's actions were contextually appropriate. Jesus and the New Testament, they say, are more relevant and prove true the claim that God is love. But it's not that simple. We can't ignore the connection between the stories and information found in the Old and New Testaments.

We also have to consider the Holy Trinity doctrine once again. It's one of Christianity's central claims, and it says that Jesus is God and God is Jesus (plus the Holy Spirit, of course). If true, this means God/Jesus/Holy Spirit created the world, created Adam and Eve, *and* killed a lot of people, including many innocent babies and children. I know that some Christians don't agree. They say that Jesus was the son of

God, literally, and there was no blending of the two beings. While that view may be easier to grasp and more logically coherent for many, it contradicts the Holy Trinity claim, which is one of the oldest and most important doctrines in all of Christianity.

There are many Christians who are simply unaware of or have somehow not fully absorbed intellectually and emotionally the depth and fury of God's wrath. For them, I present a very brief sampling of God's work, as described in the Bible:

- In Genesis, a serpent, one of God's creatures, tricks Adam and Eve into eating forbidden fruit. God's punishment is death (they were immortal before), but not just for them—for every human from that point on. This single act, eating a piece of fruit, is, according to many Christians, the reason for all the suffering and death in the world due to disease, old age, and even the gruesome predator-prey dynamic in the animal kingdom.

- With the exception of one family and a boatload of animals, God kills every person and every land creature by flooding the entire planet. This is particularly disturbing when one considers every baby and child on Earth drowning. Although the world's population was relatively small then, this would have to be considered the greatest mass murder in history. "Every living thing that moved on land perished—birds, livestock, wild animals, all the creatures that swarm over the earth, and all mankind. Everything on dry land that had the breath of life in its nostrils died. Every living thing on the face of the earth was wiped out; people and animals and the creatures that move along the ground and the birds were wiped from the earth. Only Noah was left, and those with him in the ark." (Genesis 7:21–23)

- God even killed livestock when he went after the firstborn children of Egypt. "At midnight the Lord struck down all the firstborn [children] in Egypt, from the firstborn of Pharaoh, who sat on the throne, to the firstborn of the prisoner, who was in the dungeon, and the firstborn of all the livestock as well." (Exodus 12:29)

- Not only is slavery acceptable, but God says it's okay to beat your slaves so long as you don't kill them. "Anyone who beats their male or female slave with a rod must be punished if the slave dies as a direct result, but they are not to be punished if the slave recovers after a day or two, since the slave is their property." (Exodus 21:20–21)

- Threats from God for disobedience: "I will send wild animals against you, and they will rob you of your children" (Leviticus 26:22). And, "You will eat the flesh of your sons and the flesh of your daughters" (Leviticus 26:29).
- "The LORD said to Moses, 'Take all the leaders of these people, kill them and expose them in broad daylight before the LORD, so that the LORD's fierce anger may turn away from Israel'" (Numbers 25:4).
- "And when the LORD your God has delivered them over to you and you have defeated them, then you must destroy them totally. Make no treaty with them, and show them no mercy." (Deuteronomy 7:2)
- "When the LORD your God delivers it into your hand, put to the sword all the men in it. As for the women, the children, the livestock and everything else in the city, you may take these as plunder for yourselves." (Deuteronomy 20:13–14)
- "Happy is the one who seizes your infants and dashes them against the rocks." (Psalms 137:9)
- "He that is far away will die of the plague, and he that is near will fall by the sword, and he that survives and is spared will die of famine. So will I spend my wrath upon them. And they will know I am the Lord." (Ezekiel 6:12–13)

As anyone who has read the Bible knows, there are many, many more disturbing passages that clearly indicate that God is not only violent himself but also condones and requires violence from his followers. These words and behavior are in obvious contradiction with the popular claim that God is purely peace and love. According to the Bible, he is capable of being violent, vengeful, and hateful. His Old Testament laws clearly show this. For example, there are many calls for execution for what most people today would consider to be minor offenses. Doing any kind of work on the Sabbath, even household chores for no pay, is a capital offense. Being gay is still considered to be highly controversial and is disapproved of by many Christians today; thankfully, however, fewer Christians are calling for God's biblical punishment for it, which is death (Leviticus 20:13). Even blasphemy, the act of merely insulting God, is punishable by death (Leviticus 24:16).

Many Christians don't think those laws apply to them or to our time. However, that attitude might oppose what Jesus wanted, according to the New Testament:

- "For truly, I [Jesus] say to you, till heaven and earth pass away, not an iota, not a dot, will pass the law until all is accomplished. Whoever then relaxes one of the least of these commandments and teaches men so, shall be called least in the kingdom of heaven; but he who does them and teaches them shall be called great in the kingdom of heaven." (Matthew 5:18–19)
- "Did not Moses give you the law, and yet none of you keepeth the law." (John 7:19)
- "It is easier for Heaven and Earth to pass away than for the smallest part of the letter of the law to become invalid." (Luke 16:17)
- "Do not think that I [Jesus] have come to abolish the law or the prophets. I have come not to abolish but to fulfill. Amen, I say to you, until heaven and earth pass away, not the smallest part or the smallest part of a letter will pass from the law, until all things have taken place." (Matthew 5:17)

Then there is popular belief among Christians that God sends billions of people to hell, where they will suffer unimaginable torture for eternity. From the viewpoint of a typical non-Christian, this is the ultimate in hate and violence and cannot be reconciled with the image of a loving god. Continual suffering, for all eternity, is not compatible with any sensible notion of human justice, mercy, or love. In addition to that, there is the apocalypse to contend with. Many millions of Christians believe that Jesus will return as he promised to shake up the world, dispense with the wicked, and establish the Kingdom of God on Earth. There are a few things about this, too, that contradict reasonable expectations for a god who "is love." First of all, billions of people, about 70 percent of the current world population, will suffer and then die because they are not Christians. But of the some two billion Christians, many of them are likely to perish too because they were not the "right" kind of Christian. In the end, all but a few million, perhaps, will have died horrible deaths. Mark 16:16 says that those who have been baptized will be spared, and those who have not will be damned. If true, a lot of people will be damned on Judgment Day. Presumably they will be dumped in hell to begin their eternal punishment. Jesus hardly seems like the Prince of Peace in all of this. Matthew 13:41–42 states: "The Son of Man shall send forth his angels, and they shall gather out of his kingdom all things that offend, and them which do iniquity;

And shall cast them into a furnace of fire: there shall be wailing and gnashing of teeth."

If all this violence and misery are somehow necessary, why wouldn't a loving god have made his story and claims convincing enough to all so that every sensible person could be exempt from destruction on doomsday? Skeptics ask this question and others like it not because they want to win arguments or catch Christians in a tough spot. They ask because they sincerely don't understand how this makes sense. For them, this is all a head-spinning mix of unproven claims and bizarre cruelty that does not connect in any logical way with the idea that God is love.

APOCALYPSE WHEN? Some Christians believe that "the saved" will hide at Petra in Jordan when the Antichrist rises to power. Millions of Christians worldwide believe they will vanish in an instant when the Rapture occurs. Skeptics question why, for two thousand years and counting, the end is always near but never here. *Photo by the author.*

15

WHAT DO PROPHECIES PROVE?

Sooner or later, the subject of prophecies comes up during discussions between Christians and people who are skeptical of Christianity. The prophecies that get the most attention are predictions that were supposed to have come from God. Few issues in religion draw out such strong disagreements as the claim that the Bible contains ancient, divinely inspired predictions that have already or will soon come true. But I see more than a convenient powder keg for knockdown, drag-out debates. The topic of prophecies offers a valuable opportunity for Christians to learn how skeptics think and why it is that they come to such different conclusions. Many Christians point to prophecies as ironclad proof that Jesus is real and the Bible true. Skeptics, however, look at the same prophecies and struggle to understand how anyone could be impressed by them to any degree. It's a huge point of contention with plenty of details to argue over, but perhaps the most important thing for Christians to recognize is *why* skeptics really reject these predictions as accurate or meaningful. It is not a case of nonbelievers dismissing every prophecy because of minor discrepancies or a prejudicial attitude. The problem with many biblical prophecies is that they simply do not stand out as anything special. Like well-written horoscopes or Nostradamus's quatrains, predictions in the Bible tend to be vague and therefore wide open to multiple interpretations.

Christianity has many prophecies, of course, but the most interesting ones make predictions about important events to come. To know what the future holds via a special message from God is special enough, but there is also the added value of prophecies as proof. Many Christians view these predictions as the best way to show others that their religion is indeed the right one. But no matter how impressed Christians are with Christian prophecies, most of the human population is not, perhaps because such claims are not unique to Christianity. Supernaturally sourced predictions have been around for thousands of years, even though the majority of the world has always been non-Christian. It's no surprise that Muslims, Hindus, and others aren't motivated to jump ship and convert. Why would they, when they already have their own prophecies that "confirm" their faiths? Why would somebody else's predictions be any better? The skeptic, meanwhile, sees the same reasons to doubt all of them.

Predictions are meaningless when they are so vague that they can be interpreted in many ways. This is a key problem with biblical prophecies. Despite what many people say, none of the prophecies are so straightforward that anyone could read them and conclude that they came true as predicted and that they could only have been brought about by supernatural means. Not one. It's not that skeptics are being stubborn. No doubt they would be taken aback if the Old Testament contained very specific predictions of unique and important things or events that ancient people could not possibly have known about. But we don't find anything like this.

Some prophecies predict things that were sure to happen anyway. Many Christians around the world have told me that the Bible predicted earthquakes, war, and moral decay. Then they tell me that current news headlines have proven them to be true. But these are not meaningful predictions because there have always been earthquakes, war, and complaints of moral decay. These things only seem more severe or more important than ever before because they are happening to us in our time. An earthquake in China killed more than eight hundred thousand people—in the year 1556. Wars and violence have been with us since prehistoric times. They are certainly not unique to contemporary times. It's the same with perceived problems of morality. They are nothing new. Throughout the history of civilization there have always been bad people and the younger generation has always been morally deficient, at least according to the older generation. A prediction of the Sun rising tomorrow morning is just not much of a prediction.

It's also important to keep in mind that people could be influenced by a prophecy and work to make it come true. In this case, it would mean that nothing supernatural has occurred necessarily. A very popular claim among Christians, for example, is that the creation of the modern state of Israel was prophesied in the Bible. As we know, Israel was established as an independent nation in 1948. I have heard many times that this one prediction is all the proof anyone should need to be convinced that the Bible is accurate and inspired by God. Some can't understand why this argument doesn't close the case for once and for all. But skeptics don't agree that it proves anything about God because all the evidence points to people, not God, creating modern Israel. It was a lot of hard work by Jews over many years. It was the United Nations. It was the effort and support of politicians in Great Britain and the United States. There is not and never has been anything that anyone can point to that indicates that a god created Israel with supernatural powers.

There is strength in numbers. Good skeptics know that a surefire way to make one successful prediction is to make lots of them. Make a hundred predictions, and one of them is bound to come true. This is one of the ways that psychics and astrologers are able to impress people who lack good critical-thinking skills. Confirmation bias leads all of us to remember a few correct guesses and forget the many more that were incorrect. So when a Christian or another religious person claims to have been in communication with the divine and has a prediction about the future, we have to not only assess how specific and accurate the prophecy is but also keep count of how many predictions are made and what the result of each one is. Television preacher Pat Robertson is a good example of a Christian who is very good at the scattershot approach to prophecy. He often produces a near-constant stream of "prophetic words." When some of his predictions seem to come true, as some inevitably must, he claims them as proof that he really does hear the voice of God in his head. But neither he nor any of his followers seem interested in keeping track of the number of misses.

Another problem with proof of fulfilled prophecies that appear in the Bible is that *they are in the Bible.* To describe a prediction and then claim that it came true, all within the same limited collection of ancient sources, is not good enough. Imagine if someone showed you a book, or collection of books, in which there was a prediction of an alien spaceship landing on Earth in one chapter and then confirmation that it happened in another chapter. Would that be enough to convince you? When a claim is impressive, like a supernatural prediction involving a god, the evidence needs to be impressive too.

Skeptics often wonder why religious people who stress the importance of their prophecies are so easily able to ignore or reject the many prophecies that come from other religions. One of the Islamic prophecies I heard about while in the Middle East involves the Moon and the Apollo 11 astronauts. According to many Muslims, the prophecy apparently proves that the Koran is both accurate and inspired by God based on this line: "The Moon has split and the hour has drawn closer" (Koran 54:1). From this one sentence, some Muslims claim that the Koran predicted the six Apollo Moon landings that took place between 1969 and 1972. The "split" occurred when astronauts returned with Moon rocks, which Muslims interpreted to mean that the Moon was no longer whole, since a part of it had been removed, or split. Not all Muslims, of course, but some are absolutely convinced that this clinches it. The Koran is true, Allah is the one true God, and Mohammed is his Prophet. No doubt about it, because Neil Armstrong, Buzz Aldrin, and Michael Collins split the Moon. For some reason, however, Christians, Jews, and others who believe in prophecies are not rushing to become Muslims based on this one. They are just too skeptical, I suppose.

It is important to note that even Muslims are not in agreement about this and other Islamic prophecies. Many say the line from the Koran has nothing to do with astronauts, and they attribute an entirely different meaning to it. We find this same kind of disagreement in Christianity. Prophecies are so vague and mysterious that even people who are in agreement on the god and the book often can't agree on the meaning of prophecies. So Christians shouldn't be surprised when skeptics don't get it either.

Christians who are impressed with prophecies found in the Bible might want to consider how easy it is for anybody to believe in unlikely and fantastic things or events, even when they are certainly not true. If we don't have our skeptical guard up, many predictions can easily seem to be much more than they are. For example, modern-day psychics and mediums have convinced millions of people that they can read minds, see the future, and carry on conversations with dead people. But it's very, very unlikely that they are doing any of that. For all the books, TV shows, and hype, none of them have ever proved they can do what they say they can do. Still, it's not difficult to convince someone that you are reading her or his mind or that you know the future. I know, because I have done it.

My first attempt at a cold reading was shockingly successful. Within less than fifteen minutes, I was able to make an intelligent adult woman believe that I knew very personal things about her past, her present life, and her future. I later confessed to her that I was only doing what professional psychics and mediums do. I looked her over, made some general assumptions about her and her life, and then started blurting out rapid-fire guesses while watching closely to see which ones struck a chord with her. Her predisposition to believe in psychics, susceptibility, confirmation bias, and weak skepticism did the rest. Never forget, everyone is vulnerable. One unfounded belief sets us up to fall for the next one. We all can and will embrace irrational beliefs without realizing it. That's why being a good skeptic is an endless duty and critical thinking a never-ending process.

Finally, we can't look at Christian prophecies without considering the biggest one of all: Jesus's promise to return to Earth. When the question of proof comes up, many Christians cite prophecies. They often claim that there are hundreds of fulfilled prophecies to choose from, as if they somehow are more believable when grouped together. But for the reasons stated previously, none of them are clearly stated or specific enough to prove anything. The skeptic's counterclaim to the idea that prophecies prove Christianity is the most important prediction made by Jesus himself. According to the Bible, Jesus said he would return very soon, within the lifetimes of those people he was speaking to. That was two thousand years ago. The following quote, found in Mark, immediately grabs the attention of skeptics because it seems straightforward enough to understand, and yet it clearly did not come true: "I tell you the truth, some who are standing here will not taste death before they see the kingdom of God come with power" (Mark 9:1).

Then there is this promise from Mark 13: "The Sun will be darkened, and the Moon will not give its light; the stars will fall from the sky, and the heavenly bodies will be shaken. At that time men will see the Son of Man coming in clouds with great power and glory. And he will send his angels and gather his elect from the four winds, from the ends of the earth to the ends of the heavens. . . . I tell you the truth, this generation will certainly not pass away until all these things have happened."

What happened? The generation Jesus was speaking to did pass. They are all dead. Why didn't Jesus return and fulfill the prophecy in the time frame he clearly seems to have promised? Some Christians I have discussed this with say it is not a failed prophecy at all. They say "generation" really refers to race in this context, which means Jesus said that the Jewish people would not become extinct before his return. But this seems unlikely. Much of what Jesus says in the New Testament seems urgent and directly relevant to the times. It's hardly the tone one would expect if Jesus knew the world would putter on for at least another couple of thousand years or more. And speaking of the Jews, why weren't more of them convinced by the prophecies that Jesus is said to have fulfilled when he was born, preached, and died? They were there. These were *their* predictions in *their* Torah. Sure, the first Christians were Jews, but most Jews of the day were not convinced that Jesus was the Messiah. Why not? If he was and if he did fulfill prophecies, shouldn't the Jews have been the first to recognize it?

Some scholars are certain that Jesus was an apocalyptic preacher who did make the claim that a kingdom of God would be established on Earth during his time period. Bart D. Ehrman, Distinguished Professor of Religious Studies at the University of North Carolina–Chapel Hill and author of more than twenty books, is one of those scholars. According to Ehrman, it is clear that Jesus preached that the world was about to experience a massive shift back then. The earliest sources we have for Jesus show this clearly. That detail becomes diluted more and more in later sources, however. Ehrman thinks this is because later Christians could not continue promoting an obvious error. He writes: "This move to deapocalypticize Jesus was enormously successful. Down through the Middle Ages and on to today, the vast majority of people who have considered Jesus have not thought of him as an apocalyptic preacher. That is because the apocalyptic message that he delivered came to be toned down and eventually altered. But it is still there for all to see in our earliest surviving sources, multiply and independently attested."[1]

When Christians wonder why biblical prophecies do not convince every skeptic, I hope they will understand that in most cases it has nothing to do with the credibility of the person making the claim or even with reservations about Jesus or Christianity in general. The problems for a good skeptic are simple and specific. The predictions are either too vague to be meaningful, or, if they are and do seem to have come true, it's not at all clear that they did so by supernatural means. And then there is also that apparent problem of the most important Bible prophecy of all failing to come true. Jesus said he would return and assume power over the world before his disciples died. But, as we all know, he did not.

16

HOW IMPORTANT ARE THE TEN COMMANDMENTS?

The Church, in fidelity to Scripture and to the example of Christ, acknowledges the primordial importance and significance of the Decalogue [Ten Commandments]. Christians are obliged to keep it.
—Compendium of the Catechism of the Catholic Church

The Ten Commandments are just as valid today as when God gave them to Moses over 3,000 years ago.
—Rev. Billy Graham[1]

The Ten Commandments are a big deal. To most Christians, this short list of laws found in the Old Testament is nothing less than the foundation of civilization and the crucial blueprint for a healthy and moral modern society. It is a practical guide, laid out in plain language that is timeless and applicable to all. All laws today descend from the laws written on the stone tablets Moses brought down from Mt. Sinai three and a half thousand years ago. We would be lost today without them. Many contemporary social problems are the result of our failure to remember and follow the Ten Commandments as God wanted us to.

The Ten Commandments may be ancient, but they still matter. Skeptics may not agree with either their historical supremacy or their divine origin, but these appear to be minority views. A 2005 poll found that 74 percent of Americans favor the Ten Commandments being displayed in public schools.[2] Every few years or so, a legal dust storm is kicked up over such a display in some courthouse or other government property. The argument is always the same. One side says the Ten Commandments hold supernatural significance and are a key part of our shared history, so they should be honored. The other side says that displaying the Ten Commandments in places of government business promotes religion and is therefore unconstitutional. I am less interested in these squabbles, however, than I am in why so few Christians give much thought to what the Ten Commandments actually mean.

If they are really so important, one would think that knowing them and their backstory, as described in the Bible, would be a priority. But in fact, many smart and relatively informed Christians know surprisingly little about the Ten Commandments beyond what is taught in Sunday school. For example, a 2007 survey found that most Americans can name more Big Mac® hamburger ingredients and *The Brady Bunch* children than laws of the Ten Commandments.[3]

Don't misunderstand; I'm not posing as some condescending biblical scholar attempting to scold people who aren't experts on the Torah. I merely want to point out that it should take nothing more than a casual reading of Exodus in the Old Testament to raise alarm bells in the minds of Christians because something is plainly not right. The traditional facts and presentation of the Ten Commandments we all hear in popular culture do not align with what appears in the Bible. We will explore this more in the next chapter (spoiler alert: it's not like the Charlton Heston movie), but let's first see if one traditional version of the Ten Commandments holds up to a bit of honest analysis. Christians often wonder why non-Christians don't get it, why everyone, regardless of their religious status, wouldn't want these laws celebrated and imposed everywhere. Here are some reasons why that might not be a good idea.

I. THOU SHALT HAVE NO OTHER GODS BEFORE ME.

There is an irreconcilable problem with this first law, especially in a country like the United States, which is supposed to be free and have a government that is neutral on matters of religion. This commandment blatantly conflicts with the concept of religious freedom. It couldn't possibly be a real law in any country that respects the rights of its citizens to worship or not worship as they please. One only has to consider that some two million Hindus (polytheists) currently live in the United States. How do you think they would feel about a law that says "no other gods"?

II. THOU SHALT NOT MAKE UNTO THEE ANY GRAVEN IMAGE, OR ANY LIKENESS OF ANYTHING THAT IS IN HEAVEN ABOVE, OR THAT IS IN THE EARTH BENEATH, OR THAT IS IN THE WATER UNDER THE EARTH. THOU SHALT NOT BOW DOWN THYSELF TO THEM, NOR SERVE THEM: FOR I THE LORD THY GOD AM A JEALOUS GOD, VISITING THE INIQUITY OF THE FATHERS UPON THE CHILDREN UNTO THE THIRD AND FOURTH GENERATION OF THEM THAT HATE ME; AND SHOWING MERCY UNTO THOUSANDS OF THEM THAT LOVE ME, AND KEEP MY COMMANDMENTS.

Once again, there is a conflict with freedom of religion—a right, by the way, that I'm confident most Christians agree is important. If someone wants to make a "graven image" of a dolphin or a tree and then bow down before it, shouldn't they be free to do so? If so, this law has no place in a free society. I don't know one way or the other, but I do wonder if a Christian cross worn as jewelry or prominently displayed inside or atop a building would qualify as a "graven image."

The line "for I the Lord thy God am a jealous God" seems odd to me. Why would the most powerful being in existence, the creator of the universe, and the only real God, according to many Christians, be jealous of anything? There is also a problem with God's threat to withhold his mercy "upon the children unto the third and fourth generation of them that hate me." If he has a beef with the father or mother, fine, but why carry it across generations? I think most Christians would agree that no child should be punished, or have mercy withheld from her, because of something her father, mother, or great-great grandparent did.

III. THOU SHALT NOT TAKE THE NAME OF THE LORD YOUR GOD IN VAIN, FOR THE LORD WILL NOT HOLD HIM GUILTLESS WHO TAKES HIS NAME IN VAIN.

It's not entirely clear what taking God's name in vain means. Some say it simply prohibits us from calling on God when we don't really mean to call on him. If that is the case, then this may be the most ignored law in the history of humankind. Profanity that includes "God" is common. Less offensive phrases, such as "oh, my god" and "God darn it," are even more common. Furthermore, everyone who has ever said "gosh," "golly," or "gee" might be in trouble too because those are nothing more than euphemisms for "God," and he might not be fooled by them. Again, there is a conflict with a basic right that most people support. Restricting the use of the word or name "God" violates free speech.

Some say that this commandment is about honoring oaths or contracts that have been sworn to in the name of God. However, one pastor told me that this commandment has nothing to do with spoken words or legal contracts. He said it refers instead to Christians living the way Christians should. The commandment is violated when one claims to be a Christian but fails to live morally and to observe the necessary rituals and requirements. The problem with this, of course, is that there are thousands of versions of Christianity, many with very different demands, so any law that orders people to "live like a Christian" is impossibly vague.

IV. REMEMBER THE SABBATH DAY, TO KEEP IT HOLY. SIX DAYS YOU SHALL LABOR AND DO ALL YOUR WORK, BUT THE SEVENTH DAY IS THE SABBATH OF THE LORD YOUR GOD. IN IT YOU SHALL DO NO WORK: YOU, NOR YOUR SON, NOR YOUR DAUGHTER, NOR YOUR MALE SERVANT, NOR YOUR FEMALE SERVANT, NOR YOUR CATTLE, NOR YOUR STRANGER WHO IS WITHIN YOUR GATES. FOR IN SIX DAYS THE LORD MADE THE HEAVENS AND THE EARTH, THE SEA, AND ALL THAT IS IN THEM, AND RESTED THE SEVENTH DAY. THEREFORE THE LORD BLESSED THE SABBATH DAY AND HALLOWED IT.

Again we have a law that is fine for those Christians and Jews who choose to follow it, but it's not appropriate to impose it on others. I happen to like the idea of a regular rest day in the week. I think it's wise to shut down and recharge the mind and body. But I certainly wouldn't want other people to be forced to comply with my view on this. Some people might decide they want more days of rest or no days of rest. It's their choice. And I sure wouldn't want anyone to be executed if they did some work on the Sabbath, as God calls for in Exodus 31: "Therefore you are to observe the Sabbath, for it is holy to you. Everyone who profanes it shall surely be put to death." Numbers 15:35 offers a case of the law in action: "Then the Lord said to Moses, 'The man shall surely be put to death; all the congregation shall stone him with stones outside the camp.'" His crime? He picked up sticks on the Sabbath.

God seems to care a lot about this day, and that would worry me to no end if I was a Christian. If gathering firewood could get you stoned to death, what about mowing the yard, doing the dishes, or checking e-mails? I was scolded by an ultraorthodox Jew in Jerusalem for writing with a pen on the Sabbath. Very few Christians I have encountered come anywhere near that sort of devotion. They say it's the spirit of the day that counts, not the actual absence of work. I find this to be inconsistent with the attitude shown toward other commandments. If you don't have to strictly obey the Sabbath commandment, does that mean you get some wiggle room on the others as well? If so, which ones and how much wiggle room? If not, why not?

Most Christians today, if they observe the Sabbath at all, don't do it on the day God seems to have originally intended. I have no interest in stirring up the hornets' nest that is the Saturday/Sunday Sabbath debate here, but it is interesting to note that Christians are not in agreement on the day. I have talked with enough Seventh-day Adventists to know that it's a very serious issue for some Christians, even if most do not view it as such. Seventh-day Adventists maintain that if God thought the Sabbath day was important enough to include in the Ten Commandments, then he must have wanted us to honor it strictly. They feel that the Sabbath should be observed on the "original day," Saturday, as Jews and Muslims do.

V. HONOR THY FATHER AND THY MOTHER, THAT YOUR DAYS MAY BE LONG UPON THE LAND WHICH THE LORD THY GOD IS GIVING YOU.

On the surface, this seems like a good law that we can all get behind. But it's not. The Ten Commandments are supposed to be the highest moral law laid out in black and white with no ambiguity or room for compromise, but this law shows that the commandments are anything but. Honoring one's mother and father is a great idea for families and society—except when it's not. Everyone knows that every parent is not ideal. In fact, many parents are pretty far from ideal. Every day, children are neglected, beaten, emotionally abused, and sexually abused by their parents, and many of these parents are Christians. It goes on every day. I worked as a live-in supervisor at a residential facility for abused and neglected children, so I know better than most how badly some parents treat their children. This commandment is wrong to suggest that all parents deserve to be honored by their children.

VI. THOU SHALT NOT KILL.

Again, we have a commandment that at first seems both vital to society and unassailable but upon reflection isn't so clear. Many Christians seem to be of the opinion that this commandment is conditional because some support wars and some support capital punishment. Many Christians also feel that it's okay to kill someone in certain cases of self-defense or to protect another person. These loopholes show again why the Ten Commandments aren't the crystal-clear, one-size-fits-all set of laws that many Christians say they are.

Some Christians prefer "Thou shalt not murder." It seems like it would be less ambiguous than the more popular "Thou shalt not kill." But it's not clear at all. Christians kill innocent people in wars, for example. American B17s, operated by Christian crews, dropped bombs on European cities during World War II. German aircraft, operated by Christian crews, dropped bombs on British cities. Civilians, including children, died. Was this forbidden murder or "allowable" killing, according to God and the Ten Commandments?

VII. THOU SHALT NOT COMMIT ADULTERY.

Adultery is defined differently by different Christians. Some say it refers to married people having sex with someone other than their spouse. Others say it refers to any sexual relations outside of a marriage. Either way, this commandment is not appropriate in any society that places a high value on freedom and privacy. Monogamy or celibacy until marriage may be the ideal for many people, of course, but it's something each person has to work out for themselves.

VIII. THOU SHALT NOT STEAL.

I like this one. Stealing is obviously a problem for any society that wants its people to live peacefully, so it should be forbidden. No argument with that. However, there can always be exceptions, and it's not clear if God would allow case-by-case judgments, or if stealing is forbidden in all cases, regardless of circumstances. I know that if one of my daughters is starving and the only immediately available solution is to swipe a loaf of bread from the supermarket, I'm breaking this commandment. And so would you, most likely.

IX. THOU SHALT NOT BEAR FALSE WITNESS AGAINST YOUR NEIGHBOR.

This seems reasonable, but it's unclear what God means, exactly. Does this commandment forbid me from lying to anyone about anything? Or is it some kind of legal-speak for not misrepresenting the truth in court or in formal business dealings specifically? Or does it mean that I can lie to everyone except those people who are my neighbors? What if my overweight friend asks me how she looks in her new, tight dress? Can I lie just a little bit in order to be kind?

X. THOU SHALT NOT COVET THY NEIGHBOR'S HOUSE, THOU SHALT NOT COVET THY NEIGHBOR'S WIFE, NOR HIS MANSERVANT, NOR HIS MAIDSERVANT, NOR HIS OX, NOR HIS ASS, NOR ANY THING THAT IS THY NEIGHBOR'S.

Covet means to want, desire, or crave something. This commandment could be and often is interpreted to mean that we shouldn't go overboard with desire because it may be the first step toward doing something bad that will cause us problems. Coveting my neighbor's ox or luxury car, for example, might lead me to one day steal from him or even kill him out of envy. But this is not as simple as many make it out to be. It's okay to want things. We all do. If my neighbor has a great car, I can desire it without eventually killing him. Maybe I like it so much that one day I'll make an offer to buy it. What's the harm?

The worst part of this commandment is the fact that wives and servants/slaves are listed along with oxen, asses, and whatever else one's neighbor may own. This may have been sensible and acceptable in cultures thousands of years ago, and, sadly, it still holds up in some today, but hopefully you live in a society that is advanced enough to recognize that women should not be the property of men. This commandment shows how blatantly sexist and outdated parts of the Bible are.

These are only some of the problems with the Ten Commandments that skeptics of religion think of when the topic comes up. I hope that even those who may find reasons to disagree with every point raised in this chapter can at least now better understand why many people don't think the Ten Commandments are appropriate, logical, or relevant today and why they don't want to see them displayed in public-school classrooms or inserted into government. It's not about trying to insult God, oppressing anyone's religion, or refusing to acknowledge the significant role of Christianity in society. It is about recognizing that seeking to impose the very specific religious laws of some undermines fairness for all.

DO YOU KNOW THE REAL TEN COMMANDMENTS?

The previous chapter dealt with one of the popular and familiar versions of the Ten Commandments—the laws you may have heard about in Sunday school or saw displayed on a poster or stone sculpture. This chapter will address a very different Ten Commandments—the *real* Ten Commandments. Yes, there is another set of laws set forth in the Bible that God specifically calls "The Ten Commandments." Oddly, very few Christians have heard of them.

As we explore this topic, keep in mind that nothing here is an attempt to catch Christians in a mistake. It's no surprise that most Christians don't know about the various versions and questionable aspects of the Ten Commandments. I grew up in the American South, where I often heard about the Ten Commandments but never felt the need to do any fact-checking. So I fully understand how easy it is to be lulled into a false sense of confidence about them based on hearsay from friends, family, and preachers.

The set of commandments familiar to most people is probably one or another version of the laws drawn from Exodus 20. Moses, leader of the Jewish people, met with God up on Mount Sinai and received the laws. By the way, the one-through-ten numbering of the commandments that we have come to know does not appear in the Bible. The list was formulated that way much later. That's how Jewish, Protestant, and Catholic versions can be different but still total ten.

Moses brought the laws down the mountain but then smashed the tablets in anger when he discovered that his people were partying around a golden idol. Apparently God was not upset with Moses for doing this and told him to come back up the mountain with another pair of stone tablets to try it again. Strangely, however, the laws Moses came down with the final time are very different from the ones most Christians today know as the Ten Commandments.

> ## THE TEN COMMANDMENTS, EXODUS 34
>
> I.   Thou shalt worship no other god: for the Lord, whose name is Jealous, is a jealous God.
> II. Thou shalt make thee no molten gods.
> III. The feast of unleavened bread shalt thou keep.
> IV. Six days thou shalt work, but on the seventh day thou shalt rest.
> V.   Thou shalt observe the feast of weeks, of the firstfruits of wheat harvest, and the feast of ingathering at the year's end.
> VI. Thrice in the year shall all your men children appear before the Lord God, the God of Israel.
> VII. Thou shalt not offer the blood of my sacrifice with leaven.
> VIII. Neither shall the sacrifice of the feast of the passover be left unto the morning.
> IX. The first of the firstfruits of thy land thou shalt bring unto the house of the Lord thy God.
> X.   Thou shalt not seethe [boil] a kid [baby goat] in his mother's milk.

Most Christians' immediate reaction to this list is doubt and skepticism. They feel that it can't possibly be the real Ten Commandments because many of the laws are just too weird and they can't understand why they wouldn't have heard of them before. But they are the real Ten Commandments, as the lines immediately following these laws in Exodus 34:27–28 indicate: "And the LORD said unto Moses, Write thou these words: for after the tenor of these words I have made a covenant with thee and with Israel. . . . And he wrote upon the tables the words of the covenant, *the ten commandments* [emphasis added].

God clearly identifies the Exodus 34 laws as "the Ten Commandments." He does not do this for the well-known Exodus 20 versions that many people want hung in classrooms and displayed in courtrooms. One possible explanation for this is that the laws in Exodus 34 are just add-ons meant to supplement the real Ten Commandments that are in Exodus 20. But that doesn't make sense because the Exodus 34 list of ten includes a few laws that are also in the popular version.

If these are supplemental laws, why would God make three of them repeats? A more likely reason that versions based on Exodus 20 became popular with Christians and the Exodus 34 commandments did not is because the latter includes some bizarre and obviously outdated laws. Not many people these days have much interest or need in a divine law to prevent them from boiling young goats in their mother's milk, for example.

Some Christians I have discussed this with were quick to argue that these laws were meant for the Jewish people and not Christians. It might seem like a reasonable point, as Jesus hadn't even been born yet, but how can we dismiss this version of the Ten Commandments as not applicable to Christians when most Christians claim that the other well-known versions are not only relevant today but are of critical importance and must be followed? If the Exodus 34 version is not relevant today, why would the Exodus 20 version be? There is also this line from Jesus in the New Testament: "For truly I tell you, until heaven and earth disappear, not the smallest letter, not the least stroke of a pen, will by any means disappear from the Law until everything is accomplished" (Matthew 5:18). That sounds like maybe Jesus meant for us to follow the laws of the Old Testament, including the set of laws God specifically called the Ten Commandments in Exodus 34. But most Christians know nothing about them.

A final point, and perhaps the most important, is that all this Ten Commandments business should be a lot easier to grasp if the hand of an omniscient god were involved. If the commandments really are important, if these laws really do represent some kind of turning point in our collective history that civilization and morality rest on, then why didn't God, Moses, or the authors of the Bible produce a clear and distinct list of laws that everyone who sincerely wants to know and understand them could do so? And why would so many of the laws be problematic for those who place a high value on fairness? Coveting my neighbor's wife might not be appropriate, but isn't it even more inappropriate to categorize her with property and livestock?

It is for these reasons that many people do not accept the Ten Commandments. Many Christian activists claim that those who reject the commandments do so because they want to avoid the responsibility of having to obey them. This could not be farther from the truth. Having issues with these laws has nothing to do with secret desires to make graven images, to clean house on the Sabbath, or to boil a goat in its mother's milk. It's about credibility, logic, and justice, nothing more. It doesn't take a world-class skeptic to recognize simple but important questions: Is Exodus 20 the correct Ten Commandments or is Exodus 34? If Exodus 20 is the correct version, do the Jews, Protestants, or Catholics present it in the right format? Do we have to follow each commandment to the letter? Why do some of the laws fail to account for the complexities of human life? Why do many of them seem hopelessly outdated and have no place in free and democratic societies? If God wanted us all to be aware of, comprehend, and obey a short, ten-item list of laws, wouldn't he have thought to make them a little less mysterious and a lot more relevant? Consider the situation we have today. One practically has to have a doctorate in theology or religious studies just to be able to sort out why the popular Exodus 20 commandments alone come in multiple versions.

To a sincere skeptic looking in from the outside, all of this looks suspiciously like the work of ancient people operating all by themselves without any input from a god. Laws of the Old Testament, including all versions of the Ten Commandments, seem more like something made by humans for human consumption than anything else. If this is the case, it certainly would explain the contradictions and conflict that surround the Ten Commandments. After all, confusion is inevitable when one culture transmits information to others across more than three thousand years of time. We should expect there to be difficulties in attempting to understand and appreciate laws that were produced by and for a particular group of people in their particular place and moment of history. A god, it seems, would have done better.

IS CHRISTIANITY GOOD FOR WOMEN?

Do not be ignorant of me.
For I am the first and the last.
I am the honored one and the scorned one.
I am the whore and the holy one.
I am the wife and the virgin.
I am [the mother] and the daughter.
I am the members of my mother.
I am the barren one.
and many are her sons.
—"The Thunder, Perfect Mind," an early Christian poem[1]

One cannot simply declare that Christianity is bad for women and leave it at that, as some skeptics of religion do. It's tempting, of course, given the negative words directed at women throughout the Bible, as well as the discrimination and abuse that Christian men and Christian institutions have inflicted on women in past centuries and today. However, that is not the entire story. Considering the time period, women do have a relatively high profile in the New Testament. Jesus spends time with them and even speaks to them in private and public—not something many devout Jewish men did back then. Mary Magdalene was one of his prominent disciples. Speaking to women and acknowledging their existence may not seem like much today, but the treatment of women was so bad in the ancient world, particularly in the context of religion, that it is notable.

Thanks to new research, it is becoming more and more evident that Christian women were not irrelevant handmaidens waiting in the wings while men did all the real work during the earliest days of Christianity. Elizabeth Clark, professor of religion at Duke University, thinks that women had a key role in the religion's development. Before there were churches, the early Christians met at private homes. Scholars have learned that these houses were owned by women. "I think this is significant," states Clark, "because I don't think the women who owned these houses were simply providing coffee and cookies, in effect, for the Christian community. I think that this probably gave them some avenue to power."[2] Clark adds that women are more prominent in earlier Christian writing, then become less so as Christianity becomes grounded and men establish their male-only power structure. But, she says, women still made an impact, such as in the founding of monasteries that provided aid to thousands of poor people. However, they always faced injustice. "There's not a single woman of renown in the ancient church whose story does not show enormous opposition from some of the men in the group."[3]

Karen L. King, a Harvard University Divinity School professor, finds that women were always involved, always contributing: "It needs to be emphasized that the formal elimination of women from official roles of institutional leadership did not eliminate women's actual presence and importance to the Christian tradition, although it certainly seriously damaged their capacity to contribute fully. What is remarkable is how much evidence has survived systematic attempts to erase women from history, and with them the warrants and models for women's leadership."[4]

For all the positive points, however, Christianity's role in degrading women and holding back their progress can't be ignored or forgiven if equality-minded contemporary Christians are ever to move their religion beyond its tendency to provide cover for men who treat women poorly. No Christian can simply say it's in the past and Christianity now values women as much as men, because there are still many millions of Christians worldwide who prefer the traditional view of women as second-class human beings. It should not be news to anyone, but some Christian leaders still cite the Bible as proof of women's inferiority and proper role as servants to men. The following quotes clearly show why the Bible is a reliable source of instruction and justification for men who want to oppress women:

- "Unto the woman he said, I will greatly multiply thy sorrow and thy conception; in sorrow thou shalt bring forth children; and thy desire shall be to thy husband, and he shall rule over thee." (Genesis 3:16)
- "But I would have you know, that the head of every man is Christ;

and the head of the woman is the man; and the head of Christ is God." (1 Corinthians 11:3)

- "Let your women keep silence in the churches: for it is not permitted unto them to speak; but they are commanded to be under obedience, as also saith the law. And if they will learn any thing, let them ask their husbands at home: for it is a shame for women to speak in the church." (1 Corinthians 14:34–35)
- "For the man is not of the woman; but the woman of the man. Neither was the man created for the woman; but the woman for the man." (1 Corinthians 11:8–9)
- "Wives, submit yourselves unto your own husbands, as unto the Lord. For the husband is the head of the wife, even as Christ is the head of the church: and he is the savior of the body. Therefore as the church is subject unto Christ, so let the wives be to their own husbands in everything." (Ephesians 5:22–24)
- "Of the woman came the beginning of sin, and through her we all die." (Ecclesiastes 25:22)
- "Let the women learn in silence with all subjection. But I suffer not a woman to teach, nor to usurp authority over the man, but to be in silence. For Adam was first formed, then Eve. And Adam was not deceived, but the woman being deceived was in the transgression." (1 Timothy 2:11–14)
- "And the daughter of any priest, if she profane herself by playing the whore, she profaneth her father: she shall be burnt with fire." (Leviticus 21:9)

Clearly, ideas and words like these are best left in ancient times. Thankfully, many Christians recognize this and have no interest in following the Bible's lead when it comes to women's rightful place in society. This is yet another opportunity for Christians and skeptics to find important common ground. Regarding women, a literal reading of the Bible is just not appropriate. Christians who agree should join with skeptics who care about fairness for women to challenge those who still promote the biblical view of women.

The late writer and critic of religion Ruth Hurmence Green felt that the Bible is perhaps the greatest obstacle for women. She wrote:

As long as women fail to denounce the Bible, they are in danger from it, for it has long been and continues to be their greatest oppressor. Its scriptures demean her and deprive her not only of her self-respect, but of veritable control over her body. The body makes her a slave, a piece of property and the mercy and whim of the male and in a state of total submission to her husband, who may even act as her abuser. She is regarded by the scriptures as the receptacle of the male seed and the means of reproducing the human race, and this is her only function.[5]

I don't know if progress for women depends in part on good Christians denouncing the Bible or on them simply refusing to stand by in silence when sexist Christians quote it to the detriment of women. I do know, however, that few issues relating to Christianity are as important as gender fairness. I have seen some of the worst of antiwoman sentiments espoused by male Christians in the United States and in other countries. I have heard comments and witnessed male dominance in action and was struck by the attitudes of the men, some of whom I knew personally to otherwise be decent human beings. It was troubling that they not only felt their behavior was acceptable and not something they needed to hide or be ashamed of; they seemed to feel such behavior was an obligation. It was God's will for them to lord over women, simply because "it's in the Bible." It makes no sense, I thought, good men doing bad because they think it's good. I am reminded of a quote by Steven Weinberg, winner of the Nobel Prize in Physics. About religion he said, "With or without it you would have good people doing good things and evil people doing evil things. But for good people to do evil things, that takes religion."[6]

IS IT SMARTER TO BELIEVE OR NOT BELIEVE?

Intelligence is a controversial concept, to say the least. It matters so much in so many ways, yet we understand it so little. There is not even a universally agreed-upon definition of *intelligence* within the scientific community. There is no agreement on how best to measure it or how we should fairly and productively use the measurements we do obtain. In short, human intelligence is a swirling, complex, hot-button issue that we are still figuring out. So, of course, it would have to intersect with religion at some point.

Unfortunately, confusion and unproven assumptions cloud the issue of intelligence and religion. Are religious people smarter than atheists? Or is it the other way around? Some believers think that atheists can't be too bright because they fail to see what seems so obvious to religious people. Some atheists, meanwhile, point to the popular Christian concept of faith as anti-intellectual and cite examples of how religious beliefs often contradict evidence-based knowledge. And then there are the scientists. These people are considered by many to be the smartest loosely affiliated group in the world, although this is debatable just like everything else that involves trying to measure and compare intelligence. Surveys consistently show that the rates of religious belief among scientists are significantly lower than those of the rest of society.

For example, Britain's Royal Society, a fellowship of the world's "most elite scientists," is heavily populated with atheists. As of 2008, only 3.3 percent of its members believe in a god.[1] Another study looked at America's National Academy of Sciences, also an organization of scientists deemed to be the best in their fields, and found that only 7 percent believed in God.[2]

We always need to be careful when it comes to drawing conclusions about intelligence. How do we know, for example, that scientists aren't just uniquely open about nonbelief because their subculture is more tolerant of it? Who knows? Maybe politicians have an even higher rate of atheism but we don't know because they lie about it. It's possible. Maybe highly intelligent people who believe in gods don't pursue careers in science at the same rate highly intelligent nonbelievers do. We can't assume anything.

Both of the extremes regarding intelligence and religion are wrong. Religion is not a vast domain of the dumb, and atheism is not some exclusive club for the brightest among us. Religions may have their problems when it comes to proof and logic, but any atheist or skeptic who suggests that religious belief is dependent on a dim mind is simply wrong. There are far too many exceptions. As everyone knows, there is no shortage of brilliant doctors, lawyers, engineers, artists, and writers who happen to be religious believers. Isaac Newton is arguably the greatest scientist of all time—and he was intensely Christian. He even spent a lot of time calculating a precise date for the return of Jesus (2060). Many exceptionally bright scientific thinkers have been Christians, including Gregor Mendel, Louis Pasteur, Max Planck, and Freeman Dyson. Skeptics of religion may become frustrated by people they perceive as being unable to "get it" that evidence is lacking for the existence of gods. But intelligence in general can't be blamed because the contrary evidence is too great. Skeptics may also wrongly assume that insufficient education is the ill and more education is the cure. But we know this is not the case because there are too many university graduates who believe, too many Christians with doctoral degrees running around for this to be true.

Christian universities turn out highly educated and very confident believers by the thousands every spring. And so do secular universities. Skeptics may not agree with the curriculums these graduates passed through, but no one can rightly call them uneducated after four or more years of higher education. I recall watching an interview on C-SPAN with David DeWitt, department chairman of Creation Studies at Liberty University in Lynchburg, Virginia. DeWitt is a Christian creationist who thinks the Earth and all life was created in seven twenty-four-hour days roughly six thousand years ago.[3] This is about the most absurd and extreme antiscience position anyone could hold. Numerous scientific disciplines are in agreement that life is at least three *billion* years old and that our planet formed around 4.5 *billion* years ago. Clearly DeWitt is getting this particular information from the Bible and not the scientific process. Regardless, DeWitt is a professional scientist. He is a professor of biology at an accredited university. He is a biochemist and neuroscientist with a doctorate from Case Western University. Skeptics may giggle, but they can't say he is uneducated. And it is unlikely that more education would correct his profoundly silly position on the age of the Earth and life or anything else tied to his creationist beliefs. Only an adjustment in how he thinks and how he assesses the quality and quantity of evidence would do that, I'm sure.

I must mention, however, five specific fields of knowledge that I think really can directly and rapidly erode religious confidence: anthropology, astronomy, biology, history, and—believe it or not—religious education. Like anthropology, the latter can be particularly useful in enlightening people about the reality of religion and humankind. Few religious people, immersed in just one religion out of many thousands, realize how busy we humans have been creating gods and religions over the last several thousand years. That realization alone can be jarring for some believers in relative isolation who assume their religion is significantly different and special compared with all the others. Still, no amount of education guarantees a person will emerge as nonbeliever. Remember the role of confirmation bias. It can be very difficult to destroy an entrenched belief, no matter how many contradictory facts come along.

Some Christians go too far the other way and argue that smart believers are evidence of something. They point to intelligent and/or highly educated Christians and claim that their belief in Jesus somehow proves the claim. But it doesn't, of course, for we know that very smart people can believe the most peculiar things. Some people who are clearly brighter than most are devout believers in UFOs and the wildest of conspiracy theories, for example. There does appear to be some correlation between education and belief in God, but it's somewhat tenuous. In 2011, Gallup® asked adult Americans, "Do you believe in God or a universal spirit?" Of those with a high-school degree or less who responded, 97 percent said yes. Eighty-seven percent with postgraduate education said yes.[4]

The possibility of an intelligence–religion correlation has never seemed particularly promising in my view. I have interviewed many extremely sharp people in my career. Most said they believed in a god, or else I assumed they believed based on things they said. I have had long, probing conversations with famous scientists, men who walked on the Moon, political leaders, and others. They were not idiots or fools. Likewise with atheism. I have interviewed some brilliant scientists who were atheists. For me, based on my lifetime of experiences and observations, intelligence means little when it comes to belief in a god. Don't forget that intelligence—whatever we may say it is—can be thought of as a tool or an ability that can lead or follow an individual down many different paths. A genius can play chess, invent calculus, or stay home and never produce anything. A gifted mind might take one to the Artificial Intelligence Lab at MIT or to a lifetime of daily chants and prayers in a monastery on Mount Athos. If anything can ever be shown to explain beyond a doubt why some believe and others do not, I suspect it will be found in culture, the obvious place to look, or perhaps there is some specific brain function or structure that makes some people more agreeable to the god concept than others. But I strongly doubt the key will turn out to be general intelligence.

A very interesting 2011 Harvard University study found that the *style of thinking* may be the telltale factor. The researchers controlled for education, socioeconomic status, and political orientation, and they discovered that people who are more intuitive in their thinking are more likely to believe in God and that people who are more analytical are more likely to be atheists.[5] This is not conclusive, however, because it is possible that believing in God leads people to be more intuitive, rather than the other way around.

Another study claims to have found a link between high IQs and nonbelief by looking at national IQ averages and religiosity within nations. It claims that higher IQs link well with lower rates of religious belief, and lower IQs line up with more religious belief.[6] But again, I worry that this issue is far too complex to be cracked easily. Can we really trust something like national IQ averages? It's not as if every human in every country has the same education, motivation, opportunity, nutrition, security, and so on. There seem to be too many cultural and environmental factors at play for us to be making too much of innate intelligence measurements and religion. How can we be sure that a supposedly low average IQ has anything to do with a country's high rate of religious belief? Maybe it can be explained completely by historical factors or a simple quirk of culture, such as universal religious indoctrination in schools. Or, maybe a given population is extraordinarily bright compared to others, but pollutants, war, or bad nutrition have artificially smothered innate intelligence.

When thinking about intelligence and religious belief, it is crucial for people to understand that skepticism is not a natural component of high intelligence or something that just pops up automatically as a by-product of advanced education. Skepticism is a somewhat specific skill set that has to be learned. It is also an attitude that one must consciously adopt and courageously maintain. One can be bright and still be a bad skeptic. One can be a very good skeptic without a college or high-school degree.

Many nonbelievers struggle to understand how someone can be intellectually vibrant and accomplished while holding onto ideas that nonbelievers consider to be transparently wrong. I think the answer to much of this is probably compartmentalization—something many of us do to avoid the discomfort of cognitive dissonance. That's the uneasy clash that occurs when two conflicting ideas or beliefs inhabit one brain. For example, imagine a fitness fanatic who smokes cigarettes. How can she smoke if she cares so much about health and fitness? She is able to do it because she compartmentalizes the smoking. It's walled away somewhere in her brain, just beyond the reach of reason. So while she may check the labels of food, count calories, and drink only filtered water, none of her health concerns and attention to detail are applied to smoking because her brain keeps that part of her life tucked away in another room. I think this is why so many thoughtful and sensible religious people are able to hold onto and defend unproven, extraordinary claims without flinching. But if someone wants to sell these people a house or a lawnmower, they suddenly spring into super-skeptic mode. They ask countless questions and demand proof that it's a smart purchase. Many religious people are outstanding critical thinkers and skeptics—except when it comes to their religious belief because that stays safely untouched in a "different compartment." I don't think this is healthy or safe. Nothing should be excluded from analysis and questioning. Absolute consistency of thinking may be impossible, but it's one of the most important goals for a good skeptic.

SO MANY RELIGIONS, SO LITTLE TIME. The high number of religions that exist today and the extinct religions that existed in the past make thoughtful analysis and fair comparison of their claims virtually impossible for the individual. How many Christians, for example, have researched and given serious consideration to the numerous gods of Hinduism or have visited a Hindu temple like this one in Nepal? *Photo by the author.*

IS THE BORN-AGAIN EXPERIENCE
IN CHRISTIANITY UNIQUE?

**Very truly I tell you, no one can see the kingdom of God
without being born again.**

—Jesus, John 3:5

Christians do not agree on what it takes to be "born again." Some believe that making an intensely emotional connection with Jesus in one dramatic moment is required for salvation. Others, however, don't believe that is necessary. If you want to find out what is required to be a "proper" Christian who "knows Jesus," the answer will always depend on which Christian you ask. The flexibility and diversity of the world's current most popular religion means that many such key elements of belief vary widely in interpretation. Many millions of Christians never experience the evangelical version of being born again, and they do not feel that their belief is diminished in any way without it. Some feel that a "spiritual regeneration" of some sort is important though not necessarily the most profound event of their lives, like, for example, a formal baptismal ceremony in a church, which can be more scripted and routine than a life-altering, watershed moment. Many Protestant Christians, however, do claim to have been born again in a deeply personal and spectacular manner that radically transformed their lives, made them different people, and left them with no doubt about the existence and importance of Jesus to the world.

This is no trivial sideshow. Born-again Christians tend to be the most passionate and dedicated believers, and they make up a significant portion of the US population. According to a 2004 Gallup® survey, 41 percent of Americans identify themselves as born again.[1] A 2006 Barna Group report gives a similar figure, 45 percent.[2] Whatever this phenomenon is, it clearly happens to many people.

I have never been born again, nor have I had any other kind of close encounter with Jesus. But I have talked with many people who say they have. Two things consistently stand out about their claims: there is obvious passion in their stories, and they almost always cite their born-again moment as proof that Jesus is real and Christianity is the one true religion. Because this event is so important to many Christians, it warrants analysis and challenge. Is being born again a real or imagined event? And is it evidence of a real god? I prefer to be gentle when confronting the born-again claim. While I'm not convinced these are encounters with a god, I do think many people sincerely feel they are. Millions of Christians grow up constantly hearing about the born-again experience. They are told that it is wonderful, that it feels great, and that it absolutely must happen or else one goes to hell. Given that input, what is the likely output? It is no surprise to the skeptic that many Christians report having this profound emotion, given the considerable prompting and pressure to have it.

"You don't understand," a Christian told me. "When you are born again, you *know* it's real. There is no doubt about it. You know Jesus and you are never the same again. It's powerful. It's real. I don't have any doubts whatsoever. I have a personal relationship with Jesus. I know him as well or better than I know any of my friends and family members."

"But how do you know your born-again experience was actually a supernatural connection with Jesus?" I asked. "Maybe what happened to you can be explained by human psychology, something about the way our brains work and how we think. Maybe it's all in your head. People can be overwhelmed with emotions in many different contexts and can imagine things. I'm not suggesting that you are crazy or lying. Anyone can experience something that feels real but isn't. So don't you think that a more simple, alternate explanation is worth considering?"

"It was too real," he replied. "I was born again. I felt pure joy. It was incredible, the best feeling I could possibly ever have. I knew at that moment that Jesus loved me. No doubt. There is no doubt in my mind that he came into my heart that day, and I have no doubt that it's happened to other born-again Christians. I know it's Jesus because I'm changed. He's still with me today all these years later. If you ask him to come into your heart, and mean it, you will see what I'm talking about."

I have had many conversations with born-again Christians about this, and all of them fascinated me because I felt like I was debriefing an astronaut who made first contact with an advanced extraterrestrial life-form. That's not meant to be disrespectful. I really do feel like I'm receiving dispatches from another world—and the born-again Christian thinks that as well, I suppose. Discussing the born-again experience from a skeptical perspective is challenging, however, because people are inclined to have unwarranted confidence in their senses and personal memories. They are unaware that unusual experiences—an intimate interface with a god certainly qualifies—demand a healthy dose of skepticism based on what we know about the workings of normal human brains. There are many ways in which the brain can embellish, restructure, or create an experience that is apart from reality. In light of this, it only makes sense to have doubts about stories of believers seeing, hearing, or feeling the presence of Jesus.

YOUR BRAIN LIES TO YOU

All humans come into this world with a brain. Unfortunately, none of us are issued an operator's manual that explains how it works and how we need to always be on guard against its strange but standard features that so often lead us astray. Seeing, hearing, discerning reality from fantasy, and remembering events are all things that come naturally to us and seem somewhat reliable and trustworthy. But what most people don't understand is that the way our brains perceive the world, how they go about assessing reality, and how they recall past events are very different from what our instincts and traditional common sense lead us to believe.

In order to make a fair assessment about whether or not we can trust born-again experiences as evidence of a god's existence, we have to consider how reliable and consistent we are at separating fact from fiction in our own heads. It turns out that we aren't very good at it. It is very easy for us to be fooled by the environment, by other people, and even by our own thoughts. That's why the scientific method is invaluable. It's a way of discovering, learning, and confirming reality above and beyond many of the natural human frailties such as bias and the capacity for delusion.

WHO ARE THE BORN-AGAIN CHRISTIANS?

Close to half of the American population describe themselves as born-again Christians. Following are the percentages of Christians who describe their religious identity as "born again"

Religious Tradition

Evangelical Protestant	62.4%
Black Protestant	57.3%
Mainline Protestant	16.8%
Catholic	4.7%

Gender

Male	23.6%
Female	32.8%

Education

High School or Less	33.7%
College or More	22.9%[3]

None of this is meant to disparage the human brain. It's an amazing product of the indifferent and unintelligent creative force of evolution. Thanks to this magnificent three-pound firestorm of neurons that we carry around in our skulls, our species has been able to create languages, mathematics, science, music, art, ice cream, and so on. Of course, these powerful brains also enable us to exploit and to kill one another in creative ways, too, so it's a mixed bag. Even in light of that downside, however, our brains can be described as wonderful machines of calculation and imagination. We may not be nature's fastest or strongest physically, but we are champion thinkers. Even the dimmest among us tend to have immense brain power that towers far above virtually all other life on Earth. We are special, yes, but only because our brains are.

Unfortunately, the brains we rely on for so much have weird ways of operating, many of which are not easily detectable or recognizable to us. Because of this, most people don't understand how vulnerable we all are to errors of perception, analysis, judgment, and calculation. This is why people who "see" ghosts and UFOs—or have a born-again experience—are often so stubbornly confident about what they "know." In most cases, these people are unaware of how easy it is for anyone to be misled into misperceiving things and believing virtually anything. The cold, hard truth is that if you are a human being, then you are highly susceptible to seeing, hearing, and feeling things that do not exist in reality. It is also standard operating procedure for human brains to wildly misremember even very important events of the past. Furthermore, the beliefs a person holds can and often do have a huge influence on the type of experiences he has. For example, ask yourself why it is that so many UFO believers repeatedly see alien spaceships while the world's professional and amateur astronomers never see any—despite the fact that they are looking at the sky more than anyone else. Why is it that those who already believe in ESP and psychics tend to be the only people who are impressed when some medium fumbles through a game of twenty questions?

Numerous claims of profound and powerful born-again experiences should surprise no one. They can be recognized as most likely being psychological phenomena brought on by strongly held beliefs, fueled by cultural influences and peer pressure. As they are described, there certainly is nothing about them that suggests that a supernatural being must be involved. Born-again Christians have no grounds to reject this possibility because they have human brains, and we know human brains can produce these kinds of delusions. Nothing about any of this should be interpreted as insulting or condescending. I suspect that if Christians thought more about normal brain functions and basic psychology, as well as the common occurrence of mystical experiences outside of their religion, they would be much more skeptical about born-again stories, not only others', but their own as well.

NON-CHRISTIANS HAVE GOD ENCOUNTERS TOO

If visits and personal communications from a god only happened to Christians, then born-again claims might be more compelling. But many millions of people in many different cultures and contexts have reported having experiences that are very similar. It's nothing new or unique to Christianity. Considering the broader picture of humanity may help believers see this issue with more clarity. It simply is not logical or fair to present only a subset of one religion's claims as worthy of consideration. So, in fairness, do the intense trances of prehistoric shamans confirm the existence of their gods and the validity of their magic? Do prophecies made by the priestess Pythia on Mount Parnassus remove all doubt about the gods of ancient Greece being real? Do the contorted spasms of a "possessed" animist today establish the existence of spirits in nature to a degree beyond question? What can we say is proven when a holy man prays away an evil *jinn* who had possessed the body and mind of a Muslim? Some people in the United States report emotionally charged and life-changing experiences that involve extraterrestrials abducting them. Do the sincerity, confidence, and emotional investment of alleged abductees mean that aliens are visiting the Earth? I don't think so. Born-again Christians who can recognize that these examples fail to prove anything have only to apply the same reasoned thinking and skepticism to their own claims of supernatural encounters to see how unlikely they are too.

Simply put, our brains cannot be trusted to always discern fantasy from reality. They should never be trusted without question when something extremely unusual or important is being claimed. Sincere Christians may be convinced that something amazing and real happened to them, but this alone proves nothing. It is normal human activity for people to experience unusual events, as has been demonstrated by people for thousands of years in thousands of cultures. It is for this reason that skeptics of born-again experiences should never be quick to judge believers as unintelligent or mentally ill. In the vast majority of cases, they are, I would presume, merely being human.

TRUE BELIEVERS

According to surveys, born-again Christians are more likely to believe in various aspects of Christianity than are other kinds of Christians. For example, they are much more likely than Catholics and Protestants to believe in the following:

God	97%
Heaven	97%
The Resurrection	97%
Miracles	95%
Angels	95%
The Virgin Birth	92%
Survival of the Soul	91%
Hell	89%
The Devil	89%
Creationism	68%
Evolution	16%[4]

I TRIED

Some Christians may be angered by my attempt to cast doubt on claims of born-again experiences. But it might soften their hearts to know that I once tried to become a born-again Christian. When I was around the age of thirteen, a devout and devoted Christian who was apparently working his way through the phone book called my house. The tele-missionary asked if I had accepted Jesus into my heart and been born again. When I told him that nothing like that had ever happened to me, he explained that when I died, I would not be able to go to heaven and would have to suffer in hell forever. He said it was crucial that I immediately get myself properly born again to be safe. I was, according to him, sinful and unworthy of salvation. This was a harsh message for a harmless junior-high kid who only answered the phone because no one else was home. However, I sensed the man meant well, and I was polite, so I kept listening. He told me that in order to live again after I die, I only had to invite Jesus into my heart, ask him to forgive me for all the terrible things I had done in the first thirteen years of my life, and then say the Lord's Prayer.

At first, I was just being respectful to a stranger, but then I thought, "Hey, why not?" I can't say that I was convinced by his warning, but I didn't fully dismiss the man or his claim either. So, following his instructions, I said something like "Jesus, come into my heart and please forgive me for my sins." The voice on the phone then led me through a prayer. As I recall, I was completely sincere about the whole thing. I had always had some degree of uncertainty about the actual existence of gods, and I did that afternoon, but I gave this thing a fair and honest effort. What stands out most in my memory about that phone call is the man saying something to the effect of "That's it, now you're born again. You are forgiven and will be with Jesus now and for eternity after you die." But I wasn't sold. I didn't feel anything. No sense of being in the presence of Jesus, no warm sensation, no indescribable peace and contentment, no waves of electrical stimulation surging through my body, no tremors. Nothing.

I've shared the story of my failed born-again attempt with several Christians, and most of them tell me that the explanation is simple: I didn't believe in Jesus sufficiently, therefore Jesus did not come to me. But my reaction to that is, why not? It seems odd that one has to believe Jesus is real before Jesus will reveal himself as real. Isn't that backward? Shouldn't the evidence come before the conclusion? Whenever someone holds a strong belief and then has an unusual experience that seems to confirm the belief, an internal alarm bell should go off, alerting that person to be skeptical. The reality is that the typical born-again experience does not seem to be as much of a radical upheaval to an individual's life as it is usually made out to be. It's like turning up the volume rather than changing channels—casual Christians may be transformed into intense Christians, but that's about it in most cases. As mentioned previously, believing often leads to seeing when it comes to UFOs and ghosts. Why should we think that this is any different? Christians already admit that one has to "accept Jesus" before a born-again experience will occur. To the skeptic, this sounds like one is required to give in to suggestibility, abandon skepticism, and ask no more questions. Let down your guard against irrational beliefs and something real is likely to happen? More like, let down your guard and something unreal is likely to happen.

Spurred on by that anonymous missionary who phoned me, I tried my best to initiate the born-again experience. I had doubts and couldn't fake absolute belief, of course, but I said the words and thought the thoughts with the utmost sincerity possible—and nothing happened. It was like pulling the trigger on an unloaded gun. No belief, no born-again experience.

THE PROPHECY. Did the creation of a new Israeli nation in 1948 prove that God is real and keeps his promises? Or was it solely the work of people? *Photo by the author.*

IS FAITH A GOOD THING?

Where there is evidence, no one speaks of "faith." We do not speak of faith that two and two are four or that the Earth is round. We only speak of faith when we wish to substitute emotion for evidence.

—Bertrand Russell[1]

Negatively criticizing faith in the context of religious belief can be immensely challenging because faith is held in such high regard. Few believers seem prepared to rethink or consider abandoning it after being told for years that it is positive, sensible, and essential to their religion. The marketing of the faith concept over the centuries has been so successful that pointing out problems with it can feel like a vicious attack on Mom and apple pie in the minds of many Christians. Criticizing faith has become the intellectual and emotional equivalent of kicking a kitten. Nevertheless, faith is such an intellectually corrosive concept and backward way of thinking about extraordinary claims that it must be challenged. To be clear, this chapter is not about the supernatural claims of Christianity or the existence of the Christian god. This chapter deals only with the problems of faith as a reason or justification for believing in a god. It seeks to show that faith is both flawed and undesirable because it asks people to sacrifice sound thinking in order to leap to unwarranted conclusions. Nobody, Christian or non-Christian, should rely on faith as a way to think.

Before we analyze faith, let's consider what it is precisely. As with most aspects of Christianity, there are many opinions about faith. I understand that one size does not fit all. In general, however, there are two primary definitions of faith that most Christians would probably agree with: (1) trusting in someone or something, or (2) believing/knowing that a god is real even when proof or good evidence is lacking or absent. To further confuse the issue, faith is often used as a synonym for religion. It is important to keep these definitions separate and to be consistent when trying to make sense of faith in religion. Unfortunately, many Christians seamlessly transition back and forth between the various meanings, which can be confusing in a serious discussion about faith.

Faith that a god is real is not the same as the faith (trust) one may have in a god or in friends and family, for example. The faith, or trust, that I have in my children and wife is very different from the type of faith that leads a Christian to confidently assert that her god is real. I have sufficient evidence and experience that allows me to be confident that my family will not murder me in my sleep or set fire to my beloved book collection. In that regard, I have "faith" in them. However, I don't need to have "faith" in their existence as human beings. I can say with confidence that I know they exist because I have overwhelming evidence for it; I have touched them, heard them, and seen them. My children leave trails of destruction through the house, further evidence of their existence. I don't have a place for the religious version of faith anywhere in my life. If there is evidence for something, then I'll accept it as real or true. But if there is none, I won't, simple as that. I don't want or need a concept like faith bouncing around in my head because it would lead me to declare that I know things I don't know. And that's both bad thinking and dishonest. I can still hope for things to be real or true, and I certainly can dream about anything, but faith does not fraudulently inflate my knowledge.

KNOWING WITHOUT KNOWING

The following is a typical description of faith taken from a popular Christian website: "Faith is belief with strong conviction; firm belief in something for which there may be no tangible proof. . . . Faith is the opposite of doubt. Faith is possibly the single-most important element of the Christian life."[2] The Bible describes faith as the "assurance of things hoped for, the conviction of things not seen" (Hebrews 11:1). Most Christians view faith as the route by which they are able to confidently know their god is real and know something about his role in the universe and in their personal lives—despite not having good evidence that they could share with others or submit to the scientific process. Having faith in God is considered to be a virtue, a thing to be proud of and to encourage in others.

But does any of this make sense? It shouldn't, not to a Christian or anyone else who cares about truth and reality. For their own good, everyone—including Christians—should *think* before they *believe*. Coming to important conclusions based on faith is a danger-laden cop-out. It's a shortcut, cheating in order to avoid doing the hard work of investigation and analysis. It's like trying to answer a complex math problem without doing any math. One or more gods may be real—it's possible—but we can't just say faith settles the question and move on. We must rely on good arguments and very good evidence to be sure, otherwise we set ourselves up to make mistakes and waste our time believing in things that are not real. Choosing faith over reason to decide something dishonors the magnificent thinking machine inside your skull. Using faith to figure out the existence of something is nothing more than sloppy thinking, and sloppy thinking often leads to errors and problems. Christian or not, we all should strive to be consistently sharp thinkers who come to important conclusions only after weighing the available arguments and evidence.

Keep in mind that rejecting the concept of faith does not mean one has to be an atheist. I have had discussions with Christians who recognize and admit that faith is an intellectual dead end. They still believe in Jesus, but they base their belief on a personal mix of hope and what they feel is "good-enough" evidence. This position, while not without problems, is far better than simply declaring, "Jesus is a real god because I have faith that he is a real god."

IS FAITH AN ESCAPE FROM REASON?

"Faith," as Mark Twain wrote in one of his books more than a century ago, "is believing what you know ain't so."[3] That just about sums up everything wrong with this popular justification for belief. The problem with faith is that it gives us a pass to pretend we know something without really knowing and in many cases to accept things that make no sense. It's a form of thinking that is anti-thinking. It demands that we make a decision about something important without any mental effort. How can such a process be safe, productive, or wise? If faith is the means by which we decide something without considering evidence or demanding proof, then I wouldn't rely on it to cross the street, much less to determine whether or not a god is real.

Christians and other religious people often stress the serious repercussions of their particular claims. One's "eternal salvation" is at stake, they say. If it's so serious, then how can something so flimsy and hollow as faith be allowed to enter the discussion? Are there any human activities outside of religion that place the concept of faith on a pedestal and encourage people to aspire to it? If religion's version of faith is reasonable and if it works, then why don't scientists use it to explain various aspects of the universe? "I know that extraterrestrial life is real because I have faith in its existence," says the astrobiologist. "Therefore, there is no reason to search for it by sending robotic probes to faraway planets. My faith assures me it is there." How comfortable would you be if you had a faith-reliant surgeon who said, "No need for x-rays or blood tests, I know there is a tumor in your brain, so I'm going in. Thanks to faith, I'm 100 percent certain that it's there." If faith is enough to declare that a god is real, then why not aliens and tumors too?

LET'S NOT FORGET ALL THOSE OTHER GODS

Another significant problem with faith is that it's not exclusive to one god—at least, it shouldn't be. Unfortunately for Christians who promote the faith concept, no one ever patented it, so it can be used by others too. Peter Boghossian, a philosophy instructor at Portland State University, agrees that faith in the context of religion is a substitute for thinking that no one should rely on.

> If one uses faith to arrive at a conclusion, that conclusion will necessarily be arbitrary. Like the horse in *Alice in Wonderland* that rides off furiously in all directions, faith cannot point one in a specific direction. This is because, absent sufficient evidence to justify belief, it's not possible to converge on a particular conclusion. For example, there are different faith traditions. Within each faith tradition there are different claims to truth. Muslims believe that Mohammad was the last prophet. Mormons believe that Joseph Smith, who lived after Mohammad, was a prophet. It cannot both be the case that Mohammad was the last prophet and someone who lived after him was also a prophet. At least one of these claims must be incorrect. It is impossible to figure out which of these claims is incorrect if the tool one uses to do this is faith. Faith cannot adjudicate. It cannot adjudicate because it is not a reliable arbiter of reality. It cannot help one to differentiate truth from

falsity. The most charitable thing one can say about faith is that it is likely to lead one in the wrong direction.[4]

This free use of faith, the ability to aim it at any god and any religion, should trouble the honest and thoughtful Christian because doing so sucks all power from the word. If one can allow faith to serve as the foundation or at least as a primary pillar of belief that Jesus is a god, then what happens when a Muslim says her faith informs her that Allah is real and he never had a son? What if a Jewish rabbi says he has faith that Yahweh never had a son or came to Earth in human form two thousand years ago? Would a Christian be impressed if a pagan were to cite faith in support of his belief in the gods of Mount Olympus? I don't think so.

CHURCH OF THE HOLY SEPULCHRE. The minor rumblings of one obscure
Jewish preacher two thousand years ago grew to create a massive impact on history
and become the world's most popular religion with more than two billion followers.
Photo by the author.

22

SHOULD CHILDREN BE CHRISTIANS?

I'm in a village about fifteen miles outside of New Delhi. I had spent much of the previous day standing in awe before the Taj Mahal. I had never seen such a gorgeous building. Its white marble surface sparkled, changing tones throughout the day as the angle of the Sun moved. To my eyes, the symmetry and flow of the building's lines seemed to be about as close to perfection as possible. That was a rare day of near-total immersion in beauty. The next day, however, was not.

Wandering around India alone stirs up a whirlwind of extremes and contradictions around every corner. In my opinion, no country on Earth offers more for the curious traveler. It's calming and peaceful, except, of course, when it is chaotic and exhausting. It's incredibly beautiful one moment, shockingly ugly the next. Its people are at once annoying and endearing, the best of us all, but also capable of dragging one to unprecedented lows. How can one country be so much? Many times I hated India. But I'll always love it.

After asking for a rundown on the local sights, I am informed by a friendly man that there is a madrassa nearby. I'm not sure why a Muslim school would be considered a can't-miss tourist attraction, but I decide to check it out. India's population is mostly Hindu, of course, but there are also more than 150 million Muslims, probably the second-most of any nation. On the way, a boy emerges from the rubble of an old building and approaches me. It takes me a moment to make sense of what I'm seeing. He is walking on all fours and seems twisted up in an impossible way. I guess that he is probably a victim of the polio virus, but I'm not sure. The boy smiles widely and extends an open hand, palm up. Still in shock, I don't even hesitate to scan for muggers before pulling out a wad of rupees and handing it to him. Walking on, I glance back and think to myself, "Damn, life is not fair."

I find the madrassa, and immediately I feel uneasy. A class is being taught outside in the open air. It's a beautiful day, but the children, all boys, are chanting like mindless puppets. Their teacher rushes over to greet me. He's very friendly and proceeds to give me a tour of the school.

"We use only the Koran," he explains. "Nothing else needed. Do you hear the recitations?"

"What about math?" I ask.

"No problem, we can teach anything. It's all in the Koran."

My eyes drifted over the thirty boys, ages ranging from eight to twelve, bobbing back and forth, rhythmically blurting out lines from the Koran that they have memorized. I'm shocked that this is what they do all day. I can't believe it. Surely they put the holy book away at some point and look at a few maps or maybe talk about how continental drift works, right? I asked the teacher again if all the education is Koran-based. Again, he assured me that their school does nothing with any other book or materials. He was not sheepish about this. If anything, he was bursting with pride about it. I asked in a roundabout, polite way if it was a matter of funding. Maybe the school wanted to work some biology and physics into the curriculum but just couldn't afford the textbooks. If that were the case, I'm pretty sure I would have emptied my money belt right then and there. He explained, however, that this was all by design. It's the right way, the only way, he said.

As a former teacher, my heart broke watching those kids. Two things were wrong with that scene. One, the education they were receiving was inept and incomplete, not due to some inescapable crush of poverty but because of a religious choice. Second, there was no thinking going on with regard to what they were memorizing. It was indoctrination, not education. It's incomprehensible, but try to imagine how much brain power our species squanders in this way. How many little boys spent yesterday memorizing lines from the Koran and thinking about heaven instead of learning about the stars and thinking about the future of space travel? Are our challenges so trivial that we can afford to lose potential problem solvers in this way? Oh, and by the way, where were the little girls? I asked the teacher about that too, and he said only boys go to school there. The girls, I assume, were at home cooking and doing laundry. In a strange way, they are probably better off. I know I would rather be focused on a good pot of curry chicken than on spending hours babbling line after line of text that had little or no meaning to me.

An interesting thing about my visit to a madrassa is that every time I tell the story to a Christian, I get the same response: "What a shame,"

"That's terrible," "Those poor children." Until I help them to see it, they never make the connection between what was going on in that school in India and the way millions of children are taught Christianity every day around the world. They don't recognize the link to the madrassa example because for them, such conditions seem so extreme and so obviously unfair to children.

But what about the primary method by which Christianity endures generation after generation? The religion is taught to very young children as being factual and necessary to one's life—without a hint or whisper of skepticism and critical thinking in most cases. The typical child's experience may not be to sit for hours reciting Leviticus and Deuteronomy, but the key problems are the same. A young child, from age two to twelve—thanks to the influences of nature, family, and society—is strongly inclined to accept and internalize most of whatever an authority figure such as a parent or teacher tells them. Few five-year-olds are in a position to challenge a father who tells them that Jesus, Allah, or Kali is real or that the Bible, Koran, or Bhagavad Gita is a book of pure truth. Skeptics of religion have big problems with this because it feels wrong. It seems very much like intellectual bullying.

I understand that Christians, like many Muslims and other religious adults, may feel that they are doing the right and necessary thing. To them, Christianity is the ultimate truth and source of goodness, but why not let the religion stand on its own strength? Why not let children mature to the point that they are able to think for themselves about unusual and important claims?

People often talk about contrasts and conflicts between rival religions. They almost always emphasize the wrong things. Whether Christianity or Islam dominates the future has little or nothing to with the merits or credibility of their adherents' claims. Even missionary work, marketing, and conversions are less important than the issue of childhood education/indoctrination. The religion with the adults who are the most successful at implanting it deep into the minds of impressionable and defenseless children is sure to win the popularity contest.

I recall attending a few Sunday-school classes during my childhood and being told Bible stories by a cheery woman. Moses on Mount Sinai, David and Goliath, God killing everybody in the world with a flood, the smiling lady told them all. The stories seemed far away in time and place, not relevant to me, but they were fascinating nonetheless. While other kids were sleeping or nibbling on paint chips, I was sitting wide-eyed in the front row. But it shouldn't have happened. The problem wasn't that I was told these stories or exposed to Christianity; it was the fact that the woman presented these stories as absolutely true. She never even hinted that many people in the world doubt them. I was presented the stories in the same way a child might be taught that World War II and the French Revolution took place. But there is a major difference, of course. The stories in the Bible involving supernatural events or beings have not been confirmed by historians and scientists. They are not evidence based.

It may surprise some Christians, but many atheists/skeptics, myself included, do not teach their children to not believe in gods. That would be no better than the madrassa's chanting or the Sunday school's misrepresentation of Bible stories as historical fact. When my children were very young, it never once occurred to me that I should sit them down and instruct them to reject Bible stories. In my mind, that would be indoctrination. That would be telling them *what* to think, rather than *how* to think. It made more sense to me—and seemed infinitely more fair and decent—to encourage them to think independently about religion and make up their own minds. One would think that any god with an appreciation for sincere worship and loyalty would not want it any other way.

To impose a specific belief in one god, when there are millions of them (according to various religious people), and to impose loyalty to one particular religion, when there are hundreds of thousands of them, seem like cheating to the outsider. The child is being lied to, in effect, when only one religion is placed on the table for his consideration. The parent or teacher is effectively hiding all other options from him. Why? If fairness mattered and if the minds of children were respected, adult believers would fairly and accurately present the claims of at least several religions and the biographies of several gods, and then let children make up their own minds. Better yet, just wait until people are young adults before any kind of recruiting is done. By then their minds are mature enough to at least have a chance of the independent thought necessary to weigh such matters and make decisions for themselves. Very young children ought to spend their time having fun, exploring the world, doing math and science, and reading Dr. Seuss books. Thoughts about original sin, the fires of hell, and Jesus hanging from a cross can wait for a more appropriate age.

I hope this chapter does not needlessly offend Christians. I understand that some Christians might feel like they are under attack when I say that many skeptics think all those sweet and harmless Sunday-school classes are dishonest marketing seminars designed to take advantage of innocent children. But I simply want Christians to understand that many nonbelievers view imposing Christianity on a trusting child not only as unfair to the child but also as possible evidence of a perceived weakness in the religion by its own adherents. We wonder why, if Christianity is the ultimate truth, its teachings have to be pushed in such an advantageous manner so early in life. Why not leave it until children grow up, when they are more thoughtful and less passive? Wouldn't that be more respectful to the young person and show more confidence in the religion?

I hope the Christian who recognizes what is wrong with ordering little boys to spend their days memorizing and chanting lines from the Koran will be able to recognize that at least a hint of something is amiss in the way Christianity is passed from generation to generation.

THE POWER. Are Christian faith healers such as Benny Hinn tapping into external supernatural forces, or could their acts be explained by natural psychological forces? *Photo by the author.*

23

DOES JESUS HEAL THE SICK?

O ne of the most common claims made by Christians is also one of the most extraordinary and potentially important for the world. For two thousand years, Christians have declared with great confidence that Jesus saves not only souls but bodies as well. Not all, but many Christians are certain that we have only to pray and ask for him to fix our broken bodies and restore good health. But does it work? And if it doesn't, then why does the claim persist? Finally, Christians who do not believe that Jesus heals through prayer in the way that evangelicals and others claim might ask, Why not? If Jesus is real, why wouldn't he come to the aid of, say, every Christian child with a life-threatening disease or painful injury?

For reasons we will address shortly, skeptics have little difficulty finding reasons to doubt that God heals. However, Christians should not be too defensive about this challenge. It should not be viewed as rude or confrontational to simply ask why the faith-healing claim is still unproven after all this time and to offer more down-to-earth explanations for what is going on. Skeptics are vulnerable to illness too and would no doubt embrace faith healing if they thought for a second that it would cure them of cancer or other catastrophic diseases. This is one claim everyone would love Christians to be right about.

People who are skeptical of Christian faith healing are only stating what should be obvious to all. If Jesus really cares about Christians and is able to cure them of any illness or injury, then something is clearly wrong. Look around. Our world is never short of sick and suffering Christians. Why do so many of them have to endure horrible illnesses and die young if they have the inside track to supernatural relief? Surely most, if not all of them, prayed to Jesus for help at the first sign of serious danger, so what is the problem? It's a simple question, but the usual responses from Christians are unsatisfying to the skeptic: God works in mysterious ways. Everything happens for a reason. It's

God's punishment. God likes to test us. God answered their prayers by taking them to heaven. He gave them peace and comforted them while they died. Our limited minds can't possibly understand why God does the things he does. Those who prayed for help didn't have enough faith. Sometimes God's answer to our prayers is no. We deserve to suffer and die because Adam bit a piece of fruit.

Can praying to Jesus make people feel better and even cause them to heal faster? Sure, it probably can, but so far as anyone can tell, no more reliably than praying to other gods does. The blunt reality is that there is no reason to believe that praying Christians fare better against disease, natural disasters, war, or accidents than non-Christians do. Despite centuries of claims that Jesus answers prayers related to health, no one has ever demonstrated being healed this way in a convincing manner. If such a claim had been proven, then I suspect there would be seven billion Christians on Earth today. People are not completely stupid. If one religion above all others were delivering a noticeably superior healthcare plan, there would be a stampede to sign up. If practicing Christianity really made Christians significantly healthier than Jews, Buddhists, Sikhs, and so on, wouldn't all rival religions soon fade away? It would be a colossal advantage, one the world would not ignore.

Christians who say that faith healing works should not rest until they prove their claim. Christians who are skeptical should demand that this claim be properly tested so that we might know one way or the other. If faith healing or healing by prayer is a false claim, then it's not doing Christianity any good in the long run because it weakens credibility. If true, it would change the world overnight. Imagine if prominent Christian faith healers made the effort to collect medical records from sizable test groups, record details of their healings, did the necessary follow-up work, and then published the results in reputable medical journals. In addition to saving and improving lives, the scientific confirmation of Christian faith healing would be perhaps the most dramatic and meaningful proof of Jesus's existence possible.

I stress "scientific" confirmation because the scientific process is the only way we can reliably prove important or unusual claims. Dramatic stories about random incidents are not proof. Selective compilations of "healing" events here and there are not proof. Oversight and attention to details are necessary. Experiments or studies that fail to account for bias and the placebo effect are not proof. Sometimes people take medicine with their prayers but only remember to credit the prayers if their health improves. Sometimes sufficient time passes and the body recovers, but prayers alone get the credit. Sometimes doctors make mistakes and people are not as sick as they thought they were in the first place. And sometimes people just get better for no apparent reason.

There have been some studies on intercessory prayer, of course, but they have failed to prove anything conclusive. Ideally, prominent preachers and faith healers, the ones who do the most to keep this belief going, need to apply basic science to their claims so that they can know and we can know if there is anything to them. I am sure that if I had the magic touch or was able to somehow facilitate God's healing for others, I would want it proven as fast as possible so that I could gain the medical community's approval and quickly begin emptying all the hospitals and sending sick children home to play baseball and ride their bikes again. I sure wouldn't waste time talking about it on TV or behind a pulpit. I would want to maximize the opportunity to help and save suffering people.

It makes no sense that preachers and congregations are not motivated to settle this question. It's just not enough to say "I know it's real, so I don't care about skeptics." Prove Jesus heals, and everything changes. Forget spending millions of dollars on religious satellite networks, forget sending missionaries around the world, shut down the websites, and turn off the Christian rock. Want to save souls for Jesus? Just prove that praying to him can cure AIDS and leukemia or restore amputated limbs. Do that, and it's mission accomplished.

Imagine, for example, a children's cancer hospital where only non-Christian children die. Imagine if Christians worldwide had an average life expectancy of thirty or forty years longer than non-Christians— regardless of income, living conditions, nutrition, exercise, and access to healthcare. This, of course, is not reality. The world as we find it does not seem to favor the health of Christians. If there were something to this claim, wouldn't an impoverished Christian living in rural Tanzania have better prospects of a long and healthy life than a millionaire Hindu living in a Mumbai mansion? But we know this is not so.

When a severe earthquake strikes Haiti, praying Christians get hurt and die. When a tornado rips through an Oklahoma town, praying Christians get hurt and die. When Christians in southern Sudan are attacked by military planes, they bleed just like any non-Christian would. We don't compare praying habits to determine why some people are healthier and live longer than others. We look at sanitation, nutrition, security, stress, environmental toxins, genetics, and access to modern healthcare. These are factors we can easily prove cure people and save lives. Not so with faith healing. After thousands of years of claims from thousands of religions, we still don't have proof that faith healing works. If we did, it would have been incorporated into every hospital in every country long ago. No, that's not right. There would be no hospitals today. We would all just pray ourselves healthy every day.

Another commonsense problem for Christian faith healing is that it's not unique. Virtually every religion that has ever existed makes the same claim: *Our gods will protect you. Our gods will heal you. Pray and the gods will help.* Just like Christianity, however, none of the supernatural claims of these religions have ever earned scientific confirmation. When I traveled the world and spoke with people belonging to various religions, I was struck by how many non-Christians told me that they "know" their god or gods are real because of supernatural healing. Perhaps for those Christians living in mostly Christian societies in North America, South America, and the Caribbean, it is easy to overlook the reality of the world they share with five billion non-Christians. But the fact is that faith healing does not belong to Christianity exclusively. Hindus pray for healings—and say they get it. Muslims pray for relief when sick—and say they get it. Animists and Santería practitioners pray too—with success, they say. The skeptic, wanting only to get to the bottom of the claim and figure out if it is likely to be true or not, can only conclude that something very human and very natural is going on here. No gods involved.

After all, it has been proven that we are all vulnerable to confusing cause and effect. We all have extreme biases that can mislead us when interpreting events. And the accuracy of human memory can't be trusted. The same problems that trip up people and lead them to believe in so much medical quackery out there are the same problems that can lead the best of us to innocently conclude that a prayer is the reason an illness improved. Given the way normal human brains naturally work, coupled with the influence of cultural beliefs, it is only to be expected that many millions of people would misidentify natural, real-world occurrences for magical events. In many cases, it is only skepticism and the scientific method that can protect us from being led astray by our own thoughts.

No one, skeptic or Christian, should underestimate the emotional power that a faith-healing service can generate. I attended one of televangelist Benny Hinn's "Miracle Crusades" and was shocked by the intensity of the spectacle. Even after having watched Hinn perform on television many times and thoroughly researching faith healing prior to that night, I had no idea just how overwhelming the experience could be. Viewed from up close near the stage, Hinn is more than the simple court jester many of his detractors say he is. In person, it's easy to recognize what he really is: a master showman who knows how to sway thousands by blending words, music, and belief in God. It is easy for the skeptic to dismiss it all as nonsense, but it's only fair to point out that many people really do feel something during these events.

Praying, being prayed for, or being touched by an "anointed" holy man are not trivial, meaningless acts. There is real power in the touch of a faith healer and in the words of a sincere prayer. None of this is proof of a god, of course, but it does prove something about the power of believing. Many feel the urge to conform and the desire or need to have one's faith validated. At times, during a Hinn event, the pull of the herd is strong. I know this because I felt it, and I was probably the most skeptical person in the stadium. For many, it is perhaps irresistible. The urgent desire to receive God's blessing, to be healed, and, to a lesser degree, to please the healer, must be overwhelming for some. I saw a lot that night, but I saw nothing on the stage or in the audience during "healing time" that could not be explained by simple human delusion, excitement, and the natural compulsion people have to "follow the script" when the stage lights are on them.

I felt bad for the people who poured cash and credit-card receipts into Hinn's offering buckets. I felt worse, however, for anyone there that night who might have left believing that Hinn and Jesus had cured them of a serious ailment so they had no more need to continue their medication or to make it to their next doctor's appointment. They are the ones who go off quietly in the night, far from the skeptic's eyes or Benny Hinn's touch, to suffer alone.

What the World Believes

Christianity
2.2 Billion 31.5%

Islam
1.6 Billion 23.2%

No Religion
1.1 Billion 16.3%

Hindu
1 Billion 15%

Buddhism
500 million 7.1%

Other Religions
400 million 5.9%

Source: Pew Forum on Religion & Public Life

Image by the author.

24

HOW DO WE KNOW THAT THE MAN JESUS EXISTED?

I t's a question most Christians find totally absurd. They can prob-ably muster up the patience to discuss or debate the virgin birth or the resurrection, but this? It's not even a valid question, in their minds. Of course he existed! The most numerically successful religion in history is based on this man's life and death. How could he *not* exist? But it is an idea well worth considering and investigating, if for no other reason than Jesus's importance to history and to so many people today. Nothing should be assumed or taken for granted.

I have given the existence or nonexistence of Jesus the man a lot of thought and have researched both sides of the issue. Where I stand on it today may surprise both Christians and skeptics. I am not convinced beyond all doubt that a Jewish preacher named Jesus lived in Palestine during the first century, though I suspect he probably did. To be clear, I am talking about a non-supernatural human being named Jesus who inspired a religion, not the God who performed miracles, rose from the dead, and now involves himself in the daily life of Christians. My skep-ticism about that description of Jesus goes far deeper, as it should, given that claims supporting that description are less credible. I know it's common to take a definitive stand on this matter, but, as a good skeptic, I don't pretend to know things I don't know. In my opinion, there are very good arguments on both sides of this issue. I don't think the "Jesus existed" crowd have proved their claim conclusively—not because they haven't tried or because they lack the brainpower. It's a tall order to show that one specific nonroyal, non-wealthy person from that time period lived. In fairness, the "No, he didn't exist" crowd have a near-impossible challenge to prove that there was no man named Jesus. Proving a negative is usually difficult and often impossible. The best they can do is show that there is reason for doubt, which they have done. I don't want to mislead anyone into thinking that this is an evenly weighted debate in regards to numbers. There are far more people, including scholars, who are convinced that Jesus lived than there are those who are sure he did not. Nonetheless, the challenge of confirming the existence of a man named Jesus who lived two thousand years ago is significant.

Skeptics of the historical Jesus (man) point out that there is no direct physical evidence of his existence. No clothes, no handwritten letters, no house with his name on it, no artifacts of any kind, nothing. But this is not surprising for someone who lived in that region so long ago and who was not a very prominent and wealthy person. In addition, we have no written firsthand eyewitness accounts of Jesus having been a real man. This is a significant hole. Some argue that, despite his common origins, Jesus gained some degree of local fame and notoriety, so there should be something written down by someone who actually knew Jesus. But there is nothing. If anyone did write about him, it's been lost to the past or is lying undiscovered somewhere. Some readers may be wondering why the Gospels don't qualify as a reliable written source, but the fact is few scholars believe that anything in the Bible is a true firsthand account by someone who knew Jesus personally. Even the Gospels are thought to be stories written well after Jesus's death, penned by people who never saw him. By "saw him," I mean literally saw him with their own eyes before his death, in the flesh as a human being, not in a vision as a god or spirit.

New Testament scholar Bart D. Ehrman describes himself as an agnostic. He is unconvinced that Jesus was or is a god. But he is convinced that he lived two thousand years ago. Ehrman's book *Did Jesus Exist?* is a compilation of his best arguments for the historical Jesus. While he makes an interesting case, nothing is presented that could be called conclusive proof, which is understandable, given the era. This is not like making the case for Napoleon or George Washington having lived. We can read firsthand accounts of their lives from numerous people, some who liked them, some who hated them. There are artifacts left behind. We have clothes they wore. We can visit their tombs. If we really needed to, we could even analyze their bodies, maybe try to match DNA with a sample taken from a hair off an old brush they owned. Nothing like this exists as an option for Jesus. (No, the Shroud of Turin has never been authenticated by credible scientists and proves nothing about Jesus or the resurrection.) All we have are stories about Jesus's life that were written down by people who never knew him. But this is enough, say Ehrman and other New Testament scholars. They point to the fact that it is not just one story about Jesus's life that has survived but many. Ehrman writes:

> We have a number of surviving Gospels [Ehrman names seven] that are either completely independent of one another or independent in a large number of their traditions. These all attest to the existence of Jesus. Moreover, these independent witnesses corroborate many of the same basic sets of data—for example, that Jesus not only lived but that he was a Jewish teacher who was crucified by the Romans at the instigation of Jewish authorities in Jerusalem. Even more important, these independent witnesses are based on a relatively large number of written predecessors, Gospels that no longer survive but almost certainly once existed.[1]

Ehrman makes the additional point that some of the earliest texts date back to the latter half of the first century and show no signs of authors working together. "If historians prefer lots of witnesses that corroborate one another's claim without showing evidence of collaboration," he writes, "we have that in abundance in the written sources that attest to the existence of the historical Jesus."[2]

Ehrman also points to oral traditions that kept the Jesus story going. He sees evidence in this for the historical man as well. "The vast network of these traditions, numerically significant, widely dispersed, and largely independent of one another makes it almost certain that whatever one wants to say about Jesus, at the very least one must say that he existed."[3]

What bothers me about these Jesus stories, however, is that they are not histories. They are not official records that happen to mention a "Jesus." They are not letters between friends that drop the name "Jesus." No, they are "propaganda." I don't mean that it in a negative way. What I mean by propaganda is that the stories about Jesus were written by people who said he was a god and wanted other people to believe it. The stories are nothing close to being objective and impartial accounts of past events that we can take at face value. They were produced by Christians with an agenda and could not have been more biased. This raises obvious concerns about not only factual details and miracle claims but also about the very existence of Jesus. Skeptics would be more satisfied if his name came up in less partisan texts somewhere, anywhere. Unfortunately, it does not.

Two sources outside of the Bible discuss Jesus at length: Josephus, a Jewish historian, and Tacitus, a Roman historian. Both accounts were made after Jesus's death, but each writer was convinced that he was a real man. Skeptics counter that these documents may have been tampered with and are unreliable. And there is good reason to be skeptical. In the many centuries that have passed since Jesus was supposed to have lived, any text that mentions him has been subjected to time, elements, and other factors. We can excuse the fact that all other historical writings of the time fail to mention him, because the events of his life took place so long ago that we can't reasonably expect to have a detailed and comprehensive history of that period and place. Roman histories of the time don't even mention Pontius Pilate, the most powerful person who lived during Jesus's era and in his region, so it's not surprising that they don't mention Jesus.

Ehrman points out in *Did Jesus Exist?* that virtually every New Testament and early Christian–studies expert now teaching at a university agrees that Jesus existed. This is not disputed. Expert opinions matter, of course, but let's not forget that truth and reality are not determined by a show of hands. Many times the majority is just wrong. Sometimes everybody is wrong. We also have to consider the strong bias that is surely present among these scholars. After all, who is most likely to commit to the long, hard years of study required to earn a doctorate in Christian studies? Christians, of course. People who believe in Jesus the God are far more likely to study him and his life than are, say, devout Muslims or Hindus. So the field of New Testament studies is likely dominated by people who came into it already believing that Jesus is a god. Holding this belief, at least early on, makes for a very long intellectual journey for one to end up rejecting the existence of a historical Jesus.

As someone who has spent a lot of time considering and responding to stories about UFO landings, alien abductions, Bigfoot encounters, Atlantis discoveries, conversations with the dead, and so on, I have a unique awareness of the human obsession with telling and believing stories. Storytelling is at once a great strength and weakness for our species. Stories inform us, bind us to one another as well as to the people of the past and future. We are strongly inclined to believe them when they feel good, confirm our beliefs, or inspire us. Because I am so acutely aware of how stories about virtually anything can be created out of thin air and then embraced by many people in a short time, I have no choice but to be skeptical of *stories* about Jesus serving as the proof that a man named Jesus existed. If this were any other man in question, one who did not walk on water, heal people with his touch, and escape his own death, then I could accept it so much more easily. But Jesus is more than a man, real or not. He made a huge impact on the world, one that continues to be felt, of course.

I am not sure whether or not the historical Jesus existed. My hunch is that he probably did, simply because it seems more likely to me that a real preacher stirred up some trouble and was executed, and then a few people who liked him started a new religion in his name. Another possibility is that some Jewish people just made it all up. This could be true, of course, but we'll probably never know to the satisfaction of everyone. I know better than to go too far with either of these possibilities because there is far more speculation and opinion than facts and evidence. All I can say for sure is that I don't know. In my humble opinion, this is all that anyone really should be comfortable saying, because if Jesus was a real man he was lost to the shadows of history long ago. Today, only Jesus the God remains for us to consider.

25

WHAT ABOUT ALL THE OTHER GODS?

Much of human history can be described as a gradual and sometimes painful liberation from provincialism, the emerging awareness that there is more to the world than was generally believed by our ancestors.

—Carl Sagan, *Broca's Brain*[1]

O ne of the more common errors atheists and skeptics make when talking about religion with Christians is to fall into the trap of pretending there is only one god and only a few religions up for discussion. It makes no sense to discuss Christianity in a vacuum, however, as if there isn't a vast and incomprehensible catalog of religions, a crowd of diverse gods that stretches far beyond history's horizon, and an endless stream of very different and often-contradictory religious claims. This is the same mistake that many Christians make when thinking about their own belief system. Believing inside a protective bubble may feel good, but it's not worthy of anyone who values integrity and reason. I hope more Christians can recognize the importance and necessity of understanding the religious landscape as it truly is.

I tend to believe that most Christians do not intentionally ignore all other gods and religions. I suspect their oversight is more a result of the confirmation bias that all of us labor with. Their bias is also aided by the overtly exclusive way in which preachers and Sunday-school teachers typically present information to their audiences. My hunch is that thoughtful and honest Christians don't really want to operate under a ridiculous pretext that says 99.999 percent of all gods and religions don't merit a mention when discussing or thinking about the topic of religion. If they paused and gave the matter some thought, I believe that they would recognize the necessity of including non-Christian religions and gods.

How many gods are there? I am perhaps more qualified than most to answer this question. I have a degree in history and anthropology. I have studied religion for decades. I have interviewed numerous believers from many religions. I have visited most of the world's holiest sites. I have read the Bible, the Koran, the Bhagavad Vita, and many other books relevant to religious belief, and I have attended numerous and varied religious ceremonies. So, considering my extensive background, I can reply to this question of how many gods there are without hesitation: I have no idea. I am clueless on the most important religion statistic of all—and so is everyone else, no matter what they try to tell you. Unless "a lot" is a meaningful answer, I just can't help you. I couldn't even take a wild guess to come up with a number that I could competently defend. It's definitely many, many millions; more likely, it's in the billions, if not trillions. In case any readers suspect that I am exaggerating in an attempt to try to dilute the power of their favored god, let me explain.

First of all, most gods don't expire. Therefore they shouldn't be eliminated from consideration just because centuries ago their worshippers may have lost a few key wars or suffered economic decline and were absorbed by a more dominant culture with a different set of gods. Many gods are supposed to be invisible and eternal; the fact that no one chants their names anymore or sees them anywhere aren't good enough reasons to say they are less real than gods who are currently popular. Here's something for Christians who reflexively tell nonbelievers that no scientist or atheist has ever disproved God: no one has ever disproved the existence of *any* gods. This means, of course, that gods have been adding up at an impressive rate over the last several thousand years. The farther back in time we go, the fewer people existed on the Earth, of course, but the scattered nature of human existence over most of our past meant more localized belief systems with more unique collections of gods than we see today.

Then there are the animists, who believe nature is something like a chorus of gods right before our eyes. For them, gods are found in the wind, the streams, the animals, virtually everywhere. Try tabulating that. By the way, various forms of animism were probably among the first belief systems in prehistory, but this doesn't mean animism went extinct with the rise of civilization. There are still many millions of animists around the world today.

Finally, we have to consider Hinduism. This colorful, dynamic, very old, and very popular religion is alive and well in the twenty-first century with a billion or so followers. I met several Hindus in India who explained to me that everyone is a Hindu at birth, so maybe I'm not giving the religion enough credit. Hinduism's contribution to the sum total of gods is immense, so big, in fact, that no one seems to be quite sure what it is. That's right. There are so many Hindu gods that Hindus lost count of them somewhere along the way. Estimates range from many hundreds of thousands to more than three hundred million, depending on whom you ask. No one, for the record, has managed to prove or disprove the existence of any of them.

If nothing else, it should be clear by this point that we are a god-creating species. All these gods can't be real; that would be logically impossible based on their "divinely inspired" bios. For example, there can't be a few hundred or a few thousand gods who independently created the universe. The only options are that most gods are the products of human fantasy or that all gods are the product of human fantasy. Therefore, it's undeniable that making up gods is something we humans love to do. It's something we are very good at.

NO SUCH THING AS AN ATHEIST?

Here's a shocker: There is no such thing as an atheist. That's right; Richard Dawkins and every other skeptic of religion lied to you: atheists do believe in some gods. But believers shouldn't gloat, because the only reason this statement is true is because there is no sensible and consistently meaningful definition of *god*. Technically, no educated person can accurately describe themselves as an atheist because of the fact that she or he would certainly have to concede that Alexander the Great, Julius Caesar, and Ramesses II existed, and they were gods. These men may not have met the contemporary Western standard of an immortal god with magical powers, but they were not our gods to define. Many gods have walked among us in the past, and some do today, at least according to their cultures or their believers. There is a preacher in South Florida, for example, who has been saying for years that he is a god. Jose Luis de Jesus Miranda claims to be *the* Jesus, and the people who fill his church seem to believe him. Most Christians would reject his claim, of course, but based on what? If there is no universal definition of a god, then anyone can be one in some form or another. I saw the body of the god/pharaoh Ramesses II in Cairo,

Egypt, so, unless the museum is displaying the wrong body, that god was definitely real.

So does atheism make sense when our past has been populated with many people who were declared by themselves and others to be gods? I'm being a bit facetious here, of course. But really, if some guy says he is a god—and enough people around him buy it—then isn't he a god? The reality is that the meaning of *god* is so vague and open-ended that it must be left up to whoever wants to define it. One can't even make the case that gods are only those people or beings who have demonstrated magical powers because, on one hand, nobody has ever demonstrated such powers to the satisfaction of reasonable scientific inquiry. On the other hand, many people/gods have demonstrated supernatural powers many times, according to their followers. So how can we fairly reject the unproven god claims of Hindus or animists while accepting the unproven god claims of Christians or Muslims? Christians don't get to define what a god is for everyone else. Neither do Jews, Muslims, Hindus, Scientologists, atheists, or anyone. The best we can do in the name of logic and fairness is to leave it up to various believers to declare who their gods are. Then the rest of us have to accept their gods on that long list of unproven gods. If you say somebody or something is a god, then it's a god. Such a low bar, however, says a lot about the problems with god belief.

IS MONOTHEISM MORE SENSIBLE THAN POLYTHEISM?

Not all, but some Christians, as well as some Muslims and Jews, adopt a superior attitude when they consider the claims of polytheistic religions. Why? Why is belief in one god more sensible or credible than belief in many? Is this some kind of a silent admission that god belief is silly and the silliness increases with the number of gods? I'm sure that's not a view they would agree with. But something odd is going on here. It's not as simple as some Christians maintaining that their religion is true and that others are mistaken because they don't present the same attitude when comparing Christianity to Islam or Judaism. Those religions have it wrong, they say, but not by much, emphasizing their common roots and the all-important monotheistic status. But meanwhile, people who believe in many gods are viewed as somehow primitive.

There are multiple passages in the Bible that seem to indicate that the Christian/Jewish god acknowledges the existence of other gods. He does not state that no other gods exist; rather, he says that he's jealous and doesn't want people worshipping his rivals. Remember not to confuse belief with worship. Believing that gods exist is not necessarily the same as worshipping those gods. Even if a person worships only Allah, for example, she still might think that other gods exist or existed too.

Then there are angels and demons to consider. No Christian views these beings as gods, but why not? Considering their alleged godlike powers, one can make a case that they are some sort of lesser gods. Doesn't Satan, a fallen angel, seem like a god ruling over hell? He's not so different from the ancient Greek god Hades, who is supposed to be running the underworld. Look at it this way, if one knew nothing about Christianity and heard descriptions of flying angels and demons with magical powers, it would probably seem reasonable to conclude that this is a religion with many gods who have a variety of roles and who possess different abilities, much like many other religions.

It also has to be mentioned that Christianity should be classified as polytheistic if for no other reason than the fact that most Christians think and speak of multiple gods. I understand that the doctrine of the Holy Trinity is supposed to explain how three gods combine to make one, but in practice, Christians seem to believe in different gods. Jesus did not flood the world, in the minds of most Christians. God the Father did not suffer on the cross. How could he if he was sacrificing his only son, as Christians often say?

When most people speak about religion, they speak of "god" in the singular; rarely do they use the plural. But this is not only inaccurate; it is wildly misleading. It perpetuates a misconception in the minds of billions that only one god is worth considering. Not only is this wrong but it is profoundly dismissive and insulting to other people. Hindus are modern people too. They aren't insane or stupid. Whenever a CNN report or *Time* cover story addresses religion, we can be sure that the deity concept will be described in the singular. Animists are also no less worthy of respect and inclusion in conversations about religious belief than anyone else.

The common act of ignoring or forgetting to mention the fact that more than one god inhabits the diverse universe of religious belief also disparages the intelligence of past peoples. Was Aristotle an idiot because he likely believed in many gods instead of one? Were the likely polytheists Pericles and Julius Caesar morons, unworthy of our consideration on the topic of religious belief? To speak as if only one god is relevant and important enough for discussion and debate is intellectually indefensible. It's nothing more than arrogance and ethnocentrism. It's also very convenient for Christians, Jews, and Muslims. Consider how much more difficult it becomes when one attempts to not only explain why their god exists but also why all the other gods do not. I encourage Christians to be realistic about the number of god claims. No belief system worth holding onto would need to rely on the fraudulent assumption that it has exclusive rights to the god concept. And no self-respecting believer would want to pretend that his god is the only one humans ever claimed to be real.

26

ARE CHRISTIANS HAPPIER?

The fruit of the Spirit is love, joy, peace.

—Galatians 5:22

Happiness is one of the most common associations many Christians make with their religion. They claim that feelings ranging from calm contentment to indescribable joy are gifts they receive from Jesus. This has long been a top selling point for what is the world's most popular religion today. And there seems to be more to it than just the opinion of biased Christians. Multiple scientific studies appear to back it up. Something about Christianity really does seem to bring about happiness.

There are important questions about this for both Christians and non-Christians. What exactly is going on? Are Christians really happier than nonbelievers? If so, why? Are there specific reasons for this happiness that we can identify, apart from simply pointing to Jesus? Are Christians happier than other religious people who believe in different gods and who belong to different religions? Do happy Christians prove that Jesus is a real god, as many claim? Is there anything the nonreligious can learn from Christianity that might make them happier people too?

I have no doubt about Christianity's ability to generate happiness in people. I have seen it up close with my own eyes many times and in many places. From emotional and boisterous church services in the American South and the Caribbean to more sedate but probably no less joyful moments of quiet worship in the Vatican and Jerusalem. What I am skeptical about, however, is the idea that a real god is necessarily behind it all. Maybe there is; it's certainly possible. But it seems to me that a more likely explanation is that there is something about *believing* a god loves you and something about the *process* of worshipping and interacting with like-minded believers that make so many Christians happy. And none of these things require the existence of a god.

One key reason to doubt that there is a supernatural source for Christian happiness is the fact that non-Christian religious people can be pretty happy too. I have also seen this with my own eyes. In Syria, I saw a look of pure joy in the face of a Muslim after prayer. At temples in Nepal and India, I spoke with Hindus whom I would rate about nine on the happiness scale. I once attended a puja in Jamaica that left me smiling for hours afterward and feeling good for days. I credit the people, music, and great food rather than the Hindu gods, however. I have spent time with devout Rastafarians in the Caribbean, and, while some may say they are not "real Christians," they certainly are an extremely happy bunch who spend a lot of their time praising Jesus and quoting from the Bible. Marijuana jokes aside, must the source of their happiness be a real Jesus, or could it perhaps be a real sense of community and purpose?

Muslims in America don't believe Jesus is a god and do not worship him, but that hasn't prevented them from being as content about the present as any other religious group. They are also more optimistic about the future and are more likely to say they are doing better in life than most other people. According to Gallup®, Muslim Americans predict that their lives five years from now will be at about 8.4 on a scale of 0 to 10.[1] This is higher than any other religious group in America. Gallup's Life Evaluation Index reports that 60 percent of Muslim Americans consider themselves to be "thriving" today. This is about the same percentage as Jewish Americans and is slightly higher than the percentage of Catholic Americans (54 percent) and Protestant Americans (52 percent).[2]

THE BUDDHA'S SMILE

And then there are Buddhists. There are many misconceptions about Buddhism, a religion with about half a billion followers worldwide. Probably the most common one is that Buddha is supposed to be a supernatural god. He's not. Siddhartha Gautama, the original Buddha who is supposed to have lived more than two thousand years ago, never claimed to be a god. Orthodox Buddhists revere him, of course, but do not view him as a god in the way Christians do Jesus or Muslims do Allah. To avoid confusion, I should note that there are versions of Buddhism that have incorporated gods into the belief system. This should not be surprising, however, because of Buddhism's close relationship to polytheistic Hinduism, as well as the fact that every religion, given enough time, evolves and produces multiple versions of itself. Orthodox or mainstream Buddhism, however, is technically an atheistic belief system. Followers may believe in supernatural claims such as reincarnation, but they do not have a god at the center of their spiritual life. This does not, however, seem to put a damper on Buddhists' potential for happiness. I met Buddhist monks in Thailand who glowed with extraordinary glee. I may not have left their company convinced that we all had past lives with more lives to come, but I did come away convinced that those monks knew a lot more about happiness and contentment than I did or probably ever will.

Brain researchers at University of California–San Francisco Medical Center have apparently found a way to successfully measure the happiness of Buddhists, and their conclusions match my observations in Thailand. Using brain scans, the scientists found that experienced Buddhists who meditated often were likely to be more calm and happy than most other people. They were also less likely to become flustered or angry compared with most people. Buddhist prayer/meditation apparently calms or tames the amygdala, a cluster of neurons found in the temporal lobes of the brain that process "fear memory."[3] Their religion may be godless and have nothing to do with Jesus or the Bible, but it has led them to high levels of happiness, nonetheless. According to researcher Paul Ekman, there seems to be something about practicing Buddhism that leads one to their joy and contentment.[4] Scientists at the University of Wisconsin conducted a study that yielded similar results. The Buddhists' brains showed high activity in the area of the brain that is associated with positive feelings.[5] The obvious implication for Christianity is that there may be something about the *practice* of Christianity that leads Christians to happiness. No real god required.

Another interesting thing about Christianity and happiness is that the societies that are most heavily dominated by Christians do not seem to have an edge on happiness. If Jesus really does reward his followers with superior happiness, as claimed, then one would think that the most Christian countries would be the cheeriest places on Earth. But this does not appear to be the case. University of Leicester psychologist Adrian White did not set out to address the particular issue with his World Map of Happiness, but the results are relevant all the same.

Drawing on more than one hundred studies involving eighty thousand people worldwide, White ranked countries by happiness levels. The top ten are

1. Denmark	6. Finland
2. Switzerland	7. Sweden
3. Austria	8. Bhutan
4. Iceland	9. Brunei
5. The Bahamas	10. Canada[6]

The list is dominated by nations that have some of the highest rates of nonbelief in the world. Denmark, for example, has the third-highest percentage of nonbelievers globally. Sweden has the highest ratio of nonbelievers of any nation. Canada is twentieth.[7] Bhutan is mostly Buddhist, and Brunei mostly Muslim, so we can't credit Christianity for the extraordinary happiness in those countries. Among these happiest populations, only the Bahamas is strongly Christian, with a low ratio of non-Christians and nonbelievers. At the other end of the scale, we find that the least-happy societies are all very religious with virtually no significant number of nonbelievers. These include the Democratic Republic of the Congo (ranked 176), Zimbabwe (177), and Burundi (178).[8]

Gallup's Global Wellbeing Index provides an annual ranking of countries based on the percentage of people who say they are "thriving" today and who feel good about their immediate future compared with people who say they are "suffering" and who are pessimistic about their future. *Thriving* may not be perfectly synonymous with *happiness*, but it is certainly closer to the mark than *suffering*. The index's top ten is similar to the World Happiness Map in that countries with relatively low rates of Christianity dominate.

1. Denmark	6. Australia
2. Canada	7. Finland
3. Netherlands	8. New Zealand
4. Israel	9. Austria
5. Sweden	10. Brazil[9]

Of the nations on this top-ten list, only Brazil is not ranked among the top twenty-five nations by ratio of atheists.[10] None of this proves, of course, that atheism guarantees happiness or that Christianity doesn't really make many Christians happy. But it certainly suggests that the causes for happiness and unhappiness are more likely to be natural rather than supernatural.

A study titled "Religion, Social Networks, and Life Satisfaction," published in the *American Sociological Review*, may have found the key to what makes many Christians happy.[11] "People who say they go to church every week but say they have no close friends there are not any happier than people who never go to church," explained Chaeyoon Lim, the sociologist who led the study. "People who say they go once a month or less and say they have a couple of close friends in the church they attend tend to be happier than people who say they go every week but have no close friends."[12]

"Our study offers compelling evidence that it is the social aspects of religion rather than theology or spirituality that leads to life satisfaction," concludes Lim. "Friendships built in religious congregations are the secret ingredient in religion that makes people happier."[13]

The study found that 33 percent of Christians who attend church weekly and have three to five close friends at their church say they are "extremely satisfied" with their lives. Of the Christians who also go to church once a week but who have no close friends there, the "extremely satisfied" number drops to 19 percent. It's higher for Christians (23 percent) who go to church only several times a year but who have close friends there. The percentage of "extremely satisfied" people who never attend religious services is the same (19 percent) as those who go weekly but have no friends. The key, therefore, seems to be not just going to church or believing in Jesus but going to church and being with close friends there.[14]

There may be an important life lesson in this for everyone, Christians and nonbelievers alike. Seeing close friends on a regular basis, feeling like you are a part of something important with them, and participating in a shared experience seem to be effective ways to set all of us on a path to happiness.

IS THE UNITED STATES OF AMERICA
A CHRISTIAN NATION?

Of all the tyrannies that affect mankind, tyranny in religion is the worst.

—Thomas Paine, Founding Father[1]

The claim that America is a Christian nation is controversial, no doubt, but there is a lot of unrecognized common ground between Christians and non-Christians because nobody wants a full-blown Christian theocracy for America. Well, maybe some people do, but reasonable Christians who appreciate freedom and fairness certainly don't. They don't want America to be a Christian version of Saudi Arabia or Iran. Not only would a Christian government in a Christian nation be bad for secular Americans, it would be bad for Christians as well. What sensible Christian wants government in their religion? Does the idea of Congress setting your church's agenda appeal to you? Do you really want the IRS getting involved with Sunday tithing? How about the Senate debating and voting on the Sunday-school curriculum? Some Christians fight the separation of church and state like it is a threat to religion, when in fact it's the best thing the Founding Fathers did for religion. Both secular and Christian Americans are better off living in a country with a government that is legally restrained from playing favorites when it comes to gods. Probably the key reason Christianity is thriving in America today when it is fading in so many other developed nations is because government has largely steered clear of it.

Before trying to determine whether America is or should be a Christian nation, we must first try our best to be clear about what "Christian nation" means. If it merely refers to a country with a population made up mostly of people who self-identify as Christian, then, sure, the United States is a Christian nation. But if it means America is supposed to be some sort of a theocracy, with government-enforced biblical laws, state promotion of Jesus, and Christian citizens favored above non-Christian citizens, then it clearly is not, never was, and hopefully never will be.

One of the primary reasons the American experiment has worked out as well as it has so far is that our country's Constitution has kept religion and government mostly apart. America would be a very different nation today if not for the First Amendment of the Constitution, which has kept the government mostly secular. It reads "Congress shall make no law respecting an establishment of religion, or prohibiting the free exercise thereof; or abridging the freedom of speech, or of the press; or the right of the people peaceably to assemble, and to petition the Government for a redress of grievances." Notice that the two clauses concerning religion appear first in the First Amendment. One might suspect that the framers of the Constitution tried to make it crystal-clear that, for the benefit of all Americans, government had to refrain from meddling in Christianity or any other religion.

This country's founders were not saints or superhuman, but they were smart men who knew that anything other than a secular government would likely doom America to suffer through pointless and bloody religious conflicts, both domestically and internationally. Remember, these men were highly educated and well aware of the fact that European Christians had not figured out how to peacefully and sustainably mix religion and government together, despite many centuries of trying. Based on this, I do not find it surprising that Christianity has flourished in America. A secular government has not harmed Christianity by excessively exploiting and cheapening it but instead has allowed it to thrive in a somewhat free and protected environment. Christianity is the dominant religion of the most intensely religious industrialized nation on Earth. Christians who pine for a Christianized government might consider the old adage "If it ain't broke, don't fix it."

It is obvious that Christianity and Christians have always been key factors in the formation and development of the United States. But has Christian influence always been a good thing? This is a question those who promote the Christian nation based on its "Christian heritage" never seem to give any thought to. Christianity inspired and strengthened many of the abolitionists who worked to end slavery, but it was also the first line of defense for slaveholders looking to provide moral justification for owning human beings. Christianity may motivate some men and women to love and care for their neighbors, but it has also been the motivation for others to hate, abuse, and kill their neighbors. The real Christian heritage does not stop at charity and universities. It is a mixed bag that includes prejudice, hate, discrimination, and violence as well.

Of all the arguments against the claim that the United States is a Christian nation in some historical and official sense, the most powerful one is to simply point to the one prominent place where Christianity is nowhere to be found. The nation's most important document could have forever enshrined a place in the US government for God the Father, Jesus, the Holy Spirit, and the Bible. But it does not. There is nothing in the Constitution that does so, and the omission speaks volumes. If, as some claim, the Founding Fathers were all devout Christians (they all were not) who intended for their new country and its government to be officially and meaningfully Christian in both appearance and in practice, don't you think they would have included at least a hint of that somewhere in the Constitution? After all, this was their most important contribution to the nation they founded by far. But there is nothing about promoting Jesus or any other god, nothing about favoring Christianity over all other religions, and nothing about religion being required or encouraged for citizens. Clearly Madison, Jefferson, Franklin, Washington, and the rest thought it best not to build a Christian theocracy in the New World. The Founding Fathers instead focused on creating a country with a government that would stay out of religion and allow the people to make up their own minds about what they did or did not want to believe in. They thought it would be fair, sensible, and safer to keep religion apart from government while ensuring religious freedom for all. And they were right.

The following list of quotations helps to show how absurd it is to claim that America was ever intended to be a Christian nation with a Christian government:

> **I am for freedom of religion and against all maneuvers to bring about a legal ascendancy of one sect over another.**
> —Thomas Jefferson, Founding Father and
> third president of the United States

> **As the Government of the United States of America is not, in any sense, founded on the Christian religion . . .**
> —excerpt from Article 11 of the Treaty of Tripoli,
> unanimously ratified by the US Senate in 1797

I mix religion with politics as little as possible.
—John Adams, first vice president and
second president of the United States

Because experience witnesseth that ecclesiastical establishments, instead of maintaining the purity and efficacy of Religion, have had a contrary operation. During almost fifteen centuries has the legal establishment of Christianity been on trial. What have been its fruits? More or less in all places, pride and indolence in the Clergy, ignorance and servility in the laity, in both, superstition, bigotry and persecution. Enquire of the Teachers of Christianity for the ages in which it appeared in its greatest lustre; those of every sect, point to the ages prior to its incorporation with Civil policy.
—James Madison, "Father of the US Constitution"
and fourth president of the United States, from
*Memorial and Remonstrance against
Religious Assessments*, 1785

Believing with you that religion is a matter which lies solely between man and his God, that he owes account to none other for his faith or his worship, that the legislative powers of government reach actions only, and not opinions, I contemplate with sovereign reverence that act of the whole American people which declared that their legislature should "make no law respecting an establishment of religion, or prohibiting the free exercise thereof," thus building a wall of separation between church and State.
—Thomas Jefferson, Founding Father and third president of
the United States, from his letter to Danbury Baptists, 1802

IS THE LOUDEST VOICE ALWAYS RIGHT?

Those who would still push the idea of America as a Christian nation might reconsider based on two simple points. First, it's mean. If I were on a high-school chess club and 80 percent of its members were atheists, I certainly wouldn't go around calling it an atheist chess team. Why not? Because it would imply that the other 20 percent don't really fit in and maybe aren't as much a part of the team as the 80 percent are. It unnecessarily pushes the minority into the shadows and suggests that they are inferior. That's unfair and mean-spirited. Second, the idea that America should be thought of as a Christian nation because of Christianity's positive presence and influence does not tell the whole story. Christianity's role in American history has been complex, to say the least. As mentioned previously, it's been good and bad, constructive and destructive, unifying and divisive. It is ludicrous, for example, to suggest that Christians in America have always been in sync and united by their belief in Jesus. American history is littered with sad example after sad example of Christians harming Christians, specifically in the name of their particular denomination. Any honest account of America's Christian heritage must include this persecution and violence.

David Niose, president of the American Humanist Association, believes the current calm between different Christian sects in America is a fragile peace.

> This heritage of Christian solidarity is largely fictitious, as religious intolerance and disharmony were the norm for the better part of our history. We can also understand the apparent unity we see today between conservative Catholics and conservative Protestants as something that deviates from the historical relationship between the two. No longer able to fight about whose Bible will be used or whose prayers will be said publicly, they instead join forces to fight those who prefer no public prayers be said at all. Standing together primarily to condemn secularism, even revising history to fit their agenda, there can be little doubt that doctrinal disputes and prejudices between the two factions would quickly arise if the common secular enemy were removed.[2]

Finally, I think that little more than the careful placement of a few key words here and there has led many Christians to this belief in a Christian nation. The federal government has allowed the mention of God into the most interesting places to great effect—like money and the Pledge of Allegiance, to name two prominent examples. So why wouldn't a typical American who knows little about the Constitution and the Founding Fathers, and who happens to be a Christian, be easily misled by this? It's understandable. I've heard it over and over from Christians, "Of course America is a Christian nation, just look on the money, just listen to the Pledge." But facts shed an entirely different light on the matter. For most of America's existence, "E pluribus unum" (Latin for "Out of many, one") was the primary and most popular, if not official, national motto. It appears on US coins and has been on the national seal since 1782. So when did "In God we trust" become America's official motto? Not until an act of Congress during the Cold War. The phrase had already been appearing on some coins, but, motivated by the threat of "godless communists," Congress elevated it to official motto status in 1956. Only two years before that "one nation under God" was inserted into the Pledge of Allegiance, also by official act of the federal government in response primarily to Cold War tensions. That's right, the original version of the pledge, written by a socialist named Francis Bellamy, did not contain any mention of God or religion. Okay, but what about the presidential inauguration ceremony, the oath, the hand on the Bible, the "so help me God" at the end? Surely this formal tradition dates back to the beginning of the country and shows that the founders wanted a Christian or at least a religious government, right? Not even close. Article II, Section 1, Clause 8 of the Constitution reads

> I do solemnly swear (or affirm) that I will faithfully execute the Office of President of the United States, and will to the best of my ability, preserve, protect and defend the Constitution of the United States.

That's it. There is no requirement for placing a hand on the Bible or to say, "So help me God." Once again, the framers of the Constitution could have inserted God, Jesus, the Bible, or Christianity in many places when they wrote the most important document in American government, but they chose instead to produce and sign a godless Constitution, one that would not promote religion or restrict the religious freedoms of individuals. They wisely chose to create not a Christian nation but one for all religions, or no religions, as decided by the citizens themselves.

HOW CAN WE BE SURE THAT JESUS PERFORMED MIRACLES?

Even though you do not believe me, believe the miracles.
—John 10:38

One of the most prominent features of Jesus's life, according to stories in the New Testament, is that he performed miracles. Given the charisma and courage he was supposed to have had, Jesus might have done fine without the attention-grabbing miracles he is believed to have performed. But they sure didn't hurt. Today, two thousand years later, Christians still speak of his magical powers with awe and reverence. Many Christians point to his miracles as proof that he was God, whereas others think there may be some degree of truth to them, but that they are largely meant to be taken as symbolic stories. And then we have the skeptics and nonbelievers, who suspect that they were probably nothing more than exaggerations or tricks.

In a previous chapter about miracles in general I briefly raised the idea of Jesus's more famous acts possibly being nothing more than magician tricks. This point is not meant to insult Christians. I have no idea whether or not Jesus performed tricks to fool people into believing he had supernatural powers. The possibility has to be considered not only by skeptics but also by modern Christians who care about truth and reality. We have the benefit of twenty centuries to look back on and draw from when we attempt to assess these stories. And what we find are countless holy men in countless belief systems claiming to perform miracles and many people believing them. Perhaps most of them really happened and really were supernatural events as claimed. But I strongly doubt it. In fact, we know that many are false claims and bad beliefs because there are numerous cases of prophets, preachers, and the inspired righteous being caught red-handed performing cheap tricks to fool others. I attended a small faith-healing service at a church in Tampa, Florida, where I saw a visiting preacher perform a bogus miracle right before my eyes. With all the flair of a carnival barker, he analyzed the legs of a seated man who said he was suffering back pain and declared them to be uneven. The preacher shook the man's legs vigorously, lined up the feet evenly, and then declared to the congregation that they had been miraculously aligned. People all around me gasped and cheered in approval. They bought it.

The years when Jesus is believed to have lived were glory days for miracles. Gods were plentiful, demons were around every corner, and magic was everywhere. Virtually everyone heard about miracles, saw them, felt them, and knew them. The rate of belief in them was probably higher than today. But it's not as if miracles ever went out of fashion. A 2009 Harris Poll® found that 76 percent of American adults believe in them.[1] Based on my experiences living and traveling in other countries, I would estimate that global belief in miracles is even higher. A good skeptic can't ignore the fact that most people today, from Morocco to Miami, believe in miracles. So many, in fact, that it raises the obvious suspicion that people just naturally don't think about coincidences, the way the universe works, and the ever-present danger of being tricked by a con man or misled by a delusional person. I'm not saying Jesus was a con man or delusional; how could I know such a thing about someone who is supposed to have lived so long ago? But it can't be denied that it would have been very easy to impress people with very little back then. The level of general knowledge about nature and physics was far lower than now, so people were less able to connect natural causes to weird events. Even worse, people were even less likely to have ever been encouraged to think critically, to demand evidence, and to ask smart questions. Skeptical-thinking skills, in short supply today, must have been extraordinarily rare in the general public then.

Right here in the twenty-first century, a woman in Nigeria gave birth to a horse during church services—at least that's what many people who were there say happened. The pastor in charge, Silva Wealth Iyamu, apparently sees miracles all the time, but this one surprised even him. "We have seen people vomit several things during our service but not this type of thing. God has been blessing our ministry with prophecies and miracles."[2] Probably no more than a handful of people will believe that this happened the way the pastor and others say it did (hopefully), but what if the claim was made a couple of thousand years ago? How many people back then might have believed it?

It is difficult for skeptics to understand how so many Christians can accept miracle claims as literally true. Jesus performed many miracles, including walking on water, changing water into wine, healing a woman of a fever, healing a leper, casting out demons, healing blindness, and bringing dead people back to life. Impressive as that list may seem, there is nothing unique about what Jesus is believed to have done regarding most of his miracles. Many others have claimed similar feats—and been believed by many people. I sat near the stage at a Benny Hinn healing crusade in the Caribbean and was astonished by Hinn's ability to work the emotions of the thousands present. Even as people collapsed the instant he touched them or almost touched them, he played humble and made sure to repeatedly credit God, but it was clear that there was something very special about him. He was a miracle worker in the eyes of most that night. One of the thoughts I had while watching the spectacle was how Hinn would have fared in ancient days. If he can fill stadiums in multiple countries and convince people that his fingers are some kind of conduit to supernatural healing powers today—in an age when science and reason are more advanced than ever and information is more widely available than ever—then it's not at all outrageous to wonder if he could have been seen as a god in another era.

Christians who insist on believing in the miracles of Jesus can continue to do so, of course, but I hope they understand why so many people are skeptical of these claims. Not everyone considers the Bible to be a perfect source of accurate reporting. Most of the world's people are not convinced that all its claims can be accepted without external verification, so simply pointing to a passage in the New Testament is not enough. For the skeptics, evidence is required to believe that a man once touched a dead body and gave it life. Proof is necessary before we can accept that someone calmed a storm. Miracle believers don't have to worry about anyone disproving these miracles, as they are supposed to have happened far too long ago. It's too late to interview witnesses and check the details. All a skeptic can do is show that there are reasons for doubt. In that sense, the miracles of Jesus are safer in the past than they would be today. "Even though you do not believe me," Jesus said, "believe the miracles" (John 10:38). Ironically, however, it may be easier for a skeptic to believe in Jesus than in his miracles. For we know very well how common miracle claims are, both then and now. We also know how easy it is for mere mortals to call them forth. Nothing more is required than the courage to try and an audience willing to believe.

HALLELUJAH. Many religions include rituals that often trigger profound psychological events in the minds of believers. Sometimes they are life altering. But is this proof that gods are real? *Photo by the author.*

WHAT DO EVIL ATHEIST DICTATORS PROVE?

It seems so obvious and so thoroughly damning for atheism that few believers are able to resist going there. Connecting the dots doesn't get much easier than this. Joseph Stalin, Adolf Hitler, Mao Zedong, Pol Pot. Hundreds of millions dead, because of them—and they were atheists. The lesson is right there before our eyes. How can anyone deny it? The worst crimes of the last century were committed by men who did not believe in a god. In fact, no bloodthirsty religious zealot in all of history can match the death tolls racked up by these maniacs. Okay, I get it. This can only mean one thing: religion is good and atheism is bad, very bad. Your god is real, and without him terrible things are bound to happen. It is easy to see why Christians keep bringing this up. It has all the appearance and feel of a tight and tidy can't-lose argument. It dumps the backbreaking weight of history onto the shoulders of the atheists and demands they explain their philosophical alignment with such monsters. Checkmate.

While I understand why so many believers love to play the atheist dictator card, nothing can save this argument from a minimal amount of thinking. Popular usage doesn't make it a good argument. Cringing at huge death tolls doesn't infuse it with logic. Not only is it wrong, it's very wrong for multiple reasons. As we will see, this argument is so flawed that thoughtful Christians should never use it. There are much better ways to try to make the case for Christianity.

First of all, we need to get our list of evil atheist dictators straight. One of these names does not belong. Hitler was an evil dictator, of course, but describing him as an evil *atheist* dictator is not accurate. Based on his own words, Hitler clearly seems to have believed in some version of the Jewish/Christian god. Furthermore, based on his actions and various things he took part in and condoned, he probably believed in God. To date, more than sixty years after his death, no one has been able to make a convincing case for him being an atheist. It seems very likely that Stalin, Mao, and Pol Pot were nonbelievers, but very good evidence suggests that Hitler was a believer of some sort. I am not claiming to know that he definitely was a believer, of course. He may well have been an atheist. After all, what can we really know for sure when it comes to anyone and their personal beliefs?

Nonetheless, we do have Hitler's own words, both written and spoken, to analyze, and they very clearly indicate that he believed in the God of the Bible. Of course, like virtually every other political leader in history, Hitler likely said and wrote things that were insincere but served his purposes at the time. Belief occurs in the privacy of an individual's mind, so how can we ever be 100 percent sure about the beliefs of anyone, including Hitler? What we can say for certain is that there is far too much evidence for anyone to sensibly and honestly claim to know that Hitler was an atheist. He served as an altar boy in his local Catholic church, he never outright rejected Christianity, and he wrote in *Mein Kampf*: "Hence today I believe that I am acting in accordance with the will of the Almighty Creator: by defending myself against the Jew, I am fighting for the work of the Lord."[1] But this is not the only hint that Hitler may have been Christian.

HITLER THE ATHEIST?

- It matters not whether these weapons of ours are humane: if they gain us our freedom, they are justified before our conscience and before our God.
  —Adolf Hitler, speech, Munich, August 1, 1923

- We demand liberty for all religious denominations in the State, so far as they are not a danger to it and do not militate against the morality and moral sense of the German race. The Party, as such, stands for positive Christianity, but does not bind itself in the matter of creed to any particular confession.
  —document from Hitler's German Workers' Party

- My feelings as a Christian points me to my Lord and Savior as a fighter. It points me to the man who once in loneliness, surrounded only by a few followers, rec-

ognized these Jews for what they were and summoned
men to fight against them and who, God's truth! was
greatest not as a sufferer but as a fighter. In boundless love as a Christian and as a man I read through
the passage which tells us how the Lord at last rose
in His might and seized the scourge to drive out of the
Temple the brood of vipers and adders. How terrific was
His fight for the world against the Jewish poison. Today,
after two thousand years, with deepest emotion I recognize more profoundly than ever before in the fact that
it was for this that He had to shed His blood upon the
Cross. As a Christian I have no duty to allow myself to
be cheated, but I have the duty to be a fighter for truth
and justice.

—Adolf Hitler, speech, Munich, April 12, 1922

- We have faith that one day Heaven will bring the
Germans back into a Reich over which there shall be
no Soviet star, no Jewish star of David, but above that
Reich there shall be the symbol of German labor—the
Swastika. And that will mean that the first of May has
truly come.

—Adolf Hitler, speech, Munich, May 1, 1923

- We are all proud that through God's powerful aid we
have become once more true Germans.

—Adolf Hitler, speech, March 1933

- National Socialism neither opposes the Church nor is
it anti-religious, but on the contrary it stands on the
ground of a real Christianity.

—Adolf Hitler, speech, Koblenz, August 26, 1934

- Be upright and determined, fear no one and do your
duty! If you do so, the Lord God will never leave our
people.

—Adolf Hitler, at the Oath under the Cathedral of Light,
September 14, 1936

- I, for my part, acknowledge another precept which says that man must deal the final blow to those whose downfall is destined by God.
  —Adolf Hitler, address to the Reichstag, April 6, 1942

- God the Almighty has made our nation. By defending its existence we are defending His work.
  —Adolf Hitler, radio address, January 30, 1945[2]

Hitler said some harsh things about organized Christianity, but he allowed German churches to continue to operate throughout his reign. Even at the peak of his power, he never tried to shut them down or stamp out Christianity in Europe. There simply is no body of evidence that reveals him to be an atheist. The best we can say about Hitler's religious beliefs is that we don't know what they were for sure. This means, of course, that no one can justify placing Hitler on the list of the twentieth century's evil atheist dictators.

IS HITLER IN HEAVEN?

The Catholic Church has never publicly excommunicated Hitler, and, according to the beliefs of most versions of Christianity, Hitler may be basking in heaven today. All he had to do was believe in Jesus during those final moments in his Berlin bunker in 1945 and repent his sins, which included starting a war that left sixty million dead. Unfortunately, by this same reasoning, virtually all of the six million Jewish children, women, and men he had killed are probably suffering in hell right now because it is doubtful that many of them converted to Christianity before their deaths.

Some believers dismiss all of this and simply claim that Hitler "had to be an atheist" for the simple reason that he was so bad. Regardless of what he said or wrote, the proof lies in his actions. No Christian would or could have done what he did because Christians are incapable of such behavior. His evil deeds are sufficient to make the case that he was an atheist. Setting aside for the moment how deeply insulting this is to the many millions of atheists who are decent and peaceful people, this idea leads us to an important point that should be part of any discussion about evil atheist dictators. *None of them existed in a vacuum.* A dictator does not personally shoot every rival, hang every scapegoat, stab every critic of their political system, much less enslave and murder millions.

Even if Hitler was not a Christian, so what? Virtually everyone else in his Nazi empire was. German soldiers marched off to battle with "Gott mit uns" (God is with us) embossed on their standard-issue belt buckles. Hitler's military forces included chaplains who led Christian services for soldiers, sailors, and airmen. I have seen medals, plaques, and coins from the 1930s and 1940s that unite the Christian cross with Nazi words or imagery. Hitler didn't seem to mind the presence of giant Christian crosses at many Nazi rallies. Public praying, Communion services, and other Christian rituals were common features of German culture during Hitler's reign. Marriages and funerals were presided over by priests and pastors. Christian holidays were observed under Hitler. Germans sang Christian songs at home and in public without fear of persecution. German soldiers were buried in graves marked by Christian crosses. I have seen a photo of Hitler celebrating Christmas with German soldiers. It is difficult to imagine him, given his temperament and position of absolute power, tolerating all this if he was an atheist. More to the point, the death camps of Nazi-occupied Europe were not operated by members of some evil atheist society dedicated to ridding the world of Jews before moving on to eliminate Christians. Given the region and the time period, there is no doubt that virtually all posts—from camp commander to tower guard—were occupied by Christians. So, if an imagined atheist Nazi Germany was supposed to prove something positive about God and Christianity, then what does the Christian Nazi Germany that existed in reality prove?

DOES ATHEISM LEAD TO MASS MURDER?

Moving on from Hitler, it seems like there still could be plenty of trouble for atheism here. Men such as Stalin, Mao, and Pol Pot issued orders that caused the deaths of many millions of people. They crushed dissent and smothered freedoms. And they did all this while not believing in a god. Many Christians see a rather straightforward and undeniable equation here: No belief in a god + evil leader = mass murder. The claim is that the absence of belief in Jesus directly caused or at least made possible the horrible behavior of these men. But here's another equation to consider: Belief in Jesus + evil leader = mass murder.

The truth, what history really shows us, is that both equations work well. This means, therefore, that Christians cannot make a sensible case that the absence of belief in Jesus equates to murderous leaders, not when so many leaders who believed in Jesus behaved terribly too. Much of European history is a blood-soaked mess—orchestrated and executed by Christian kings, queens, and popes. The exploration and conquest of the Americas and the Caribbean was no better. A vile fusion of murder, abuse, and exploitation was standard operating procedure for Christian rulers, governors, military officers, and business owners in the New World. In US history, numerous Christians plotted, organized, and executed genocidal campaigns against Native Americans. Christian politicians and slaveholders ignited America's bloodiest war in hopes of preserving their right to own human beings. If, as so many Christians claim, a few evil atheist leaders mean atheism is bad, then what does the considerably longer list of evil Christian leaders mean for Christianity? History clearly shows that people are capable of being good or bad with or without belief.

BODY COUNTS

Over the years, I have had many interesting conversations with Christians about atheism and dictators. I have found that some Christians like to cite the number of dead, as if body count is an objective measure of evil. It's not. I understand the impulse to think this way, but just because the atheist Stalin killed more people than some of the worst Christian kings and popes, that does not necessarily mean he was a more despicable human being than they were. Yes, Stalin killed more people than the Christian inquisition. Mao Zedong's policies directly or indirectly killed some fifty million people, far more than can be pinned on Pope Urban II for launching the Crusades. Therefore, goes the reasoning, the atheist Mao must be more evil than the Christian leader who started a series of wars that led to the deaths of maybe two or three million people.

Comparing raw body counts is meaningless, however, because there is no consideration given to historical context, overall population at the time, and—most importantly—the weapons technology available during different periods. Most of history's Christian rulers who were prone to large-scale violence had to make do with armies that were armed with little more than swords and spears. Stalin, on the other hand, could use or threaten to use bombs, ships, submarines, warplanes, tanks, machine guns, and pistols in order to impose his will. Is there any doubt that more than a few Christian kings, queens, and popes would not have hesitated to slaughter many millions if they had possessed such power? Many Christian leaders demonstrated their willingness to commit mass murder and to abuse their power. What more would they have done if they had twentieth-century weapons? The Knights Templar, an elite fighting force of Christian warriors in the Crusades, were vicious fighters known for preferring death to retreat in battle. Do you think their belief in Jesus would have restrained them from using nuclear weapons if they had them?

President Harry Truman was by all appearances a devout Christian, but this didn't stop him from ordering the dropping of atomic bombs on two cities during World War II. He provides us with two historical examples of a Christian using an immensely powerful weapon against civilians. (The argument can be made, of course, that these bombs saved many more civilian lives by hastening the end of the war.) So there is no reasonable basis to think that many Christian leaders of the past would not have used the most lethal weapons of mass destruction available to impose their will on enemies. Imagine medieval warlords with stockpiles of modern weapons in their castles. I have never heard one credible reason to believe that they would show restraint because of their Christian beliefs, not when so many of them showed little or no restraint with swords and axes. Anyone willing to cut a man in two with a blade would have no problem cutting him down with a 50-caliber machine gun. The Hundred Years' War, fought in the fourteenth and fifteenth centuries, pitted English Christians against French Christians. Given the brutality shown by both sides, I can imagine that the death toll would be much higher than the estimated three million who died if twentieth- or twenty-first-century technology was available to the rulers. How many Christian military officers would have hesitated to use napalm against their opponents if they had it? How many would have thought twice about seeding the landscape with landmines? Not many, I suspect. Again, our past is filled with murderers and warriors who killed people and waged wars—regardless of whether or not they believed in Jesus.

HOW MANY WOULD A CHRISTIAN STALIN HAVE KILLED?

It is also fair to speculate about how many more people Stalin, Mao, or Pol Pot might have abused and killed if they had sincerely believed in God. Maybe they would have killed fewer people, but they might just as easily have killed more. Imagine if those men were driven not only by a lust for power and control but also by the need to fulfill some divine plan they sincerely believed in. Blending a popular religion such as Christianity with their agendas—as many leaders have done throughout history—probably would have made killing even easier for them. How much more motivated might these men have been if they were confident that a god was on their side and that they would be rewarded for their actions after death? How much easier would it have been for them to inspire or coerce subordinates to murder for them if they had exploited religion's proven ability to unite one set of people against another?

It is necessary to face a critical truth about both atheist and religious mass murderers: *Regardless of whether or not they believe in a god, very bad people who have absolute power are prone to killing.* If we can point to examples of both religious and atheist mass murderers, then doesn't it seem appropriate to view this as more of a human problem than one that can be defined by the presence or absence of belief? To be blunt, Christians can't have it both ways. If an atheist's reign of terror proves something positive about Christianity, then the numerous bloodbaths throughout history that were presided over by Christian leaders must prove something negative about Christianity. There is a fundamental imbalance here. While many Christians attempt to support the case for the existence of their god and the necessity of their religion in society by pointing to murderous leaders who were atheists, I would never point to every murderous leader who happened to be a Christian and argue that his or her actions prove that God does not exist and that Christianity inevitably leads to evil. What I can say confidently, however, is that the many examples of evil deeds by Christian leaders and their subjects across the centuries show that this religion is not the guarantee of high moral behavior that many say it is. Furthermore, it's fair to highlight the role of Christianity if a bad person specifically stresses that they are killing in the name of Jesus primarily—and we have many examples of that. It is difficult, if not impossible, however, to find historical examples of bad leaders who were motivated to kill in the name of atheism primarily.

Don't forget that atheism is merely the absence of belief in a god or gods. It is not a club, a philosophy, or another religion. Some atheists say there could be gods; some say there is no possible way gods are real. Some atheists are nice, some are mean. But none of that matters to the basic status of being an atheist or a believer. Anything attributed to an atheist beyond that is subjective and irrelevant to the issue of evil atheist dictators. I may be an atheist just like Stalin was in the sense that neither one of us believed in any gods, but beyond that, what do we have in common? Nothing. I don't think people with whom I disagree should be murdered or sent to prison camps. Unlike Stalin, Mao, and Pol Pot, I think free thought is a crucial freedom that should be universally protected by law. All people should be able to believe or not believe as they wish. We could not be farther apart philosophically. This is why the constant attempt to draw a line between evil atheist dictators of the twentieth century and all atheists today is ludicrous. Skeptics often point out that Stalin and Hitler both had mustaches too. Should we worry about a connection between mass murder and facial hair?

In a fascinating way, many evil dictators became gods and spawned their own religions. They clearly had no problem with religion—so long as they could write the narrative, make the rules, and be the god everyone feared and worshipped. North Korea today is a glaring example of how bizarre a cult of personality can become. Officially, this country is an atheist state that technically has no religion within its borders. But that's not really true. The reality is that North Koreans do have a religion and they do worship a god. The people there seem to literally believe that their late "Great Leader" Kim Il Sung is more god than human. They pray to him, they thank him when good things happen in their lives, they fear him, and they perform rituals that are nearly identical to those of more traditional religious god belief. I remember watching a National Geographic documentary a few years ago in which some blind North Koreans had their eyesight restored by visiting doctors from another country. Upon having their bandages removed and seeing again, the North Koreans ran right by the doctors and began screaming praise and gratitude to large portraits of Kim Il Sung and his son, Kim Jong-il, that hung on the wall. The manner in which they waved their hands and shouted was very familiar to me. I've seen it many times in many churches.

Now we come to the real meat of this question. What do the crimes of atheist dictators in the twentieth century prove about Christianity? They prove absolutely nothing about the validity of Christian claims or those of any other religion. And, of course, the crimes of these men prove nothing about atheism. Atheism, remember, is simply the absence of belief in a god. It is not a philosophy, a way of life, or a collection of rules and doctrines. Don't make the mistake of confusing one or two prominent atheists or some atheism organization with what atheism is. Virtually all Christians agree on at least a few important things such as Jesus being a god and the existence of heaven. But there is nothing that virtually all atheists have in common apart from not believing in any gods. Typically, atheists tend to be less offended than they are confused when Christians link them to Stalinist purges and Cambodian killing fields. Atheism just does not seem to lead to bad thoughts and deeds the way many Christians say. For the record, I don't know any atheists who admire Stalin's behavior or worldview. I don't know a single skeptic who feels intellectual kinship with Pol Pot. I have never met one freethinker who believes it is right to lock people up for what they believe or do not believe. But I do know many Christians who share several specific and important beliefs with Jim Jones, David Koresh, Pope Urban II (instigated the Crusades), and Joseph Kony (African warlord). They, too, believed or believe that Jesus is the only way to heaven, that the Bible is God's word on Earth, that the Ten Commandments should be obeyed, and that Christianity is the one true religion. This doesn't mean all Christians condone their actions of, of course, but there is common philosophical ground here, far more than what a typical atheist shares with evil atheist dictators of the twentieth century.

30

IS THE UNIVERSE FINE-TUNED FOR US?

While traveling around the world, I have asked many people belonging to many different religions what made them so sure their various gods existed. One of the most common answers I heard is that the universe and the Earth are far too complex and too beautiful to have "just happened by chance." A god—*my god*—must have done it, they explained. Again and again, people told me that it is preposterous to suggest that natural processes hung the stars and planets just so. Only God could have established this wonderful oasis of life we live on. Only God could have set the orderly laws of physics in place so that we could live and thrive. If the conditions on the Earth and in the universe were even minutely different, no life could exist, they say. But life does exist in this profoundly complex universe that clearly is designed to accommodate it. And if there is design, then there had to have been a designer: God, of course.

This "argument from design" is a very appealing idea that strikes a chord for billions of people. It's been around in various versions for some time and shows no sign of going away anytime soon. The design argument is, of course, the basis for the biology-centered intelligent-design movement that many Christians want incorporated into science classrooms. One of the most popular presentations of the general design idea was put forward by a British Christian philosopher named William Paley (1743–1805), who presented the so-called watch analogy. He wrote of finding a watch and, due to its complexity, being able to recognize that it was designed by an intelligent creator. The universe being far more complex than a watch, he argued, tells us that God must exist.

Christians should be aware of why skeptics are unimpressed. Many people reject the design argument because it has some very big holes in it. Before peering into some of those holes, however, it is important for Christians to understand that the problem is not that the argument points to God. Good skeptics just want figure out what is real and true.

For example, I am fascinated by the universe. Everything related to space excites me. I want to know all I can about the origin of the universe, its structure, the possibility of extraterrestrial life, and what the future holds for everything. If God made the universe and runs it, then I want to know that too, of course. I'm certainly not opposed to an intelligent designer of the universe—if that is the reality. I just can't believe something like that until it's proven. This attitude is not unique to me. Far from it. Skeptics tend to be very open-minded to extraordinary ideas. The only catch is that, without evidence, skeptics don't become believers.

MY HABITABLE ZONE OR YOURS?

The claim that it is no coincidence that the Earth occupies a very special place in space, the perfect distance from the Sun for life to flourish, is not nearly as impressive as one might initially think. Sure, the Earth is in what we call the "habitable zone" and our existence depends on it, but so what? Skeptics ask why its location should be viewed as evidence that a god intentionally placed it there. Plenty of planets in our solar system and throughout the universe are *not* in what we would describe as the "habitable zone." Does that mean they are evidence *against* the existence of gods?

What about the Moon? As far as we know, it has no indigenous life. Does that mean God designed it to be lifeless? He didn't want life to exist there, so he made sure by giving it the characteristics of a lifeless world? If this is the position of some Christians, then it would mean everything is proof of God because all one has to do is point and say, "That's the way it is because God wanted it that way." If we find microbial life on Mars, will it mean God must have designed Mars precisely to harbor microbes but nothing else? And if there is no life on Mars, are we to conclude that God designed that planet to be lifeless? This is bad reasoning because it simply credits God for everything without proving it or at least demonstrating some connection.

Seth Shostak is the SETI (Search for Extraterrestrial Intelligence) Institute's senior astronomer. He's a sharp-witted, interesting scientist who has been thinking about extraterrestrial life since at least the age of ten. For the last several years, however, he has been doing much more than simply thinking about that exciting possibility. He has been actively hunting for ETs and engaged in researching where life might exist beyond the Earth. Shostak has heard this claim about our planet being so special that only supernatural design can explain it many times, and he is not convinced by it.

> In a galaxy with a trillion planets, the latest estimate, could ours somehow be special? Could Earth be the only locale for—if not life— then intelligent life? This is the opinion of some, who point out that our world is blessed with such beneficial characteristics as a large moon, plate tectonics, a magnetic field . . . not to mention liquid oceans and a salubrious atmosphere. But there's no reason to think that these attributes wouldn't be shared by many millions of other worlds in the Milky Way. So the fact that our planet is so favorable to life is a matter of chance, and doesn't imply that there was some plan involved. After all, if you have a winning lottery ticket, is it correct to look around at all the losers, and claim that someone planned for you to be a winner? It could just be the luck of the draw.[1]

WAIT, WHAT IS LIFE, ANYWAY?

We need to be careful about arrogantly assuming that we have life all figured out and know just what is required for it to exist. This may be news to some, but scientists can't even agree on how to define *life*. That's right; the definition of *life* is not even settled yet. We have so much more to learn. At this time we know something—far from everything—about life on precisely one planet. That's not a very impressive sample size. If it turns out that there is life elsewhere in the universe, it could well be that our concept of what constitutes a habitable zone doesn't mean much to anyone or anything other than humans and dandelions. It's hardly a crazy idea, for example, that there could be life-forms in our galaxy or another that wouldn't last ten seconds on Earth because their habitable zone requirements are far different from ours. Maybe total darkness, intense radiation, and a waterless environment are the bare minimum for 99.999 percent of life in the universe. Maybe we are the freaks of the universe. Based on some of the extremophiles that have turned up on our planet in the last few decades, it wouldn't surprise me if we one day find out that life-forms elsewhere go about their business in ways very different from ours.

In short, we still don't know enough about the universe or life itself to make grand assumptions about the Earth being special and the universe being intelligently designed for "life." What if it turns out that we're all there is? Imagine if nobody is home but us. What would that say about the idea that the universe was made for our comfort and enjoyment? So much empty space and deadly radiation, so many hostile environments. That is a universe that would look much less like it had been intelligently designed and much more like an indifferent one that just is.

There is no denying that creationists and design believers grab your attention when they say that the fit for life as we know it on Earth is just too convenient and too perfect to have been a random stroke of luck. After all, so much fell into place that was to our advantage: Earth's size, the abundance of water, the stabilizing presence of the Moon, the makeup of the atmosphere, and even Jupiter as the protective big brother that may have saved us from many asteroid strikes by drawing them away from us. If any of these things and many more factors had not been place, we simply wouldn't be here. The skeptics' response to this is simple: *Then we wouldn't be here.* This is not complicated. If things were different, they would be different. The skeptic reasons that life fits fairly well on Earth because life evolved on this planet in this planet's environment. The reason there are so many air-breathing animals, Sun-dependent plants, and marine creatures here is because there is air, lots of sunshine, and plenty of water here. If there were no air, no sunshine, and no oceans on this planet, then all those life-forms would not exist, at least not in their current form.

An additional point to be made is that Earth is far from perfect for life, including us. Keep in mind that failure, also known as extinction, is the normal and expected result of existence. An estimated 98 percent or more of species failed and are now gone. The environment was too harsh, too fast-changing, or too competitive for them to survive. This is one of the first things a skeptic thinks of whenever a Christian claims that the Earth is intelligently designed and perfect for life. If our planet is fine-tuned for life, then why does life have such a hard time here?

YOU CALL THIS BEAUTIFUL?

One of the more striking differences of opinion among Christians is their assessment of the world's current state. Some Christians say the world is "fallen," hopelessly contaminated by rampant sin and near the end of a long slide to the apocalypse. But others see only beauty, or at least so much beauty that it can't be an accident. There could never be so many wonderful waterfalls, gorgeous sunsets, and cute puppies if not for God having made them that way. Interestingly, I know some Christians who simultaneously hold both views! They say the world is pretty much a lost cause, soon to fall apart completely—and also too beautiful to be an accident.

I once showed an image of the famous Eagle Nebula to a colleague of mine at a newspaper where we worked. His immediate response was to say, "How can anyone look at beauty like that and deny that God is real?" But is the Eagle Nebula beautiful? Yes, I think that famous Hubble image of it is beautiful, but I'm not so sure I would feel the same way about it if I found myself adrift in the middle of it looking for a place to land. This is one problem skeptics have with the beauty-proves-design argument. Beauty is subjective. It's opinion tightly framed by context and perspective. Jupiter is a gorgeous planet, but I wouldn't want to get too close to it. I feel the same way about lions in Africa. Beauty is not an objective, quantifiable thing that can be easily measured like the temperature, so it's not going to be reliable evidence for the existence of a god. Subjectivity issues aside, however, there is plenty of horror and ugliness in the world to counterbalance, if not bury, this argument anyway.

If a beautiful sunflower is somehow supposed to be evidence of the Christian god, then what is a parasitic worm that eats children's eyeballs evidence of? Let's be honest, nature (or God, if you prefer) may serve up some dazzling sunsets for us, and few would dispute the joy a thousand wildflowers in a field or just one kitten can stir in our hearts, but what about all the horror that lies beneath the surface? The inorganic beauty of some rock formations, mountain ranges, and shorelines may please our eyes, but there are also the inorganic earthquakes, hurricanes, tornados, and flash floods to consider. Beauty that comes to us in organic packages pleases us, no doubt, but we can't let it distract us from recognizing the way life really works on this planet. There is a never-ending slaughter of pain-feeling creatures. Every moment of every day, animals are being stalked, captured, and eaten alive by other animals. At best, we can say that ours is a planet with great beauty *and* ugliness. It is a mix, I would suggest, that looks every bit like what one should expect from a world run by the indifferent and unintelligent forces of nature.

CENTER OF ATTENTION

Perhaps the more important question has less to do with radiation levels, atmospheric gases, or planetary orbits and more to do with the maturity of humankind. Could it be that the design argument's popularity is tied to a deep-seated fear of irrelevance and insignificance? This belief that the universe is tailor-made for life and the Earth designed with humans in mind sounds suspiciously self-centered, something that comes quite naturally to us. As toddlers remind their parents every day, it is only human nature to assume that the world revolves around us—until we grow up and admit otherwise.

"The universe was made for me." This extravagant claim sounds similar to something a child would say, one who wants to feel special. I'm not claiming to know that it is, but doesn't the design argument sound like the squeal of insecurity? Saying that everything was designed for me is perhaps a quick antidote for scary thoughts about being an accident flung by nature to some cosmic backwaters. That may not be a pleasant thought for some people. But should it be the more likely reality, why not face up to it and decide to make the best of our circumstances?

31

COULD WE DESIGN A BETTER WORLD?

W hat if you were a god or possessed extraordinarily advanced technology that enabled you to create both a world and the life to live on it? Would you do it? Well, let's just assume that you would, because the really interesting questions are, What kind of a world would you create and what kind of life?

This is a valuable thought experiment because it can lead us to think in new ways about the Christian god's alleged achievement of creating the Earth and all its life. If he is omnipotent, then he could have come up with an infinite variety of creations. For the skeptic who is unconvinced that there are any creator gods in the first place, this is an opportunity to try to do better. Trying to outdo a god might seem arrogant, even rude to some, but it's not meant to be. This is just harmless imagination for the purpose of hopefully gaining new insight on religious belief. For Christians, this is a chance to think more deeply about why God would have made things the way they are. Nothing wrong with that.

Many thoughts immediately come to mind. First of all, why does space have to be so cold and forbidding? Why not make the universe one big, inviting atmosphere that is more agreeable to fragile air-breathing humans? Why not make the open space of the cosmos user-friendly? No deadly radiation, no asteroids or even micrometeorites, not even a surprise gamma-ray burst to worry about. Imagine being able to set sail across the solar system, across the galaxy in open-air space rafts, feeling the warm, gentle breeze of solar winds in your hair. But wait, this is going too far. This is not supposed to be an exercise in dreaming up a Willy Wonka fantasyland with chocolate-milk rivers and lickable wallpaper. We want to create at least a vaguely realistic Earth and fill it with life-forms somewhat similar to what exists now, only better, if we can.

The first thing I would do as a creator god would be to come up with a planet that is much less volatile than the current Earth. Earthquakes, tornadoes, hurricanes, floods, landslides, volcanoes, tsunamis, windstorms, wildfires, and severe droughts might serve positive or necessary functions in the big picture of planetary processes, but I'm a god, so I can predict that they won't be much fun for the life-forms I intend to create. Therefore, I think I'll create a more stable, quieter planet. On the Earth that God is believed to have created, natural disasters are routine and the cost in human and nonhuman life is high. Even though we know these events are inevitable, people still die. In 1556, an earthquake in China killed more than 800,000 people. Floods in 1931 may have killed up to four million. A 1970 cyclone killed from 500,000 to a million Bangladeshis. In 1976, an earthquake killed as many as half a million people in Tangshan, China. More recently, an earthquake in Haiti claimed 230,000 lives in 2010, and tsunamis in the Indian Ocean killed an estimated 250,000 people in 2004.[1] These are just a few of the worst. Natural disasters have taken many millions of lives throughout human existence, too many to reasonably estimate. I could not possibly let such destruction and misery occur on a regular basis in a world I created. It's simply too much suffering, too many deaths for my conscience. If I'm designing the planet, then I would have to find a way to do it that eliminated earthquakes, floods, tornados, and other such lethal spasms.

LIFE FOR THE LIVING

As far as life goes, I would want to arrange that much differently as well. The first thing I would do would be to establish an ecosystem that does not require some life-forms to take in nutrients by clawing, stabbing, stinging, strangling, poisoning, crushing, or chewing other life-forms. It is possible. Perhaps I could make all animal and microbial life dependent on plant food. Then I would make sure to create plant life in a way that ensures that it feels no pain. My world would be a peaceful land of vegetarians. There would be no stalking, no horror of the hunt, and no one would ever be eaten alive. Of course, this would make the evolution of my creations very interesting. Without the pressures of predator-prey competition, I might end up with a planet of intellectually dim grazers. A frighteningly boring outcome but well worth the gamble considering the misery that would be eliminated.

Another important issue that I would pay particular attention to would be infectious disease. As the creator of a vast web of life, I certainly would not want to launch a seemingly infinite army of microscopic invaders toward the rest of my creations and leave them to suffer illness, pain, and death. If I deemed it necessary to fill my world with a thick soup of germs, I would do something to ensure that a constant state of biological warfare is not the result. Maybe I would beef up the immune systems of my creations or somehow engineer the genes of the microbes so that they did not quickly evolve into the tormentors and killers of all life, as we see on our Earth.

Perhaps most people never pause to think about it, but we really are in a state of constant war against bad bacteria and violent viruses. Microbes do much that is good for the world and for us, more than we know, I'm sure, but the bad ones have tortured us relentlessly throughout our existence. Every day hundreds of millions of people around the world are disabled in some way because of germs and parasites. For example, at any given moment a third of the human population is infected with worms. Of these people, some three hundred million are severely ill—50 percent of which are children.[2] The protozoa that cause malaria are particularly vile. Half the world's people are threatened from it, and hundreds of thousands die each year. Troublesome bacterial, viral, and parasitic species combine to kill more than two million people per year—mostly children—by contaminating drinking water.[3] I understand the importance of microbial life to the greater ecosystem here on Earth, but since I'm a god in this thought experiment, I'll find a way to create my world without such mayhem from microscopic monsters.

If I make life too safe and easy for my creations, I might end up with too many of them because they would live too long. But overpopulation could be avoided by tweaking reproductive rates. I might even decide to eliminate death altogether. Physical space shouldn't be a challenge. If I went to all the trouble of creating a staggeringly large universe, then why not let the most intelligent of my Earth creations live long enough to develop the capability of intergalactic travel? Then they can explore and settle a hefty portion of it, making good use of the trillions of other planets I made.

WOULD MY CREATIONS BELIEVE IN ME?

I'm not sure that I would bother with a worship-style religion for my more intelligent creations. Simply watching them evolve and progress would be satisfaction enough. I certainly don't imagine that I would feel a need to bath in their gratitude and reverence for my awesomeness every day. I also think that I would want to at least give them a shot at standing on their own without constantly looking over their shoulder for help from me. If, however, I did decide to let them know about me, I would be sure to do it in a way that left virtually no chance of confusion and conflict. The worst thing I could do would be to cast myself as unnecessarily elusive and mysterious. That would generate doubt. Many would believe I was real, and many would not. I would have enough foresight to recognize that this could lead to tension, disunity, and possibly even wars over uncertainty about me and my intentions for my life-forms. If I decided to communicate with them, my first step would to make every one of them certain that I exist. Only after that would we move forward.

What would I say? Maybe my awesomeness would be too over-whelming for casual conversation, so I might use a few of them to serve as messengers. No, on second thought, prophets are too risky a proposition because some of their peers are likely to have doubts about them. And that is understandable; how could they be sure these weren't false prophets just making up messages or distorting real ones? Probably the best way short of direct communication with all would be to give them something in writing. Again, the first step would be to prove legitimacy to them, so I would be sure to include something in the text that no one of them could possibly know. I would make this proof so clear and significant that none would doubt its authenticity. Maybe I would present the schematics to an energy-producing machine that is a trillion years beyond their current technology. Or perhaps I would give them the gift of a wormhole that allows them safe and fast travel to other galaxies and maybe a detailed map of the entire universe too. That should do it. Okay, now what? What would I tell my creations?

Maybe I would just give them some suggestions to help them along the way. I wouldn't want to call them laws. That's too pushy. I want my beings to stand on their own two feet as much as possible and think with their magnificent brains. I would hope they would recognize the wisdom in my words and decide to act accordingly rather than line up like obedient robots. Orders and threats wouldn't be the best path, for sure. So I would probably offer some simple suggestions and leave it at that. Maybe something like this:

THE CREATOR'S TEN RECOMMENDATIONS

    I. Forgive
   II. Be curious
  III. Help others
  IV. Improve yourself
   V. Think independently
  VI. Enjoy the ride until it ends
 VII. Be nice; be really, really nice
VIII. Don't harm anyone or anything
  IX. Dream, imagine, and try new things
   X. Create things the universe has never seen before

I know what you're thinking. Sure, it's easy to create a universe on paper, but go ahead and try, and you'll see that it's a lot harder than it looks. I'm sure it is. But even if my world and my life didn't turn out to be as calm, creative, and peaceful as I had hoped, it's difficult to imagine how I could end up with something worse than the world and system of nature we have here on our Earth. The planet is in constant flux. It never ceases to shake, explode, blow, and flood with no concern for us. The natural world is a blood-soaked orgy of violence and agony. Deadly monsters stalk all life, from without and within. Yes, there is great beauty and wonderful cooperation to be found all around, no doubt. But the constant stream of suffering and untimely deaths that stain the global ecosystem make it impossible to fully celebrate and enjoy those positives. It's as if no one cares about us, except us.

SEARCHING FOR SMILES. Many Christians claim that Jesus is the key to true happiness and contentment. But what about happy Buddhists? *Photo by the author.*

32

WHAT HAS ARCHAEOLOGY PROVED?

I'm a big fan of archaeology. I have a degree in anthropology, have taken archaeology courses, and have gotten my hands dirty on many occasions. I once rescued from its Caribbean dirt tomb an eighteenth-century bottle. Although the find was not particularly valuable—monetarily or historically—it physically connected me to the past for a brief moment that I'll never forget. Archaeology is special. We all should appreciate the invaluable job it does of filling in so many blanks of the past. It's scary to think how little we would know about ourselves and our story without professional archaeologists and paleoanthropologists checking the words of history and answering so many questions about our distant past. No less important, they give us even better questions to ask.

All this fondness and respect I have for archaeology has a dark side, however. I become more irritated than I probably should when I see what I perceive to be the misuse or abuse of this important scientific discipline by people who should know better. It's saying a lot these days, but nothing on television bothers me as much as pseudo-documentaries that attribute unproven claims such as the ancient alien astronauts or the Bermuda Triangle to the work of real scientists, often archaeologists. As a former science teacher, I know firsthand that children are especially vulnerable to these programs. They end up with wildly distorted views of history and the world they live in today. It's not like we are doing so well as a species that we can afford to have the intelligence drained from our youth this way. As you probably can already guess, I also don't like it when the good name of archaeology is hijacked by people who hope to use it to prove the claims of their religion. People do this in the name of many religions. But none do it with quite the enthusiasm, and missteps, of those who place archaeology in service of the Bible.

Biblical archaeology might seem like a great idea at first glance, but it's terribly flawed and risky at every turn because there are so many con artists out there who are eager to fake artifacts and cash in on the excitement that always surrounds anything that can be connected to Jesus or a Bible story. And then there are people who might mean well but who are so biased and determined to prove their Christian beliefs that they are rendered incapable of doing proper scientific work. Meanwhile, there are many professional archaeologists who may happen to be Christians or followers of some other religion but are fully capable of doing real archaeology just fine. They understand that conclusions are derived from evidence and not the other way around.

Why "biblical archaeology" anyway? The name alone rings alarm bells in the skeptic's mind. In archaeology, one can't force the artifacts to conform to a religion no matter what the artifacts are and still claim to be a scientist. Too many people who describe themselves as biblical archaeologists are amateurs who are more interested in confirming their religious beliefs than they are in illuminating what actually transpired in ancient times. Too many fans of biblical archaeology seek to attach their religion to a proven scientific method of discovery without really respecting or embracing that scientific method. If there were such a thing, would a typical Christian be inclined to trust the work of "Scientology archaeology," which sought to confirm Lord Xenu's genocidal campaign against humankind seventy-five million years ago? Imagine if a bunch of wild-eyed atheists started a movement called "atheist archaeology" and ran around the Middle East with trowels trying to find things that would disprove religious claims. I for one would be very skeptical of their work because I would suspect that they would probably be a bit too committed to reinforcing their prior conclusions at the expense of ethics, professionalism, and science. Archaeology should be done by people who are curious about the past in a way that drives them to reveal it—no matter what that past may turn out to be.

I encourage Christians and everyone else to be good skeptics when thinking about archaeology and religion. If you are honest, then you don't want your religion propped up by lies and nonsense masquerading as science, right? Be on your toes. Chances are, you will encounter one of the routine news reports that seem to pop up every year about some new amazing discovery in the Holy Land. The headlines scream "Jesus tomb found!" or "Shroud of Turin authenticated!" Don't take the chance of trusting an overly enthusiastic headline writer. Make the effort and check the story. Usually the text of the report itself will give it away as much ado about nothing. If not, do a web search and see what credible, professional archaeologists are saying about it. The track record for these major finds is not good. The Garden of Eden and Noah's Ark have been "found" repeatedly, for example, but for some reason we still don't know where they are or if they even exist. I once interviewed two Mormons for a feature article on their religion, and one of them dropped the line I've heard many times: "Archaeology has confirmed many of these claims." The problem is, I always check, and, no, archaeology hasn't confirmed their most important claims, not for Mormonism or any other religion. If anything, archaeology has been devastating to the claims of the Mormon religion. For example, the Book of Mormon's description of horses, cows, goats, pigs, wheat, and barley existing in the New World thousands of years ago conflicts with the evidence-based archaeological record that is clear about them arriving after European contact no earlier than five hundred years ago.

Most Christians don't closely follow the work of those who describe themselves as biblical archaeologists. However, many do carry around in their heads the unjustified belief that biblical archaeology has confirmed Christianity and proven many of its claims. And they are right, but only to a very small degree. The problem is that while biblical archaeology has contributed to our knowledge of Jewish and Christian cultures in ancient times, it has done nothing to confirm or prove any of the *supernatural* claims made by these religions. This is the crucial point that too many people miss. Finding evidence of people who lived thousands of years ago in the Middle East is not the same as finding evidence of God, miracles, angels, and demons.

The cold, hard reality is that nothing has ever been found that proves a supernatural claim made by any religion. There is no such artifact, no such evidence found anywhere, ever. But when a boat is discovered at the edge of the Sea of Galilee that dates to the first century and is promptly named the "Jesus boat" and put on display, some people draw the wrong conclusion and assume its existence somehow supports the claim that Jesus performed miracles and rose to heaven. It does not. It's a boat used by people in ancient times. I have seen the Dead Sea Scrolls and was impressed by them. Their age alone is awe-inspiring. As I stared at the text, I imagined a hand so long ago moving delicately across the parchment more than two thousand years ago to leave behind a trail of words. But there is nothing magical about these documents. They are important, no doubt, precious to many millions of people. They offer invaluable insights to a part of our shared past. But they prove nothing supernatural, nothing about the existence of a god. I saw many ancient structures in Rome and Athens, including many magnificent artifacts in museums there. But none of it amounted to evidence for the existence of Jupiter, Zeus, or Athena. Such spectacular finds illuminate only dead people, not living gods.

Christianity's importance to Christians comes from the claims it makes about supernatural events, supernatural beings, divine messages about heaven and hell, and predictions about God's plan for the future. If Christianity were just a story about Jewish people who lived a couple of thousand years ago and one human Jewish preacher with a bunch of disciples, it wouldn't be a big deal. It certainly would not have more than two billion followers today. What makes Christianity interesting, exciting, and vital to so many is that it claims to be the one true source of stories and information about a real god. And not just a god, but a god who once walked with us, and will again one day after the world is turned upside down. It also claims to offer the only path to heaven. This is big stuff, but nothing any archaeologist has ever found can even remotely be called proof for any of those claims.

Over the years, I have adopted a routine response to that moment in a conversation when Christians tell me that archaeology has confirmed the Bible or proved the reliability of Christian claims. I don't correct, lecture, or argue. I just ask a simple question: What is the most important archaeological discovery? Sometimes there is a moment of awkward silence. Usually they mention the Dead Sea Scrolls, the Walls of Jericho, and, of course, Noah's Ark. To that I reply that the Dead Sea Scrolls prove only that ancient people could write. The Walls of Jericho prove only that ancient people could build stone walls. And the repeated discovery of Noah's Ark proves only that biblical archaeology is overrun with amateurs, some of whom lie.

If Christians want to know more about the lives and practices of the ancient Jews and earliest Christians who shaped their religion, then they should follow *real* archaeology in the Middle East and support *genuine* scientific excavations conducted by professionals with respectable academic credentials. This is the way we learn, not by supporting or even paying attention to people who are unethical or who lack the training and sensibilities to produce sound work. Nobody likes to be misled or lied to, even if it feels good for a fleeting moment. On this point, I think, most Christians will agree.

WHY ISN'T EVERYONE A CHRISTIAN?

A simple question that both Christians and non-Christians might wish to consider is why Jesus can't convince the world. The majority of people are still not sold on his existence or his story two thousand years after he walked the Earth, performed miracles, and rose from the dead. For centuries, Christian missionaries, warriors, explorers, and settlers have traveled to virtually every place on the planet to share the good news with locals about Jesus dying for their sins so they could be saved from hell and live in heaven forever. Nations with populations that are dominated with Christians—such as the United States, Great Britain, Germany, France, Spain, Portugal, and Italy—have wielded immense power and influence over almost every other nation on Earth. They have shared or imposed many aspects of their culture, including, of course, Christianity. Literacy rates have risen dramatically over the last thousand years. Today, a majority of the world's population is capable of reading the Bible, a book that is widely believed to be the all-time bestseller. For a century, countless Christian radio programs have aired around the world. Over the last few decades, Christian television networks have used satellites to cover the globe with their pitches. Christianity is now some two thousand years old, and at this point, it's reasonable to assess how successful this belief system has been and to try to figure out why more people are not convinced that it's true.

Christianity's central doctrine tells us that the purpose of Jesus's life and brutal death was to provide salvation for all—or at least for all those who would embrace the opportunity to be saved. We are all born flawed sinners who will inevitably do bad things, according to traditional Christianity, but Jesus is the gracious escape clause. He is our path to peace of mind in this life and to heaven in the next. He died so that "we" may be saved. But if "we" refers to us—the people of the world—then something is very wrong here, because it didn't work.

According to Christians, Jesus came and went in the flesh some twenty centuries ago. He was tortured and crucified so that we could be saved. But "we" weren't saved and "we" aren't being saved. Most of us are hell-bound, at least we are according to the claim that says Jesus is the only way to salvation. What went wrong? Why didn't Jesus's message and method work? Why is it that the large majority of people of every generation since Jesus's time went to their graves as non-Christians? Clearly there is a big problem here.

When I ask Christians about this, the usual response is "free will." God gave us the ability to make our own decisions, they say, therefore, some people will always reject Jesus. It's their choice, right? No, this is not a good explanation because it misrepresents the reality of what is going on in the heads of non-Christians. By the way, because doctrinal and ritual disputes are so common and intractable, *non-Christian* here refers to those who do not self-identify as Christian rather than those Christians who fall short in the eyes of other Christians—because, of course, all Christians are apostates in the eyes of at least some, differing Christian sects.

Contrary to what many believe, the many billions of people who were not Christians throughout history and are not Christians today did not reject Jesus as a god who is the only way to heaven. They just weren't or aren't convinced by the story. Yes, one can reject organized Christian religion, oppose Christian people, and even turn away from the idea of Jesus. But all this is very different from rejecting or opposing a real god named Jesus.

I suppose there are some people somewhere who refuse to think of themselves as Christians even though they do think that Jesus is the one true God, that the Bible is accurate, and that there is no way but through Jesus to enter heaven. But how many of these people can there be? Not many, I would think. They would be an aberration with a mindset that is far different from most other non-Christians. The common claim that all non-Christians chose their status suggests that billions of people have turned their back on a god they knew to be real. This view is inaccurate, but one can easily see why it is so popular. If most of the world's people refuse to believe in Jesus and suffer severe consequences as a result, it's their fault. No blame can be assigned to God for failing to supply humanity with a convincing story.

There is a problem with the idea that one chooses to believe in Jesus. A typical atheist, for example, doesn't really "choose" to be a nonbeliever. She is a nonbeliever because she is not convinced that Jesus or any other gods exist. This is a very important point. Christians often confuse not believing in Jesus with rejecting Jesus, but the two are very different. If Zeus turned out to be real, would it be fair to charge today's Christians with rebelling against him? No, they think he is an imaginary god, made up by ancient Greeks. They don't think he is actually there to rebel against. It comes down to one's position on knowing whether or not a god is real. I can offer myself as an example. I was never directly harmed by Christianity or anyone representing Christianity in an official capacity. I may be troubled by some of the things done in the name of Christianity in a general sense, but I have no personal ax to grind, no animosity for it based on my own experiences. The reason I am not a Christian is because, to my knowledge, no one in two thousand years has been able to prove that Jesus is a god. I don't reject Jesus. I don't think he's there to reject in the first place. This means, of course, that I am not choosing to turn my back on Christianity in some bold or foolhardy act of rebellion. I'm stuck at the gate, not even in the game. I can't turn away from something or someone I haven't even found yet. I can walk away from Jesus no more than I can walk away from Oz or Middle Earth. The problem is not that I don't want to "know" Jesus or live a Christian life. My problem is that I'm unconvinced that the important claims are true. If I did believe the claims, then I would be in a position to choose to be a Christian or to reject Jesus. This situation is the same as the one faced by Muslims, Hindus, Sikhs, animists, and virtually all other non-Christians. Most of them are not in a position to accept or reject Jesus because no one has convinced them that he's real.

WHAT'S WRONG WITH THE STORY?

The basic problem that hinders the core claim of Christianity is the same one almost all religions face. The key claims are unproven by any reasonable standard, especially for something that is supposed to be so important in this life and beyond. There simply is insufficient evidence to balance the story's extraordinary claims. Calling on "faith," believing without proof, is not a reliable route to Jesus because many people are already leaning on faith to give them confidence in some other religion. Embracing Christianity can be very difficult for people who are not led into Christianity during childhood and who do not have a personal religious/psychological experience that convinces them (as people experience in numerous other religions). Those who insist on thinking before they believe or have already been convinced by another religion tend to require more than a story before they can accept Jesus as a real god with the only keys to heaven.

Yes, many Christians feel that Christianity has been proven true based on their feelings, but this doesn't hold up to fair and honest scrutiny. Sensing a personal connection to Jesus or experiencing a profound event that makes Jesus seem very real doesn't do it. Sensing gods nearby and "encountering" them is such a common claim across time and cultures that it carries little to no weight as evidence of anything other than routine occurrences for human beings. Answered prayers, miracles, fulfilled prophecies, divine visits, and visions may impress those who experience and interpret them, but they are all next to meaningless as proof that Jesus exists because thousands of other contradictory religions have claimed and still claim the same "proofs" for their gods. If it doesn't work for them, it doesn't work for Christianity. Christians are rightly unimpressed by Hindu miracles and Scientology cures. They don't jump ship and convert over such claims because they are skeptical enough to have doubts. So why should non-Christians react any differently to their claims of miracles and divine cures?

THE GREATEST STORY NEVER PROVED

Let's consider what the goal of God/Jesus was. According to most versions of Christianity, he wanted to provide a way for people to escape the innate sinful nature that had already condemned all of us to hell before we even learned to walk and talk. Jesus was the ultimate sacrifice. His death somehow absorbed our guilt so that we could all have the opportunity to avoid hell and make it to heaven. All we have to do is repent our sins and accept Jesus as our exclusive lord and savior. Unfortunately, the event, or the story of the event, has been a colossal failure. Clearly something went terribly wrong because far more people have died without Jesus in their hearts than have died with him. If God wanted to show mercy on humankind and save the maximum number of people who were willing to play by his rules, then the verdict has to be epic fail.

If Christianity is accurate, then hundreds of billions of people are suffering eternal torment in hell—not because they rejected or rebelled against Jesus, but because they never heard the story, or if they did, they were not convinced by it due to the absence of good evidence. Many of the billion Hindus alive right now have surely heard of Jesus, but few of them will ever stop believing in their gods and embrace Jesus as the only way to heaven. They don't do this out of spite or because they fear they can't measure up to the standards of Christianity. No, they remain Hindus because they were influenced by family and culture to believe in Hindu gods and to practice Hinduism. In fact, due to the universal trait of confirmation bias, a typical Hindu is likely to give many reasons why Hinduism is the most sensible religion of all. Christians who struggle to understand why everyone does not "come to Christ" have only to reflect on why it is that they do not rush to Ganesha. After all, Ganesha and other Hindu gods have performed miracles, answered prayers, healed the sick, and made their presence known, too—well, at least that's what millions of Hindus have been saying for thousands of years.

Many Christians point to the Bible as a work of perfection. They say that this collection of divinely inspired books is the most important vehicle for communicating truth that has ever existed. It is God's message for all of us, a guidebook for how to live and how to defeat death itself. No book comes close to matching its ability to transform lives and to inspire. It gives hope to the hopeless and turns heathens toward heaven. Really? One could argue that the Bible is the most overrated book in history. After all, its primary purpose seems to be to transmit the story of God in order to save more souls. Wielded by believers, it has convinced many people in many places, no doubt. Overall, however, the book has failed. Widely available in print and online, there is no indication that the majority of the world's people will be Christianized in this century or the next. The Koran may well be the most popular religious book by the end of this century. If the Christian god wanted a book that would catch the attention of the world and convince most people of a story that is true and important, then he missed with this one.

As with all extraordinary religious claims, evidence is the sticking point for anyone who decides it's wise to think before believing. Why, for example, should anyone believe that all supernatural elements of the Jesus story are true when so many other stories make equally unusual claims? If you believe that Jesus rose from the dead and the tomb was empty, then why not also believe that Joseph Smith met an angel in New York and that Mormonism is the most perfect form of Christianity? Mainstream Christians can't really charge "lack of evidence," can they? Why don't all Christians accept the claim of divinity made by Florida preacher Jose Luis de Jesus Miranda? For years, he has been saying with a straight face that he is the Messiah, and he has a church full of believers backing him up.[1] It is certainly the absence of good evidence that stops most Christians from accepting this man's claim. Why not just have faith that he is? Clearly Christians care about evidence sometimes. Like all reasonable people, they want proof for extraordinary claims before they jump onboard—except when it comes to the core claims of the religion most of them were raised to believe in. This inconsistency is perhaps difficult to recognize and no easier to correct, but all thoughtful Christians should give it a lot of thought.

Christians might ask why there must be so much uncertainty and mystery surrounding the all-important Jesus story. If the Christian god loves us and wants us to know him, then why make the story so easy to doubt? After all this time, two thousand years later, the story still can't convince even half the people on Earth. This is where we must place the ball in God's court. If he wants us to know him, then why doesn't he simply introduce himself to us? It should not be much of a challenge for the creator of the universe to come up with a way to ensure that all people—regardless of family, culture, or time period— are aware of his existence. Jesus could appear for all to see and allow for scientific confirmation of his existence. Or perhaps he could simply project himself into our brains in a way that left no doubts. Once global awareness is achieved, then, for the first time ever, it really would be up to individuals to decide if they want to follow, worship, reject, rebel against, or ignore him—and suffer the understood consequences.

WHAT IS THE PROBLEM WITH EVOLUTION?

During a visit to East Africa, I enjoyed a moment of solitude by allowing my imagination to run free. Far from the cities and close to a wild Earth that was once all we knew, I "see" prehistoric humans cooking meat over a fire they made. One cracks open bone with a stone hand ax. They chatter back and forth, making a noise I don't understand. I only know that it's definitely language. It fills the evening air, like beautiful music in a vast concert hall. Based on their low foreheads, heavy eyebrow ridges, and stone tools, my guess is that they are *Homo erectus*. It's maybe half a million years or so before my time. They're obviously people, but not quite anatomically modern. A mother tussles with her energetic baby. He is a handful, but she manages to keep him within arm's reach without too much effort. I'm not sure, but I think I heard the mother giggle. An older child picks up a stone tool. She smashes small sticks, one after the other, pausing only to admire her work. Meanwhile, an adult male stands at the edge of their camp. He looks powerful and athletic. If there were a prehistoric Olympics, this guy likely would be a champion decathlete. I sense that he's confident and bright. He stares up at passing clouds. Is he analyzing the weather, finding animal shapes in the clouds, or simply allowing his mind to wander and dream like I am? Maybe he is wondering what the world will be like half a million years from now. Far away, I see more people. They are running at a very slow pace, perhaps trying to track an animal to exhaustion. Or maybe they are just trying to get somewhere. Despite physical differences and the vast span of time between us, everyone I see is familiar to me. I haven't met these people, but I do know them. They are family, mine and yours.

Sadly, my personal moment of time-travel tourism during a safari in Kenya, though based on solid science and hard evidence, is highly controversial. Because of Christianity, many people think such a scene is silly fantasy at best or dangerous heresy at worst. Time machine or not, my imaginary visit could never have happened, say millions of Christians. In their view, all life today is as it was when it was spontaneously created a short geologic moment ago. There has only ever been one form of human on Earth, and we are it. There could not have been hominids or anything else in the distant past because there is no distant past. The world is less than ten thousand years old, some say. Furthermore, the idea of modern humans evolving from other human species and prehuman species over millions of years is not only impossible but insulting as well. Oddly, the Bible's claim that the first human was made from dust or dirt is not objectionable. No matter what people believe, however, life has evolved—including us.

The evidence that has been amassed behind Darwin's discovery is now so abundant and diverse that it can be described as overwhelming. It's too much; it can't be sensibly denied. The fact of evolution is as solid and sure as anything in science can be. Remarkably, however, nearly half of the adults in America disagree. A 2012 Gallup® poll found that 46 percent of the population thinks that their god "created humans in their present form at one time within the last 10,000 years."[1] Gallup also found that this belief rises with church attendance. Nearly 70 percent of those who attend church weekly say they hold this belief. It should be clearly understood that the problem with evolution is religious and cultural. It has nothing to do with science. Those who have a problem with evolution are mostly people who trust science, happily embrace most of its discoveries, and rely on the technology it produces throughout much of their daily lives. They hit the brakes and refuse to proceed, however, when it comes to what the same scientific process says about how life changes across generations. This is a stance that is unnecessary, however.

The evolution of life and an Earth that has existed for four and a half billion years are among the most basic and trustworthy facts of all our scientific knowledge. This is according to virtually all the world's professional scientists, many of whom are religious, by the way. Museums and laboratories around the world are stocked with millions of fossils that point directly to a long and complex story of ever-evolving life. The extensive fossil record that we have so far only makes sense in light of evolutionary theory. I can't state it any more clearly than to say that the evidence forcefully and completely contradicts a spontaneous creation of all life in present form less than ten thousand years ago. One might as well believe that the world was created last week.

Christians who have a problem with the theory of evolution need to understand that it is not controversial within science today. Scientists disagree and debate over the details, but no credible professionals reject the fact that life changes via genetic mutations and natural selection. Evolution is controversial only outside of science. Antievolutionists are not really fighting against atheists and scientists; they are fighting against evidence and reality.

If millions of fossils telling a clear tale of evolution over billions of years don't convince you, there is plenty more to consider. Microbial, insect, and even fish evolution have been *observed*. Vast and important fields of activity such as medical science and modern agriculture routinely rely on the reality of evolution to get things done. Healthcare and food production are life-and-death issues—and our working knowledge of evolution is key to their success. There is even evidence inside of us all. A "reading" of our DNA spells out the same conclusion: life evolves. Against all reason, however, some people continue to insist that the Earth is young and evolution is wrong. Why?

The reason many Christians reject evolution is because of their particular kind of Christianity, of course. It is not because they are all hopelessly dumb or uneducated. I know and have encountered many people who are bright and educated yet still have the motivation and the nerve to defend this intellectual dead end. They do not become evolution deniers after making a careful assessment of the evidence with an open mind. Typically, the more devout evolution deniers have not utilized knowledgeable sources to learn about evolution. They haven't read evolution books by credible scientists who are experts on evolution. If they did all this, they probably wouldn't find themselves in the strange position of denying one of the strongest theories in all of science.

Unfortunately, those Christians who tend to reject the foundation of modern biology tend to do so because of the questionable sources they rely on and the people they trust have misled them into believing that evolution is synonymous with atheism or an anti-God position. I recall having a chat/debate about evolution with a friend who ran through several points as if she was reading through a grocery list. None of it was impressive. I finally asked her where she was getting this stuff from. She told me she had recently read something on evolution by Chuck Colson. Yes, her understanding of evolution had been informed not by an expert on modern biology but by some political hatchet man from the 1970s. Colson, now deceased, had been special counsel to Richard Nixon before serving time in prison for his role in the Watergate scandal. While in prison he said he had a born-again experience and had become a devout Christian. I'm not suggesting that Mr. Colson was not an intelligent person, but why on Earth would anyone attempt to learn about evolution from him?

Sadly, my friend's experience is far too common. Many curious and well-meaning Christians turn to nonscientists to learn science. Former child TV star Kirk Cameron carved out an adult career as an evangelical evolution denier. Today he is on TV, in books, and all over the web "educating" millions of curious Christians about the most important aspect of modern biological science. It's no wonder that many good Christians end up with bad facts when they rely on all the wrong sources.

The problem with evolution lies with religion and culture, not with science. That's why all the battles over evolution happen not in laboratories but in school-board meetings, political campaigns, and courtrooms. The question of whether or not life evolves has been answered. The problem is that some people erroneously think they aren't allowed to accept the answer. Before getting to why it's okay for Christians to accept modern biology, let's make sure we know what evolution is.

WHAT EVOLUTION IS AND WHAT IT IS NOT

Evolution may seem like an impossibly complex concept to some. And in a way, I suppose it is. After all, we are talking about a multibillion-year process that involves trillions of living creatures on, above, and under the Earth's surface. But it's also a surprisingly simple concept, too. Evolution is change. That's the key, really. It's about animals, plants, and microbes changing each generation. What's to deny? If one can accept that, everything else is mere detail.

The shuffling of genes from generation to generation—plus genetic mutations that can be positive, negative, or neither—injects variety into life. This always-changing landscape of species is then favored or hindered by the current environment to some degree. Those life-forms that happen to have a batch of genes that are favorable for the moment might enjoy an advantage that allows them to survive and reproduce more successfully than the others around them. If so, they may well pass on these new traits to their descendants who then repeat the process. Over millions and billions of years, it's easy to imagine how this can lead to astonishing biodiversity—just like we see here on Earth today.

FIVE BAD REASONS WHY SOME CHRISTIANS REJECT EVOLUTION

- **Evolution is "just a theory."** Don't be confused by the way popular culture defines and uses the word *theory*. In everyday speech, a person might say, "Excuse me, but I think your dog may have swallowed my cell phone. But I'm not sure; it's just a theory." The use of *theory* in science is very different. In fact, it's about as far away from a hunch or wild guess as one can get. In science, a theory is a strong, well-thought-out, tested, and precise explanation of something in the natural world. In science, theories are backed up by a vast body of facts, observations, and experiments.

- **The evidence is lacking.** No, it's not! The theory of evolution is one of the most well-established and thoroughly proven theories in all of science. Numerous fields of study and a staggering amount of evidence have confirmed it. Evolution does not teeter on one fossil or the ideas of one scientist.

- **There are gaps in the fossil record.** Of course there are gaps! The only way to eliminate all gaps in the fossil record would be to discover the fossilized remains of every creature that ever lived—an impossible task. But there are not so many gaps that we can't see what has been going on for the last four billion years or so. The fossil record we have looks just like the theory of evolution predicts it should. If, however, we found bird fossils that dated to four billion years old and five-thousand-year-old triceratops fossils, then the theory of evolution would have some explaining to do. But so far we haven't.

- **Evolution is evil.** Some Christians promote the idea that evolution is an evil concept and that simply teaching it to children inevitably leads to everything from drug addiction to violence and general moral decay. Some also point to Hitler's Aryan superiority nonsense as proof that evolution is evil. This is nonsense. In World War II, Nazi bombers relied on gravity to deliver bombs from the belly of their planes to the rooftops of European cities. Should we therefore ban the teaching of gravitational theory to students because it is linked to killing? The best response to this bizarre claim is to simply state the obvious: We are responsible for our actions. A scientific theory does not justify the murder or abuse others. Some people were bad before Darwin and some people are bad after Darwin. Blaming him is silly.

- **I can't accept evolution if I'm a Christian.** The real obstacle to full public acceptance of modern biology is a false choice between Jesus and evolution that many Christians wrongly think they face. Of course evolution is going to lose almost every time when it's put like that to a typical devout believer. But here's something these Christians rarely hear: It's a lie. The choice is bogus and doesn't have to be made. One can be a Christian without denying the fact that life evolves. This is not my opinion or a guess. Many millions of Christians around the world prove it true every day by accepting the reality of evolution and keeping their belief in Jesus too.

I hope readers noticed that there was no mention of the Christian god or any other gods in this brief description of evolution. This is because evolution has nothing to do with religion—until religious people go around saying that it does. The theory of evolution is about how life changes over time. It is not a statement or belief about religions and gods. All that stuff is external baggage that gets dragged into the picture by some believers and nonbelievers. There was a time in history when the Earth's orbit around the Sun and its position in the universe was a matter of intense concern. It carried profound implications for Christianity, said many Christians. Much like the evolution of life, however, the Earth's location was never a question for theologians, priests, and preachers. It was a question for science to answer.

Just as belief in Jesus did not wither and die when it became obvious to all that the Earth revolves around the Sun, the acceptance of evolution will not destroy Christianity. Virtually all Christians today have no problem with the fact that the Earth is not at the center of the solar system, our galaxy, or the universe. There was a time, however, when it was profoundly important to deny this in the name of God. Now, not so much. Christians realized that the scientific explanation of where the Earth spins in space need not be a deal breaker for them. They figured out that they could have their Jesus and a realistic grasp of basic astronomy, too. In much the same way, belief in Jesus doesn't have to live or die on the theory of evolution, no matter what some preachers and antievolution activists claim. Jesus and Darwin can coexist in the same mind. We know this is true because millions of Christians around the world accept modern biology and still manage to practice their religion just fine. Today, if a Christian tells me they can't accept evolution because of their religion, I ask them to explain how it is they can accept the Earth revolving around the Sun. It's the same non-problem. Christians do not have to deny evolution.

It must be made clear, however, that the theory of evolution is not compatible with every version of Christianity. It really is hopelessly irreconcilable with the forms of Christianity that demand radical anti-science and anti-reality positions. One simply cannot, for example, believe that the world is ten thousand years old and claim to be in line with modern science at the same time. There are also "old-world creationists" who accept the real age of the Earth but still deny that life evolves. And then there are those Christians who say they accept that some life evolves—germs, for example—but not larger life-forms like us. This is like saying that the laws of physics are real—but they only apply on weekdays. Or that gravity is a real phenomenon—but only during daylight hours. It makes no sense. There is also no proof to accommodate the belief that God guides evolution. Maybe he does, but it's an extraordinary claim with no evidence.

My friendly suggestion to Christians who struggle with evolution is to accept that their religion, like all others, can and does adapt to new knowledge. The more we have learned about ourselves, our world, and our universe, the more all religions have changed. It may seem that religions are fixed and unchanging. Preachers often claim that their religion is the same as it was in ancient times, but this is never true. Much like life, every religion evolves. Incorporating new discoveries and self-correction are not bad things to be denied or avoided. To the contrary, they are often evidence of strength and wisdom. The willingness to make necessary adjustments if better evidence arrives is precisely why science works so well. Can't we all agree that change is good when it turns us away from mistakes to set us on a better course? And why would this not be as true for religion as anything else?

35

IS IT BETTER TO BE SAFE THAN SORRY?

My Christian friend slowed the pace of his words. His voice strengthened. Perhaps feeling a bit fatigued and frustrated by my barrage of polite questions regarding his religion and all others, he decided it was time to go in for the kill. He pulled an ace card and slammed it on the table, hoping to stump me once and for all. "Look, even if I'm wrong, so what? My life is better because of my belief in Jesus. I've been a better person thanks to my Christian faith. What did I lose if I'm wrong? But if I'm right, what have I gained? I get eternity in heaven. Atheists, on the other hand, lose everything in the worst way possible." I can't remember if he added, "It's better to be safe than sorry," but that's what he meant.

That wasn't the first time I'd heard the "better safe than sorry" argument, of course, and I'm sure it won't be the last. But it was one of the more polite recitations of it. My friend resisted going into great detail, as many do, about how I would burn and suffer in hell forever if my "choice" turns out to be wrong. Nor did he say that my life as a non-Christian is somehow substandard and immoral by definition. The implication was there, but at least he didn't feel the need to spell it out. So, what's wrong with this claim? Does it make sense to bet your life on Christianity because it's a low-risk and high-reward gamble? On the surface, this seemingly clever claim appears reasonable as an argument to believe in Jesus and become a Christian. But it's not, and here's why.

Despite its popularity, the safe-bet argument for Jesus has multiple flaws and is far from the game winner many Christians think it is. First of all, it presumes that one can become a sincere Christian in the same way one decides to sign up for the local bowling league or join the Rotary Club. It's not that simple. Many Christians seem to misunderstand what is going on inside the atheist's mind. Atheism, remember, is the *absence* of belief in a god. No belief. No gods. An atheist is not a person who knows Jesus is a real god but chooses to turn away from him anyway. An atheist is unconvinced that Jesus or any other supernatural gods are real. To the atheist, there simply are no gods to mistrust, to dislike, to hate, or to reject. Imagine if you were invited to join a nude volleyball club that meets on Saturn on the second Saturday of each month. Would you spend much time pondering club dues, time commitment, if it sounds like fun, if you are likely to mesh well with other members? No, it's unlikely that you would worry about any of that stuff until someone first convinces you that there really is such a club that meets on Saturn. That is the first step.

In the same way, an atheist doesn't feel inclined to worry much about hell, heaven, praying, church, and so on because he or she is stuck at the first step, unconvinced that Jesus is a real god. Therefore, even if an atheist were to accept the idea that being a Christian is a safe bet, she or he couldn't take that bet without first crossing the bridge to belief. This is also the case for most of the world's non-Christian religious people. They may believe in a god or gods, but they don't believe that Jesus is the only way to heaven, so it's just not that easy for them to switch lanes and become a Christian, even as a safety measure or a smart bet. Perhaps many Christians are so supremely confident that their religion is true that they find it difficult to imagine how people just don't get it. But the fact is there are billions who don't think Jesus is a god. They are not stupid or stubborn, just unconvinced by the evidence and arguments. These people cannot just decide to "be Christians" in order to play it safe. They first have to be convinced that the most basic claim made by the Christian religion is true.

THE JESUS BOOST

What about the part of this claim that says a Christian's life is better simply because that person believed in Jesus? Even if Jesus is not a real god and the Bible's claims are wrong, can a person's life be enhanced nonetheless? Of course it can. If being a Christian provides someone with some of the motivation needed to live a positive and productive life, then it worked for them and that's a good thing, I suppose. If Christianity helps someone beat drug addiction, excel in a career, or find the strength to be a great parent, then it has done well by them and I certainly wouldn't deny credit where credit is due. However, we shouldn't overlook that fact that many people do all these things and more *without* Christianity. It should not have to be said, but many atheists and many non-Christian believers are highly motivated, good, productive people. They are outstanding parents, they have overcome addiction, and they soar at work, and so on. If we are honest and look around at humankind as it really is, then we clearly see that Christianity is by no means the one necessary ingredient for a good life. I think that most, if not all, Christians who credit Jesus and the Bible for leading them to a wonderful life sell themselves short. I suspect that they are stronger and more capable than they know. I believe they could have overcome obstacles and achieved great things without the inspiration of that particular religion or any religion because so many people do.

CHRISTIANITY'S COST

The idea that nothing is lost by being a Christian—even if Christianity turns out to be untrue—fails to consider the finite span of a human life. A good run these days is about seventy or eighty years. That might seem like forever to a child or teenager, but in the context of the universe, the planet, and all of human existence, it's not much. Unproven claims of life after death aside, the only thing we know for sure is that each one of us is a relatively brief flash of existence. The quality of human lives varies greatly, of course, but in the absence of great pain and suffering, a life can be perceived as precious and beautiful, every moment of it worth appreciating. Therefore, to suggest that spending thousands of hours worshipping, reading the Bible, thinking and talking about Christianity is "no loss" even if the religion is wrong doesn't ring true. Much is lost. Time would have been wasted for little or nothing. Energy would have been squandered and money misspent. Yes, many positive things can come out of adhering even to untrue religious claims, as we see around the world in various contradictory religions today, but most benefits of religion can be experienced without religion in a much more efficient manner. Socializing, charity work, prayer (as a form of relaxation or meditation), connecting to history and tradition, a sense of belonging to something large and important, even moments of transcendence can all take place without religion or supernatural beliefs of any kind.

SO MANY BETS, SO LITTLE TIME

The final problem with the "better safe than sorry" claim is that Christianity and atheism are not the only two bets on the table. There are literally hundreds of millions of gods and hundreds of thousands of religions to wager your life on. Imagine one of those casino roulette wheels with several hundred million black and red spots for the little ball to land on. Not exactly great odds. Given that scenario, I wouldn't bet ten cents, much less my life. Even *within* Christianity all is not as simple as some would have us believe. There are tens of thousands of versions of just this one religion. And, according to people who adhere to them, the differences are extremely important and carry severe consequences pertaining to the afterlife. So, which of them is the safe bet? Catholic or Protestant? Eastern Orthodox or Oriental Orthodox? Baptist or Pentecostal? Mormon or Methodist? Jehovah's Witness or Seventh-day Adventist? Christian Scientist or Church of Christ? Any choice you make immediately condemns you to hell, according to millions of very confident Christians who say they have scripture, revelation, and common sense to back them up. What are you waiting for? Step right up and bet your life.

The easiest way to illustrate the problem with the "safe bet" claim is to turn it around on the person making the claim. I doubt very many Christians would be very impressed by a Muslim who politely explained that there is but one god, that worshipping Jesus is heresy, and then closed by saying, "If Islam turned out to be wrong after you had believed in Allah and followed the Koran faithfully, you would have lost nothing. But if it is true and you did not believe in Allah, then you would lose everything. It is better to be safe than sorry." Just as a typical Christian is unlikely to lose sleep over the threat of an Islamic hell or become a Muslim in order to "play it safe," an atheist is unimpressed by the Christian call to play it safe and worship Jesus.

36

WHY DID GOD SACRIFICE HIS SON?

**For God so loved the world, that he gave his only begotten
Son.**

—John 3:16

**In fact, the law requires that nearly everything be cleansed
with blood, and without the shedding of blood there is no
forgiveness.**

—Hebrews 9:22

F ew stories have been told more often than the one about the god
who sacrificed his own son so that all the people of the Earth could
be saved. This story, presented as historical fact, has captivated countless people across the centuries, inspiring them to believe in Jesus, to
love him, and to feel confident that they would live beyond death in paradise with him. But the story has problems. Besides the fact that there
is no evidence beyond the Bible that it happened as Christians believe,
there is an even greater challenge to making sense of it.

Why? That is the first question that comes to mind when I and
many other skeptics hear about the crucifixion of Jesus. Why would
God have needed such an event to provide a path to heaven for us? If
our creator felt we were inherently flawed and needed saving from ourselves, why not just fix us or help us fix ourselves? If it is forgiveness
for our sins that is required, why not just forgive us and be done with
it? Why did Jesus have to be tortured and killed before we could go to
heaven? Who made up these rules, anyway? Let's not forget, it was God
who was supposed to have created the world and set up the entire scenario. Heaven and hell were his ideas, presumably. It seems odd, but at
some point were his omnipotent arms tied, giving him no choice but to
stage a human sacrifice in order to save humankind from a punishment
that he was handing out?

It has been my observation that Christians rarely question the basic framework of this important story. I believe they should, however. It ought to be discussed often and openly because Jesus's death is central to the entire religion. It demands simple questions, not blind acceptance. After all, this story is important to everyone on Earth. It is the foundation of a religion that has made a huge impact on world history and continues to influence contemporary culture. Many know the story, but how many can explain it? God gave his only begotten son. Jesus died for us. Okay, but why? Why was this necessary? Couldn't God come up with a better way to deliver an escape clause to us, one that didn't involve a savage human sacrifice? And was it really the sacrifice it has been built up to be?

WOULD I SACRIFICE MY SON FOR THE WORLD?

What does it mean to sacrifice your son? It's a powerful and disturbing idea that captures anyone's attention. I can't imagine anything more difficult than to sit back and allow your child to be killed when you could have prevented it. However, if I was confronted with a situation like God apparently had before him two thousand years ago, I would offer up my son's life too, and without much deliberation. I don't say this lightly. My son struggled with health issues in childhood, and I could have lost him, so I have an extraordinary appreciation for his presence in my life now. Not a day goes by that I am not relieved and grateful that I can reach out and hug him. That said, I would submit to him being tortured and executed—but only if I was given the same deal God the Father had when he gave up his son, Jesus. God "sacrificed" his only son so that present and future generations could be saved and go to heaven. This means my son's crucifixion would save many billions, potentially trillions of people into the future. Certainly there would be plenty of motivation to help humanity. However, I would still struggle with the fact that he would die young and be taken from me.

But wait, that's not how it would happen. Just like God, I would know that I would see my son again, safe and sound, within a matter of days. Sure, signing off on my son's execution would be tough, but given the overall deal—potentially trillions of people saved from eternal torture, including my son, who will be with me forever—how could any father not agree to it? It would be a no-brainer.

Here's another imaginary scenario to ponder: What if the tin-pot dictator of some small country announced that he was going to conduct a human sacrifice in the central square of his capital city, and the victim was to be his own son who had committed no crimes? How do you think this news would be received by the world? I'm pretty sure most people, including Christians, would call this dictator evil, crazy, brutal, unjust, murderous, and so on. But wouldn't that be holding a dictator to a higher moral standard than God? What if the dictator said he had to do it, otherwise every citizen of his country would have to be executed? His son's ritualized death would be the only way the nation's people could be spared. The obvious question would be "Why?"—the same question I ask about the human sacrifice that Christianity is based on. Why would anyone with ultimate power make up rules that condemn everyone as guilty, including children and babies, and then come up with a barbaric human sacrifice as a way to circumvent those rules? If a dictator or a god really wanted to save people from his own wrath, couldn't he just pardon them and leave it at that?

WHO'S ON THE CROSS?

Another basic problem with the God-sacrificed-his-only-son story is that it's not at all clear who was actually supposed to be on the cross. The concept of the Holy Trinity is important to the story of Jesus's death because so much is made of God the Father sacrificing his son, who was later resurrected and reunited with his father in heaven. Keep in mind that priests and preachers have been telling this story for many centuries to stir emotions. "Try to imagine how much God loved us for him to be willing to give his only son," they say, over and over. However, the Holy Trinity claim makes it unlikely that God the Father sacrificed anything at all.

According to the doctrine of the Holy Trinity, the Christian god is three unique beings rolled into one. There is God the Father, Jesus, and the Holy Spirit. They are different but somehow the same. This has been explained to me several times by laypersons, Protestant preachers, and Catholic priests, but I still struggle with it. I am told that the one God takes three different forms, sort of like water becoming ice, vapor, or liquid. But even as there may be three versions of God, it is important to keep in mind that there is only one God in Christianity. This presents what should be an obvious problem for the crucifixion story: How did God the Father sacrifice his only son, Jesus, when the two of them are the same divine being? If Jesus was on the cross, does it mean all three of them were there together? If God the Father and Jesus are the same, then what does it really mean to sacrifice your son if your son is actually you? I am not trying to nitpick or exaggerate the importance of a minor detail. The Holy Trinity is a key doctrine in Christianity, and it seems to me that it has a lot to do with how we should feel about the claim that God "gave his only begotten son" so that we could be saved. What exactly did he give up? Did God sacrifice himself on Earth temporarily and then rejoin himself in heaven? If so, it doesn't seem like much of a sacrifice.

WHY DIDN'T IT WORK?

Finally, there is the biggest problem of all with the story of God sending Jesus to suffer and die in order to save us: it didn't work then and it's still not working. If Jesus is the only way to heaven, as the Bible states, then the crucifixion was mostly a tragic failure two thousand years ago, and it's mostly failed every generation since then because a majority of the world's people are not Christians. They either didn't hear the story of Jesus's sacrifice, or they did but were not sufficiently impressed by it to believe in him. Yes, Christianity is the world's most numerically popular religion with an impressive two billion followers. But five billion is an impressive number too, and that's how many people are not Christians today because the story of God's sacrifice failed to convert them. That's a lot of people for Jesus to have suffered and died in vain for. And this is only the number of non-Christians currently alive. When you add all the non-Christians who have lived in the past and those non-Christians who presumably will live in the future, the tally of lost souls soars. They say Jesus saves, but apparently not very well.

Here we are, in the twenty-first century, and most people are still unconvinced that Jesus is a god who grants access to a life after death in exchange for exclusive worship. It is not sensible to dismiss the world's non-Christians as too stupid or stubborn to take advantage of this offer. Obviously there are billions of people outside Christianity who are intelligent, thoughtful, and sane who would not turn their backs on something so important to their well-being—*if* it made sense to them. In the majority of these cases, isn't it more likely that the problem is with the credibility of the claim and not with the doubters? Most people are simply unconvinced that the story is true. Don't blame them. Blame the message.

THE SEARCH. For two millennia, Christians have sought a connection with the divine and say that Jesus is the way. But why do a majority of the world's people remain unconvinced? *Cathedral de Notre Dame, Paris. Photo by the author.*

DID GOD DROWN THE WORLD?

T he story of the Great Flood and Noah's Ark is one everybody knows. God flooded the world and killed most life on it. Although he knew how the humans he created would turn out in the future, God was disappointed enough by their disobedience and bad behavior that he decided to drown them all in a global flood. God wanted to wipe the slate clean, initiate the ultimate reboot of humankind—but not completely. He spared one old man, Noah, and his family. He instructed Noah to build a ship that would keep them safe.

God also told Noah to keep onboard "two of every kind" of animal. They, like Noah's family, would be spared in order to repopulate the planet after the waters receded. After forty days of relentless rain followed by months of Noah and his passengers drifting around, the waters receded enough for the ark to come aground atop a mountain. In our post-flood world, all land animals and all people alive today are descended from the ark's passengers.

HISTORY OR MYTH?

Skeptics tend to view this tale very differently than Christians do. Skeptics think of it as a genocidal horror story (God *killed* almost *everyone* on Earth), while many Christians view it as a demonstration of God's grace (he *loved us* so much that he gave us another chance). Subjective interpretations aside for the moment, the most simple question of all is, Did this really happen?

First we have to specify whose flood story we are addressing. Not every Christian believes that every detail in the Bible can be trusted. For some, the biblical story of Noah's Ark is not to be taken literally. They regard it as a sacred tall tale, loaded with important meaning, perhaps, but definitely not as an accurate account of a real event. Maybe it did happen, they suggest, but probably not on the scale or in the exact way recorded in Genesis. However, these Christians appear to be in the minority. According to an ABC News poll, no less than 60 percent of Americans believe that the Great Flood happened *exactly* as described in the Bible.[1] They think it was global and that virtually all land life everywhere was annihilated. This is significant because, if true, it means a majority of Americans are in near-total disagreement with some of the most fundamental conclusions of the geological and biological sciences. For this flood to have occurred as they claim, science would have to be very, very wrong about many, many things. Some skeptics view the Noah's Ark belief as a secondary issue and not worth significant attention. I disagree. It needs to be challenged because it is so antithetical to what we know about the Earth, nature, and our own history.

PERCENTAGE OF AMERICAN ADULTS WHO SAY THE NOAH'S ARK STORY IS "LITERALLY TRUE"

All	60
Catholics	44
Protestants	73
Evangelical Protestants	87
Non-Evangelical Protestants	50[2]

YOU CAN'T HIDE A GLOBAL FLOOD

Even among Christians who agree that the flood happened more or less as the Bible says, there is disagreement over when it happened. Some Christians say the flood happened "a long, long time ago" and leave it at that. Some say it happened less than ten thousand years ago. Still others are more precise and declare with certainty that it happened in a specific year. I spoke with a woman who was a follower of Harold Camping, the California man who predicted the world would end on a specific day in 2011. She told me the flood "definitely" occurred in the year 4990 BCE. "No doubt about it," she declared.

If one had to choose among these views, "a long, long time ago" would be the best option because the flood could not have happened a mere ten thousand years ago or less. Ten thousand years is an extremely thin sliver of time in geology. It's certainly not so long ago that modern geologists would not have confirmed the flood. A global flood would have been an extraordinarily massive event in the Earth's history with a colossal impact. It would have left behind a very clear and obvious record. Evidence for it would be everywhere, and the world's geologists would be the first to see it. Just imagine the vast sedimentary layer that would be left after such a deluge. Millions of tons of dead plants and animals would settle into one very distinct layer that no geologist—or public works department backhoe operator, for that matter—could miss. There is just no sensible way such a flood could occur without leaving such obvious proof. Credible professional geologists have found no evidence of a global flood occurring within the last ten thousand years, the last hundred thousand years, or even the last hundred million years. Furthermore, credible professional archaeologists have found no hint of a global flood that wiped out every human society on Earth at once.

Some Christians who believe the flood story have suggested to me that there are scientists who "know the truth" but won't admit it because it contradicts their godless beliefs or they are afraid of losing their jobs. This is nonsense. If just one geologist anywhere could prove this event occurred, or at least find enough good evidence to make a serious and compelling case, then she or he would instantly earn superstar status in academia and would surely be a big hit with the general public as well, given the religious implications. Fame and fortune await the geologist who can confirm Noah's flood. Yet so far there is nothing. Sure, there are creationists who claim to have evidence and claim to have proven that the flood occurred. But their work to date has not survived the scientific process. Every one of their key claims is rejected by virtually all professional geologists.

The scientific silence on the Great Flood described in the Bible is not only from geologists. Paleoanthropologists, microbiologists, archaeologists, biologists, marine biologists, herpetologists, and many more scientists in many more disciplines would have discovered glaring signs of a global deluge that caused the death of virtually all life a relatively short time ago. The bottom line is that this claim of a global flood taking place at any point during the time period in which we have existed is unproven and so unlikely that it is not taken seriously by geologists and others who best know the Earth. The genetic and fossil evidence is very strong that anatomically modern humans are about 150,000 to 200,000 years old. If a flood happened—and we were there to see it—then it would be easy to prove. The fact that no one has come close to proving it means it almost certainly did not happen.

HOW DID NOAH DO IT?

There is no doubt that severe localized floods were common in ancient and prehistoric times, just as they are now. Floods can take many lives and have always been a threat to many forms of life. Some floods can be catastrophic to a particular area, so much so that victims may find the destruction difficult to comprehend and explain. It is not hard to imagine, then, that an unscientific and mostly illiterate population who suffered through a major flood thousands of years ago might have imagined that it was a worldwide disaster. For them, given their extremely limited perspective, it was.

Regardless of when the Noah's Ark story is supposed to have happened, we also have to try to understand how it happened. Claiming that eight humans, two giraffes, two gorillas, two elephants, and so on boarded a boat to ride out a global flood and then repopulate the world may make sense to children in Sunday school, but adults should be intellectually responsible enough to ask a few simple questions. First, how did all these animals get onboard? What about the oceans between continents? How did South American sloths make it across the Atlantic in order to board the ark? They move pretty slowly. What about the koalas in Australia? The penguins in Antarctica? Some say that the continents had not yet separated and the animals simply walked across the land. But this violates the well-established time line of continental drift by many millions of years. The best response I have heard to the question of how the animals got aboard is that it was a miracle. The wild animals from the far-flung reaches of the world were transported and temporarily tamed by God. The problem with that, however, is that trying to explain something by simply citing magic is not really an explanation at all.

Another simple and fair challenge to the flood story deals with the number of species that would have boarded the ark. Most Christians who favor a literal interpretation claim that Noah's vessel was between four and five hundred feet long. That's no dinghy, for sure, but could it have been large enough to accommodate two members of each species of all land life? Not even close. The number of species on our planet is staggering. It's such a big number, in fact, that nobody even knows what it is. To date, scientists have only been able to make estimates. Globally, there are probably somewhere between ten million and one hundred million species of life. Scientists still routinely find new species and will likely continue to do so for a long time. All other challenges aside, if someone wanted to gather two of every species today and put them on a ship, that ship would probably need to be the size of Australia.

Many ark believers are quick to point out the precise wording in Genesis when questions arise about how so many animals could fit on one ship. Indeed, Genesis does not claim that Noah's boat provided sanctuary for a male and female of every *species*. (There was no such classification system then.) It says there were two of every *kind*. So the argument goes that Noah didn't need to board, say, two each of the hundreds of thousands of species of beetles; he only needed to provide safe passage for two.

But there are problems with this explanation. The world we see today is filled with numerous, distinct species of beetles, as well as rodents, primates, lizards, ants, and so on. How can these creatures exist if all land life today is descended from the species carried on the ark? How did two ants lead to many thousands of ant species? The only explanation is that they must have mutated and adapted, and maybe some isolated population had different reproductive success rates in different environments.

Wait, this is beginning to sound a lot like evolution, and those who promote a literal interpretation of the Noah's Ark story tend not to like the idea of speciation via evolution. No need to worry about that, however, because six thousand years or even two hundred thousand years would not be nearly enough time for two of every "kind" to evolve into the dense and diverse abundance of species we see on Earth today. It couldn't have happened.

Let's not forget the people. For the story to work, Noah's eight-member family would have had to give rise to all the great civilizations of the last five thousand years or so. Think about this. The Babylonians, the Egyptians, the Greeks, the Romans, the Aztecs, the Maya—all sprang from that one family in one specific place in perhaps as little as a couple of thousand years? Impossible, say the world's credible professional geneticists, archaeologists, historians, and anthropologists.

THEY FOUND NOAH'S ARK—AGAIN!

Much like Bigfoot and Atlantis, people keep discovering Noah's Ark again and again—but they never really do, of course. Scarcely more than a year goes by without some report about a person claiming to have found the ark being published. But these reports are never followed up with a presentation of the big discovery to the world. Something always happens somewhere between the announcement and the confirmation. The ark, it seems, is just one more holy grail for pop culture to keep reaching for and never quite grasp. I can remember hearing about the discovery of Noah's ship when I was a child, and I've heard or read about many more ark discoveries since then.

The reason the ark is repeatedly "discovered" yet never produced is that the non-archaeologists who make these claims are motivated by religious belief and are not sufficiently guided and restrained by the scientific process. The result is that a piece of wood on a mountaintop or a rock formation becomes the ark in the minds of those determined to find it. Unfortunately, many people are misled by the inevitable irresponsible reporting that follows and end up believing that the ark has been found. I have encountered many Christians over the years who confidently tell me that the ark has been found and therefore the story is confirmed. My polite way of handling this misinformed view is to simply ask the following questions: Who found it? Where did they find it? Where are the ark or ark artifacts kept or displayed?

The usual response I get is that "they" found it on Mount Ararat in Turkey, and that's all. But if "they" really found it, wouldn't we all know "their" names? Howard Carter found King Tut's tomb in 1922, and he is fairly well known today for that discovery. Indiana Jones is an archaeologist who doesn't even exist in real life, and everybody knows him. Don't you think we would all know the name of the person who led the team that found Noah's Ark and scientifically confirmed one of the most important stories in the Bible, as well as one of the most important events in the history of our planet?

THE REAL MEANING OF THE NOAH'S ARK STORY

Whether or not Noah and his ark existed, it seems clear to me and many others that this is a gruesome story of death that raises questions. Beyond the factual challenges, why is it so popular? Why are there so many cheery illustrated children's books about the flood, and why do so many of them include smiling cartoon animals and a jolly Noah waving from the deck of the ark as if they are on a pleasure cruise rather than escaping planetary mass murder? Why is this deeply disturbing story a staple of Sunday-school curriculums? I am aware that many Christians view it as proof of God's love for us. Yes, he could have killed eight more people and wiped us out completely. But he didn't. He gave us another chance. This is nice spin, I suppose, but let's take a realistic look at what God did, according to Genesis.

He flooded the planet with torrential rains. No dry ground any-where. He drowned all land life, except the fortunate "two of every kind" and Noah's family. Drowning is not a nice way to go. Inhaling water is terrifying and painful. The CIA subjected alleged terrorists to waterboarding because drowning is a perfect storm of unbearable fear, panic, and agony. Try to think about everyone on Earth, save one family, treading water in a desperate attempt to keep their heads above water, only to eventually tire and sink. Imagine all their desperate screams before they go under and their lungs fill with water. Many would have clung to debris and floated for days before slowly succumbing to dehydration or hypothermia. The population would have been smaller then, of course, but it's still a disturbing number of people dying in one horrible moment.

Let's say God was justified in flooding the world because all the adults were hopelessly wicked and disobedient. Let's assume that every one of them deserved their painful deaths, even though this all-knowing deity knew before he created them that they would behave precisely the way they behaved. But what about the children? What did the babies do wrong? Imagine every infant on the planet drowning at the same time. Try to visualize thousands of little child corpses bobbing in the waves for days and weeks. And what about all the animals, especially those that experience fear and feel pain similar to us? The chimps, orang-utans, gorillas, monkeys, elephants, horses, dogs, puppies, cats, kittens, rabbits, and so on would have all died horrible deaths too. Why? Wouldn't a compassionate god have left a few islands somewhere so that animals of higher intelligence could have been spared? Skeptics are not being belligerent when they ask for explanations from those who promote this story as both factual and positive. They just don't get it. Remember the Indian Ocean tsunami in 2004 and the tsunami that struck Japan in 2011? Imagine that same level of terror and destruction occurring every place on Earth on the same day. Regardless of whatever bad behavior or slack worshipping habits people were up to, it is difficult to understand how everyone apart from one family could have deserved such a brutal end inflicted by a god described as just and loving.

38

WHY DO BIRTH LOCATION AND FAMILY MATTER SO MUCH?

I f I were a Christian, one of the biggest concerns I would have about whether or not my religion is true would be the simple question of why the place one is born matters so much. If the Bible is correct and Jesus really is the only way to heaven, then the whole system seems profoundly unfair. A baby born into a family of Christian evangelicals in a small South Carolina town, for example, would enjoy an extraordinary advantage over a baby born into a Muslim or Hindu family in Yemen or Mumbai. If one's choice of a god and religious affiliation truly does carry with it implications that determine an eternal fate after death, then why don't all people have equal access? Sure, many people around the world are aware of Christianity, more today than ever, but how difficult must it be for the majority of people in those societies where Christians are few or nonexistent? How tough must it be to go against the currents of family and culture to embrace a foreign religion? For most, it's probably not even a matter of emotional strength and determination. More likely they never even consider becoming Christians because of their upbringing by family and society, which imposed a different god belief on them. They have no compulsion to become Christians because they feel they are already doing the right thing.

The number of new Christians is growing in some places—China, for one—but the fact remains that the easiest and most common route to Christianity is to be born into a family of Christians who live in a society made up mostly of Christians. But this should worry Christians. Why can't Christianity attract more people? Why does it rely so heavily on exposing/influencing/teaching/indoctrinating/coaching/proselytizing (choose your word) children to keep filling its ranks? Why can't Christianity simply stand on the merit of its claims and let adults make up their minds about whether or not the claims are true?

The fact that Christianity is currently the world's largest religion means little when one considers that the vast majority of today's

Christians were told to believe in Jesus, dream of heaven, and fear hell from the earliest days of their childhood. What might the religious landscape be today if all children were taught about ten or fifteen of the most popular religions in an unbiased manner? How do you think the numbers might sort out a generation or two later? How many American children would end up being Buddhists or Muslims then? Christianity might still end up top—it does have some universally appealing features—but it is very unlikely that the direct parent-to-child transmission of belief would survive such a scenario.

Islam may pass Christianity as the world's most numerically large religion of this century, but if this happens, it won't be because Islam makes more sense, has more evidence, or is more logical and likely to be true than Christianity. Adult conversions are a factor, but the primary reason for Islam's current rise is simple population statistics. It's primarily about birthrates. Thoughtful Christians ought to give some thought to how it is they find themselves adhering to the same belief system that they were exposed to in childhood and were encouraged to accept. It's unlikely to be a coincidence. That baby born in South Carolina might have ended up a Christian anyway, even if she had been born in rural Pakistan—but I doubt it.

My polite challenge to Christians is this: Why no comparison shopping? How can you be sure Jesus is the right or best answer if you haven't given Mohammed a fair hearing? How can you place trust in the Bible as the supreme book of important truths if you never read the Koran? What does it mean to claim that Jesus answered your prayer and is therefore real when ancient Greeks and Romans said the same thing about their gods thousands of years ago or when contemporary Hindus say it today about their gods? Multiple studies have exposed most American Christians as being grossly ignorant about not only their own religion but all others as well.[1] They shouldn't feel picked on, however. Religious ignorance is a global problem and sadly is a common source of fear, mistrust, and hate. I am sure that if the world's Christians had a half-decent understanding of at least several contemporary religions and a few extinct ones, they would gain a much improved perspective on world history, current affairs, and their fellow humans with whom they share the planet today. The common lack of curiosity about other religions that I have observed from too many Christians is puzzling. If one is already convinced that there is a supernatural dimension to our universe and that one or more supernatural beings are real, why wouldn't you be curious to know what the majority of the planet has to say about this? Remember, no matter what your religion is, the majority of the world believes differently. No one religion, including Christianity, has been able to convince most people that it is true.

It may be a disturbing thought for some Christians but I think it's a thought worth having. Imagine if you were a little boy born into a loving family that would do anything for you. You were cared for, protected, nurtured, and loved unconditionally. And every family member is Sikh. Yours has been a Sikh family for more generations than anyone can remember. Upon birth you are labeled a Sikh too. Barely a toddler, you are told glorious stories, taught to pray, to worship, and how to dress. No haircuts for you and certainly no Sunday school at a church either. Honestly, what are the odds that Christianity would penetrate such a fortress of loving indoctrination? It might happen, but it's very unlikely.

Often when I am doing a broadcast interview about science and skepticism, the host or a caller will ask me about Jesus or God. Because of my cultural location in the West, it's always "God," never gods, always Jesus, never Mohammed or Buddha. Before answering, I try to squeeze in the fact that half the world's population doesn't believe in the Jewish/Christian/Islamic "God" and more than two-thirds of the world is unconvinced that Jesus is a god. Sometimes these basic truths derail the conversation completely. If I am able to get it in, I add that if I were on a TV or radio show in Saudi Arabia or Pakistan, Jesus would probably never come up, but Allah and the Koran certainly would. It is clear that culture rules when it comes to religion. Anyone who travels the world with open eyes can't miss this. Conversely, however, a skeptic of religion is a skeptic of religion regardless of family or cultural location. Adherence to basic critical-thinking skills and the resolve to demand evidence when confronted with unusual or important claims does not change according to society or time period. Skepticism is good thinking, always and anywhere. That's what makes it so powerful and so valuable.

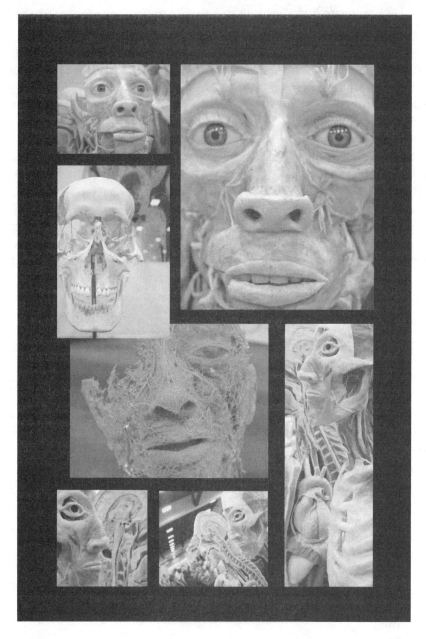

BEYOND NATURE? The structure and processes of the human body and other life-forms have led many to conclude that only a god could account for such complexity. The primary problem with the intelligent-design claim, however, is that it asks us to surrender the quest for knowledge. It proposes a final answer based on our current ignorance, as if we will not continue to learn and discover more. *Photos by the author.*

39

WHY DO CHRISTIANITY AND SCIENCE SO OFTEN COME INTO CONFLICT?

F or many centuries, a strange war has raged between science and Christianity. People have physically suffered and even died on the frontlines of this conflict as scientific discoveries unsettled the foundations of faith. Sometimes the cost is not a human life but all human progress. Why must there be this conflict? Who exactly is fighting and what do they hope to achieve? Must Christianity and science forever clash, or can a way be found that would allow them to coexist peacefully in the same universe?

Of course peace is possible. We see the evidence for that. There are millions of Christians who embrace science. Many respected professional scientists are Christians. They certainly don't seem to have found any irreconcilable differences that forced them to choose one over the other. Conflict is not inevitable for every Christian. Science is not antireligion, anti-god, and pro-atheism. Science is anti–false claims, anti-delusion, and pro-reality. If a religion doesn't pretend to know things about nature that it can't prove and that do not conflict with evidence-based conclusions, then there shouldn't be a problem with science. But too often religion goes too far. Religious people make extraordinary claims they can't prove, and they deny scientific conclusions that were earned the hard way, by collecting evidence and testing. Many versions of Christianity do not directly prohibit accepting science as a reliable method of discovery and a body of ever-changing knowledge. Unfortunately, however, others do. Serious problems do exist between Christianity and science because some versions of Christianity choose war. Those Christians think faith can and must defeat science-based reason. They think belief is better than skepticism. For some religious people, the basic attitude of science: "doubt is good, question everything" is considered an attack on their religion rather than the best way we have to sort out reality from fantasy. So, here we are, in the twenty-first century, still caught in the crossfire between faith and fact, between belief and knowledge. Far from being trivial, this clash does significant harm to the world. And we all suffer for it.

When thinking about how all humanity pays a price for the clash between religion and science, it is too easy to point to a few cases of religious parents neglecting the health needs of their sick child because they think prayer works better than medical science. It is too simple to point out the energy and countless hours wasted by politicians and other leaders who think they must serve not only people but gods too. The greatest cost of all, however, is the loss of infinite constructive dreams and thoughts—the kind that could change our world for the better. Every time we are misdirected from the reality around us and the challenges before us by unproven religious claims, some of humanity's intellectual treasure is squandered. We lose ideas every moment of every day with little or no acknowledgment of doing so. They go unmissed because we cannot see what might have been. When Christianity, or any other religion, hinders science and scientific thinking, we all lose.

In another chapter I described my visit to a madrassa, where I saw young boys memorizing and reciting lines from the Koran. It deeply saddened me because I felt like healthy minds were being lost or at least crippled right before my eyes. I felt those innocent boys had been condemned by a religion to die a sort of mental death and then go through life as little more than faithful zombies. Maybe some of them will find the opportunity and the strength to break free and live, but how many? For me, this is the cost of the war between science and religion. When religion wins total victory, children are lost and humanity has been diminished. Boys who could have been taught about the universe and encouraged to think in bold new ways were instead effectively lobotomized in the name of a god. I know this may sound harsh to some, but that scene haunts me. Sacrificing children in this way is not only bad for them; it's bad for the world.

I once visited a Christian school that also seemed committed to turning out graduates who would never think critically or produce thoughts that might challenge and change the world for the better. Although it did not appear to be even remotely as mechanical and dehumanizing as the madrassa I visited, the Christian school was not shy about its goal. From the posters on the wall to the textbooks to the repeated prayers of students, it was clear the curriculum was

God first, and everything else a distant second. I am not suggesting that no devout Christian or Muslim can have original thoughts or rise up to change the world in positive ways; many have done just that throughout history, of course. I am referring to those who are left so numb and disengaged from reality by the worst madrassas and Bible schools that they are unlikely to ever awaken for the rest of their lives.

Imagine if, starting tomorrow, no adult Muslims, Christians, or Jews discouraged any children from thinking independently and freely. What if instead all the world's children were taught how to think like little amateur scientists? What if they were taught math, science, and literature, and were told to dream of anything they wished and to have no fears about straying off the path of tradition, so long as it did not harm themselves or others? Of course, some religious people would warn that these children would be doomed to immoral and destructive behavior without Bible or Koran instruction and an imposed god belief. But we know better, because we have only to look at countries with extraordinarily high rates of atheism, such as Sweden and Denmark, to see that children can be just fine with a secular family life and education. So what might happen? No one knows for sure, but I suspect that in twenty years all those free-thinking, skeptical, science-literate young adults coming online would be the profound boost for humanity we need to move us closer to solving our biggest problems.

I have taught science to children, and the joy I saw in their faces, the excitement that explodes from their eyes, taught me that they want to learn. They want to know. I don't think they want to be indoctrinated into some adult's truth. Sure, kids need structure and security, but children want to discover the truth on their own. They want to explore reality on their own as much as possible. They can think if we allow them to. But hundreds of millions of children around the world are never given the chance to think independently and to develop their minds fully. Their potential will never be realized. This is a price we pay for the science and religion clash. And it's far more important than squabbles over evolution, funding stem-cell research, or the age of the Earth. Those are but symptoms of the real problem.

A cease-fire might be too much to hope for any time soon, but I'm optimistic that we can help reduce the intellectual carnage of this sad war simply by teaching people what science is. Too many Christians think science is their enemy because it is rigidly anti-God and aggressively arrogant. Nothing could be farther from the truth. First of all, science can't reasonably be accused of arrogance, not when every scientist freely admits there are more questions than answers and that nothing in science is written in stone or in indelible ink. This, after all, is the one field of human activity that admits to and builds on near-constant failure. Errors and dead ends are the rule and not the exception. Better evidence that shows previous conclusions to be wrong is not viewed as a catastrophe to be avoided as is so often the case in politics and religion. In science, better evidence is an opportunity to get it right, to get closer to a better answer. Mistakes and radical revisions are not only tolerated in science; they are expected.

As for the anti-god charge, science has no particular agenda regarding gods and religions. It is a tool, a process. It's the best way we have to get at the truth and find correct answers. There is nothing better than the scientific method for weeding out error, lies, and nonsense. How does any of this equate to being anti-God (or anti-gods)? If Jesus is a real god, then science—by definition—cannot be anti-Jesus because science is concerned with all things that are real. Science, done properly, has no agenda other than revealing reality and uncovering mystery. Trust me, if scientists found good evidence for the Christian god that could be tested and had predictive value, they would produce the Theory of God and publish their work for others to check. Their first move most certainly would not be to ignore or bury that proof because science is committed to some dogmatic antireligion position. No, they would be ecstatic over yet another great achievement by the scientific process. They would gain instant fame and fortune and would rightly be hailed as heroes who added to our understanding of the universe.

Science should be viewed as the enemy of Christianity only if Christianity is opposed to truth and reality. If, however, a particular version of Christianity is accurate in its claims, if it is true and real, then why would it be in conflict with a system designed to seek truth and reality? The followers of that version might be disappointed or frustrated that science has so far been unable to confirm Christian miracles, a global flood, heaven, hell, or resurrection. But they should not interpret the absence of scientific proof for scientific assault. Maybe it is not science in general that some Christians don't feel comfortable with; rather it is this absence of validation from science that bothers them. After all, is there any doubt that even the most extreme fundamentalist Christians—such as those who are activists against the teaching of modern biology in public schools, for example—would be overjoyed by news of scientific proof of Jesus's divinity? It is likely that they would become the world's biggest fans of science instantly and champion the scientific process for the rest of their days.

I hope all Christians hear the good news that science and skepticism are not necessarily their enemies. Science and skepticism may be at war with irrational belief, yes, but if our worldview is clouded by lies, honest mistakes, or delusions, then science is the solution we want, right? No one wants to be deluded and wrong, I hope, so no one should reject the scientific process that works so well at rooting out and exposing delusion and error. If your claims are true, science will not tear them down. Those who find themselves at war with science should ask what it is exactly that they are fighting against. Everyone not opposed to truth and reality can count science as an ally and not an enemy.

THE GOD MAKERS. The number of gods that humans have believed in over the last several thousand years is staggering, numbering in the hundreds of millions. Does our apparent knack for inventing gods have implications for Christianity's claims? *Photo by the author.*

40

WHY DO PEOPLE GO TO HELL?

Whosoever was not found written in the book of life was cast into the lake of fire.

—Revelation 20:15

He that believeth and is baptized shall be saved; but he that believeth not shall be damned.

—Mark 16:16

Few Christian beliefs are as fascinating as the one about a place called hell. Even heaven, serving up round-the-clock goodness for all eternity, seems like it might become a bit boring after the first few trillion years or so. But hell offers constant excitement for residents in the form of weird demons and endless agony. Never a dull day in hell.

The world's two billion Christians do not agree about what hell is, where it is, how one ends up there, or if it even exists. Most Christians, however, clearly do believe there is a place somewhere that is very bad and should be avoided at all costs. In 2009, the Harris Poll® found that 61 percent of all American adults believe in hell.[1] That's 14 percent less than believe in heaven but still a majority of all Americans. The only way to stay out of hell, say many Christians, is to "repent your sins and accept Jesus." That sounds simple enough. But it's quite the challenge for any sincere skeptic in the habit of asking for reasons to believe. It can also be difficult, I imagine, if one was raised by a non-Christian family in a culture that promotes and reinforces belief in Islam, Hinduism, Sikhism, or some other contradictory religion. But without Jesus as your god, it's off to the lake of fire for you, no exceptions.

Some Christians say there are exceptions. Jews and very young children who die early deaths, for example, might get a pass. Then there are Christians who believe that hell means nothing more than being apart from God/Jesus after death. There is no fiery dungeon, no endless agony. I've taken the time to explore these opposing views, and I have asked Christians about each position. The usual response is to launch a barrage of Bible excerpts that seem to support their respective positions and leave it at that. In short, some say hell is in the Bible so it must be real, while others say Jesus is way too nice to be so mean. In the end, of course, opinions and competing Bible quotes rarely settle anything, which is why there are more than forty thousand versions of Christianity one can choose from today.

I suspect that much of the disagreement between Christians on the specifics of hell comes down to personality types. The tough, hard-nosed sort of Christians are happy to talk about all the suffering and screaming of the damned. They know it's an effective way to scare people and get them to pay attention to Jesus's message of love and forgiveness. The other type of hell believer represents the increasingly popular "Oprah-fication of Christianity," meaning everybody is going to be OK; all roads lead to heaven; God is love, therefore he would never send anyone to a place of never-ending pain—regardless of what the Bible actually says. At worst, say the optimistic Christians, hell is a halfway house where one takes a crash course in self-improvement before proceeding on to heaven. It's sort of like a time-out: not fun, but not so bad. I can't offer an opinion on which side makes more sense because I think they both are wrong. There are numerous problems with the concept of the Christian hell, but for me, one simple point stands out: in all of history, no one has ever produced any good evidence for its existence. None.

TO HELL AND BACK

In addition to circular arguments based on Bible quotes that prove nothing, there are eyewitness accounts from people who claim to have died, gone to hell, and then returned. While not as numerous as stories about people dying and visiting heaven, hell stories do exist. Bill Wiese, a Southern California realtor-turned-evangelist, has a great one. In his 2006 book, *23 Minutes in Hell*, he describes his brief journey to the lake of fire in graphic detail. While sleeping on the night of November 22, 1998, Wiese says God/Jesus suddenly snatched him from his bed and dropped him into a burning-hot jail cell located in the middle of

ry day. If you're really interested, you can search for "recording of
1" on the Web, but I already listened to it so you don't have to waste
ir time. It's mostly a garbled mess, though you can hear some muffled
eams. According to the tale of the tape, Russian geologists drilled a
e nine miles deep into the Earth somewhere in Siberia and managed
breach the lair of Beelzebub. Ooops! Once they had unintentionally
nctured the roof of hell, however, horrible screams of tortured souls
ured out, which they recorded. The story is great and the tape is fair.
e only problem is that the entire thing is an obvious hoax.[3]

HICH HELL?

ere's something atheists never worry about that Christians might
'ant to give some thought to: Which hell do the damned have to go to?
ew believers consider it a problem, but there are many hells, according
ɔ the world's believers, past and present. Does the soul of an atheist go
ack and forth between all of them for eternity? Or is the infidel's soul
ivided equally and shared among the various hells at once? Hindus
re in trouble with both Islam and Christianity, for example, so which
ell do they end up in? Do Christians really get to go to heaven, or do
they have to go to the Islamic hell for failing to worship the one true
god who has no son? And do devout Muslims who kept the pillars of
their faith have to go to the Christian hell for not believing in Jesus?
Or could it be that we are all in trouble and will end up together with
Hades down in the underworld of ancient Greek religion?

Christians who respond to such suggestions by claiming that there
is only one hell—theirs, of course—need to explain how they know this.
After all, there is no more or less evidence for other hells than there
is for the Christian hell. There are even great stories of non-Christian
hells. There are sacred scriptures in the texts of other religions that
mention non-Christian hells, too. And the current popularity of belief
in the Christian hell means nothing because more people throughout
history have believed in non-Christian hells than have believed in the
Christian hell. So if a non-Christian or lapsed Christian is told to fear
hell, an appropriate response might be either "Which hell?" or "Why
fear just one?" I often tell Christians who warn me about the lake of
fire that I will begin to worry about their hell when they begin to worry
about all the others.

hell. Two huge reptilian-humanoid demons greeted [
smashed Wiese against a wall, breaking some of his b
the other creature began shredding his flesh with i
always taken care of my body by eating right, exercis
in shape," says Wiese, "but none of that mattered as m
destroyed right before my eyes." While this was goin
could hear the desperate screams of "millions." Wiese
fire that was one mile wide and filled with suffering pe
him were spiders, maggots, worms, and snakes. The air
putrid, rotten smells. Fortunately for Wiese, Jesus inter
him back to his bedroom, where his wife discovered hin
floor next to the bed.[2] Since then, Wiese has devoted a
warning others that hell is real and Jesus is the only one
us from ending up there.

I'm amazed that unsubstantiated stories like this appe
Christians. (Wiese's book was a *New York Times* bestselle
been well received on most of the prominent Christian tele
I suppose if Christians already believe strongly in hell, th
an unproven and unlikely story about it can feel rational.
problem with Wiese's story and all others like it should b
to Christians as it is to everyone else. There is a complet
anything remotely resembling evidence. A good story is ju
enough when it comes to extraordinary claims. When some
was abducted by aliens in his sleep or abused by harpies in th
the night, or that he woke up on the floor next to his bed cryi
he just visited hell, a bit of skepticism is called for, to say
Dishonest people lie—we know this. Honest people can have
nightmares that feel very real—we know this. Mentally heal
can have powerful hallucinations that distort reality—we k
Isn't it far more likely that one of these down-to-earth possibili
be behind Wiese's story? Maybe he really did visit hell for twe
minutes that night like he says. But until Wiese or anyone else
up with something better than a mere story, no reasonable pers
accept such a claim as fact. Even Wiese himself has plenty of 1
doubt the hell story, if only because of the well-known ability of t
to produce realistic fantasies that can fool the best of us.

Some hell believers might point to more tangible evidence,
an actual audio recording of the damned screaming in the lake
Yes, such a recording really is out there, probably winning c

WHERE IS THE LOVE?

The ideas that God/Jesus forgives and that Christianity is a religion of love are very important to most Christians. However, the concept of hell seems to contradict these claims. Why would God/Jesus create or allow such a place to exist, much less allow the majority of people on Earth, generation after generation, to go there and suffer forever? If Jesus is the only way to heaven, and if hell is the alternative, then a lot of nice people must be in hell right now. Sorry, Gandhi. Too bad, Einstein. Tough luck, Mark Twain. Meanwhile, anyone can dodge hell—no matter if they spent a lifetime murdering, raping, and robbing people—simply by "repenting their sins" and "accepting Jesus" twenty seconds before they die. Maybe it's just me, but I don't like any justice system that could place a Catholic Hitler in heaven and a Jewish Anne Frank in hell.

A typical defense of the hell concept is that it's the individual's choice to avoid it or not. Nonsense. According to mainstream Christian doctrine, I will go to hell and swim in fire forever. But I'm not *choosing* it. I just don't think hell is real, nor do I believe that the supernatural claims of Christianity have been proven. I'm not stupid. If I thought for one second that hell was real, I would try my best to avoid it. All that wailing and gnashing of teeth does not appeal to me in the least. But many Christians make it sound like hell-bound nonbelievers are merely being arrogant or recklessly defiant and therefore get what they deserve. But I and many other skeptics do not reject Jesus and the existence of hell in the same way I might reject membership in the Girl Scouts or the Ku Klux Klan. I believe the KKK exists, for example, but I don't feel that it's a good fit for me, so I don't want to join it. This is significantly different from my view of Christianity. The important claims of Christianity have not been proven to my satisfaction, so I can't sincerely "turn my life over to Jesus." I couldn't even if I wanted to because I am not convinced that he exists. Why would God/Jesus set up a system that severely punishes people who are skeptical and who are merely trying their best to align themselves with reality? And does the punishment fit the crime? Eternity is a long time to be tortured. Even lowly, mortal justice systems here on Earth are more compassionate than that. If flawed and corrupt humans can find it in their hearts to show mercy, why won't Jesus issue pardons or at least give time off for good behavior? Some Christians say he does just that, of course, but many, many more say hell is forever.

My children are perfect angels—except when they're not. There have been the rare moments when it was necessary to punish them. I may have taken away a favorite toy for a day or two or made them go to their room and think about their behavior. But never once, no matter how mad I was, did I consider punishing them *forever*. Even if my children committed unthinkable crimes, such as playing catch with my *Cosmos* DVDs or breaking one of my museum-quality replica hominid skulls, I am sure I could find it within myself to forgive them— after, say, twenty years or so. I'm not even a god, just an imperfect human, but I can't imagine ever being so brutal and unforgiving that I would want to punish them for eternity. Yet we are asked to believe that "God is love" and would do this with his children. Either Jesus is far less loving and forgiving than his followers claim or they are mistaken about this place called hell.

CAN ATHEISTS BE TRUSTED?

The fool says in his heart, "There is no God." They are corrupt, their deeds are vile; there is no one who does good.

—Psalm 14:1

Atheists are a problem, say many Christians. They don't think Jesus is a real god, and they don't believe the Bible. So where do they get their morals from? Do they even have morals? How can anyone trust these people if they don't think they have to answer to a higher power? In the mind of an atheist, there is no right or wrong. They can do anything they feel like doing, justify any action, excuse any evil. For them, everything is a meaningless free-for-all. In light of all this, how can we view them as equals? How can we fully embrace them and allow them to participate in society? Atheists can't be trusted.

Since 2009 I have been in communication with an evangelical pastor who has twenty-five years of experience in the pulpit and became an atheist a few years ago. He says he struggles with the "hypocrisy and cognitive dissonance" required to maintain his position as a professional preacher while he seeks a secular job. His congregation is unaware of his current belief status. He described for me what most Christians he knows think of atheists. "They think they are fools and the worst of enemies," he explained. "Atheists are people who have been completely deceived and captured by the evil forces of Satan. This can be seen as harmful to the extent that it perpetuates the mentality of fearing anyone who is 'not one of us.' All groups do this somewhat, but religious fear and suspicion resulting in hatred has been shown to be the cause of much bloodshed."

Not every Christian feels this way about atheists, of course. But enough do, unfortunately, to make nonbelievers one of the world's most unpopular demographics. In America, for example, atheists are considered to be similar to *rapists* in the minds of many religious people! This is not an exaggeration. A scientific study actually found that when many test subjects who believed in a god were given a description of a criminally untrustworthy individual, they selected atheists and rapists as representative of the description, but not Christians, Muslims, Jewish people, feminists, or homosexuals.[1] The same study found that trust is the primary issue many people who believe in a god have with atheists. It's not that they necessarily dislike them or are disgusted by them, as is the case with many groups that face intolerance. Believers just feel they can't trust nonbelievers.[2]

Christians can easily be relieved of their concerns, however. All they have to do is get to know a few atheists or discover that many of the people they already know are atheists. Like all irrational prejudices, the traditional fear and distrust Christians have for atheists is based on a dreadful brew of bad information and no information. Probably every Christian on Earth, from Albania to Zimbabwe, has at least one atheist friend, family member, or coworker—many just don't know it because so many nonbelievers feel the need to hide their skepticism of the dominant religion of their time and culture to avoid rejection, harassment, persecution, or worse. If more Christians would simply recognize and admit that many millions of people around the world today are living nonreligious lives and living them well, attitudes likely would change. Virtually all atheists, agnostics, humanists, nonbelievers, nonreligious—whatever the label—are regular, everyday people. They are far more concerned with finding love, holding a job, paying the bills, having fun, raising children, and being nice neighbors than they are with nitpicking the Bible and debating Christians. It is their normalcy and decent lifestyle that keeps them off the radar. Most are just too busy living good lives to worry about Christians who think they are little better than rapists.

NOT SO DIFFERENT

Christians have no problem professing their skepticism of all other gods. Many Christians are excellent critical thinkers with impressive skeptical powers. But where does it all go when it's Christianity that comes up for scrutiny? Truth is, we are all skeptics. It's just a matter of consistency and degree. I always move toward this common ground when discussing belief with Christians in order to show them that we are not so distant from one another after all. I agree, for example, with Christians who recognize that Islam makes extraordinary claims that no one has ever proven to be true. I agree that the Koran was almost certainly written by human hands alone, with no help from a god. Like Christians, I, too, think that the gods of Hinduism are much more likely to be the creations of human hopes and fears rather than real beings who inhabit our universe and interact with us. Catholics and I sing the very same tune regarding the credibility of Joseph Smith's story and the Book of Mormon. I'm in sync with Protestants who don't think the current pope has a special pipeline to God. Presumably all Christians think the gods of ancient Greece were made-up characters. Me too! We only part ways when it comes to Christianity. The key is that I don't change my thinking process based on which extraordinary claim happens to be in front of me at a given moment, but Christians do. The very same skepticism and demand for evidence that leads me to doubt the existence of the Sumerian god Anu are what stop me short of believing that the Christian god is real. If Christians only applied the same reasoning they use on other gods and other religions, they might feel differently about Christianity—and atheists.

One thing Christians often miss about atheists is the fact that they are not a homogenous group. Nonbelievers are very diverse and come in a wide variety of packages. For example, have you heard of a religion called Raëlism? Raëlians are atheists who don't believe in traditional supernatural gods but do believe that technologically advanced extraterrestrials came to Earth long ago and created modern humans after one of them had sex with a prehistoric hominid. Raël, the group's founder, says he knows all this because he met some aliens in the woods in 1973 and they told him. The Raëlians have never presented any good evidence to support their claims. I—like most atheists, I'm sure—don't feel a philosophical kinship, intellectual connection, or emotional bond with Raëlians, atheists though they may be.

The absence of god belief does not unite all atheists or even make them compatible. How silly it would be to think that everyone on Earth who doesn't believe in trolls (A-trollism?) has essentially the same intellectual makeup, the same character and moral compass. A typical atheist is no more comfortable being lumped in with Joseph Stalin and Mao Zedong than a typical Christian is being categorized with David Koresh and Jim Jones. Christianity is too big and too diverse to make assumptions about every Christian's morality or trustworthiness, right? To think that assumptions can be made with atheists based solely on their atheism is illogical and unjustified. Any generalizations and blanket dismissals of huge swaths of humanity are almost always a bad idea. To write off millions of nonbelievers because they don't belong to your club or because some nonbelievers did bad things is indefensible. It would be no different than a non-Christian refusing to trust or associate with all 2.2 billion Christians for no other reason than they are labeled Christians.

THE PROBLEM WITH PREJUDICE

Perhaps it would help if more Christians admitted that common negative feelings toward atheists are just another form of prejudice, little different from other forms they likely recognize as wrong. In the United States it seems that atheists currently are in a place where black people, women, and gays were decades ago. A University of Minnesota study surveyed popular attitudes about atheists and confirmed what many nonbelievers already know. A large portion of the population distrusts atheists and wants nothing to do with them. The researchers write:

> It is striking that the rejection of atheists is so much more common than rejection of other stigmatized groups. For example, while rejection of Muslims may have spiked in post-9/11 America, rejection of atheists was higher. The possibility of same-sex marriage has widely been seen as a threat to a biblical definition of marriage. . . . In our survey, however, concerns about atheists were stronger than concerns about homosexuals. Across subgroups in our sample, negative views of atheists are strong, the differences being largely a matter of degree.[3]

The numbers given in the study are discouraging. Asked to identify the group that "does not at all agree with my vision of American society," 39.6 percent of participants selected atheists, putting them at the top of the list. They were well ahead of the next group, Muslims (26.3 percent), followed by homosexuals (22.6 percent).[4] Americans also have strong feelings about whom their children marry. More than three decades after the 1967 *Loving v. Virginia* Supreme Court case that made interracial marriage legal, 27.2 percent of Americans still don't want their son or daughter marrying a black American. Some might call that slow progress, but it's a lot better than the 47.6 percent of Americans who say they would disapprove if their child wanted to marry an atheist. Muslims were a distant second at 33.5 in the problem-marriage category. The study also found that older people are more likely to reject atheists and that Americans with more education are less likely to reject atheists. Interestingly, the study revealed that some people associate atheists with illegal drug use and prostitution, while others see them as "rampant materialists and cultural elitists." This suggests that regardless of the atheist's place in society—street hood, or penthouse millionaire—he or she is thought to be actively degrading or destroying it.[5] The researchers conclude that America's Christian majority sees atheists as people who are something more than mere intellectual skeptics of religion. They are the scapegoats of the day:

> Americans construct the atheist as the symbolic representation of one who rejects the basis for moral solidarity and cultural membership in American society altogether. Over our history, other groups have, perhaps, been subject to similar moral concerns. Catholics, Jews, and communists all have been figures against which the moral con-tours of American culture and citizenship have been imagined. We suggest that today, the figure of the atheist plays this role—although we emphasize that this is for contingent historical and institutional reasons, and we also emphasize that this is the case regardless of the morality and patriotism of actual atheists.[6]

Is this really the problem? Atheists are so distrusted because Christians think they not only reject belief in gods but also turn their backs on America? Again, knowing a few atheists would do wonders here. Atheists strap on helmets, pick up rifles, and put their lives at great risk in the military for America—and do so without the comfort of a belief in an afterlife. Yes, there have been many atheists in foxholes. I know atheists who wouldn't dare take a penny off the sidewalk for fear that the rightful owner might return to look for it. The perception that atheists are immoral and somehow less American than Christians is not just wrong; it's outrageously wrong. After all, America's prisons, like those in most of the rest of the world, are not overflowing with atheists but with people who believe in gods. Some atheists do bad things, of course, but no religious person has ever presented credible and compelling evidence that shows nonbelievers commit crimes at a higher rate than religious people. All there have been are bad assumptions and worse lies.

Many Christians believe that religion is the best or the only answer for just about every social ill and individual problem, so it stands to reason that they would think anyone who isn't religious would be highly vulnerable to running off the rails. According to one study, 85 percent of Americans believe that if parents were "more deeply religious," they would do a better job of raising their children. With more religion, crime would go down, say 79 percent of Americans, while 69 percent believe that greed and materialism would decrease if people were more religious.[7] But are any of these reported assumptions about religion versus atheism true? Remember, just because many people may believe something doesn't mean it's necessarily real. What is certain is that no one has ever proven any of these beliefs about religion's ability to improve people and societies. There is no proof, for example, that parents who believe in a god are better at parenting than those who do not. There is no proof that more religion leads to less crime in a city, state, or country. In fact, a lot of good evidence points in the opposite direction. The states with the lowest rates of violent crime, for example, are Maine, Vermont, and New Hampshire. These are also the three least-religious states in America. The state with the highest murder rate and incarceration rate is Louisiana, the fourth-most-religious state in America.[8]

It is difficult to come up with an accurate figure for the number of nonbelievers in America and worldwide. Many people who do not believe in gods do not self-identify as atheists because they don't understand the term or don't want to be associated with it given all the negative baggage that comes with it. Many people say they are nonreligious and have little or nothing to do with traditional religions, but they still do believe in some version of a god or "higher power." A study published in 2012 by the Pew Research Center reports that 1.1 billion people globally describe themselves as nonreligious or unaffiliated with a religion.[9] This is a huge number, about one in six people or 16 percent of the world's adult population. It's too many people to ignore, too many to reject, definitely too many to generalize about when it comes to moral behavior and trustworthiness.

In the United States, atheists/nonbelievers are growing while the number of those who say they are religious is declining. According to the Global Index of Religion and Atheism, 73 percent said they were religious in 2005, but only 60 percent said the same in 2012. Those saying they were "convinced atheists" (whatever that means) rose from

1 percent to 5 percent. Globally, 59 percent of the world says they think of themselves as religious, and 36 percent think of themselves as either not religious (23 percent) or "convinced atheists" (13 percent).[10]

It is in everyone's best interest, Christians and atheists, to understand one another, to cooperate, and to get along as well as possible. Looking past the propaganda and the imagined canyon between them, Christians and atheists are more alike than different. Remember the common ground. Remember your shared skepticism and, most important, your shared humanity. Where the complexities of tribes, nations, and gods may divide us, one simple reality is always close at hand, ready to sober us up if we accept it: We are first human beings who share one world together.

WHY HASN'T THE BIBLE CONVINCED MORE PEOPLE?

The Bible is special. It's one big book created out many little books. Far heavier than its weight, it is less a collection of stories than a compilation of warnings and promises. Almost every time I look at one, even a new one on a bookstore shelf, I can't help but think about all the years and mileage on it. The words have been so many places, seen so much. I sense they must be tired. It's staggering, really, to consider what the Bible has caused and been a part of, and what it continues to mean to people today. So many smiles, so many tears. So much reverence, so much disgust. So much life and creation, so much death and destruction. It is immeasurable goodness intertwined with unimaginable evil. This is a book that has brought peace while fueling wars. It reveals God's entrancing love while simultaneously exposing his repulsive hate. It has defended the slaveholder and inspired the abolitionist. It has spread the brightness of literacy into darker regions and has been used to dim the creative light of humanity.

For many believers, the Bible often is exhibit A in the case for Christianity. For many nonbelievers, it often is exhibit A in the case against Christianity. However, I remember staring at the beautifully illustrated Book of Kells, displayed in Dublin's Trinity College Library, and thinking to myself that the Bible is a part of us all. Accurate or not, divinely inspired or not, the Bible is a very human book, and it belongs to everyone, Christian and non-Christian alike. Some of us may reject the Bible as completely true and despise many things done in its name, but we cannot sensibly think ourselves separate from it.

The stories of the Bible moved from tongue to tongue throughout the ancient world. They were printed by the first European presses and carried everywhere by saints and sinners, missionaries and warriors. Astronauts have read the Bible's words more than two hundred thousand miles from Earth. Today, the Bible has been digitized, advertised, and globalized. Its impact is difficult to overstate. Still today, people argue about how individual lives, families, schools, and governments should be "more biblical." Most people have no idea how many of its phrases have seeped deep into our common language. The following all come from the Bible: *by the skin of our teeth*; *bite the dust*; *at wit's end*; *blind leading the blind*; *a fly in the ointment*. See, there's nothing new under the Sun (that one is from the Bible too: Ecclesiastes 1:9). Its themes, lessons, and warnings have been plagiarized and bastardized by authors, playwrights, and filmmakers. Its ubiquitous reach runs so deep that it becomes almost invisible. But, recognize it or not, it's always there.

As the tangible foundation of the world's most popular religion, the Bible has been adored and defended by monks, madmen, geniuses, and fools. The original text, written by unknown authors, has been translated from Hebrew, Greek, and Latin into multiple English versions. It's long and complex, not an easy read for most from cover to cover. Love it or loathe it, however, one has to respect its ability to win hearts and minds around the world generation after generation.

But all good skeptics know that popular success doesn't necessarily mean a claim is true and real. Not every *New York Times* nonfiction best-seller is an accurate, true, and meaningful book. The Koran is pretty popular too, but Christians have no problem applying skepticism to its claims. So is the Bible just a book or something more? Is it perfect? Can we determine if it really is the inspired word of God? Is it filled with the laws and moral guidance civilization depends on? Does it contain accurate predictions about what our collective fate is to be? Does it reveal to us the only way we can beat death and access heaven? To all those questions, many people say yes, of course. But many more say no, and Christians should be aware of some of the reasons why. It's an important question for every Christian to consider: For all its emotional punch and staying power, why has the Bible failed to convince the majority of people alive today?

Those who are skeptical of Christianity may be surprised by the absence of a lengthy list of biblical contradictions, horrors, and bloopers in this chapter. Sorry to disappoint, but I have no interest in dissecting the Bible here. There are entire books and websites dedicated to that very thing, and they do it very well. (If interested, try the *Skeptic's Annotated Bible* at http://www.skepticsannotatedbible.com.) The book you are now reading aims to bridge the gap between Christians and skeptics. I want to show Christians why so many people are skeptical about their religion, and I want to show nonbelievers that a single criticism of the Bible is superior to all others. I don't think attacking bits and pieces of the Bible's content helps with that goal as much as simply pointing to the big picture does. The Bible's greatest problem is not that it often makes God look like a deranged, bloodthirsty maniac, or even that it contains numerous errors. No, the real reason the Bible hasn't been able to convince everyone everywhere that Jesus is the only path to heaven is that it is poorly written and structured. Virtually everything about it is wrong if its purpose is to speak for God to the world.

I'm a mere nonreligious mortal, about as far from a god as one can be. But I still think I could do better than the Bible if I had a few divine powers of my own and wanted to guide the hands of humans to write a book that would serve as the ultimate moral beacon and guidebook for all humanity. First of all, I would avoid flowery language, metaphors, and anything else that might in any way confuse future generations or be misinterpreted and misused by bad people. Poetry is wonderful, but it doesn't work for everyone, especially across cultures and over centuries. I would use short, crystal-clear sentences because I'm omniscient and would know that my words would be translated into different languages over thousands of years. I would never be so careless as to pass on lengthy passages that could be easily misunderstood and misapplied. I would feel a profound sense of responsibility to get it right and to avoid giving aid and comfort to the worst of my creations. The last thing I would want would be for some people to do evil things and justify them with my book. I definitely wouldn't include any outdated rules and advice for owning slaves, beating servants, or killing people for minor infractions.

Most important by far, I would include proof, lots of proof. It matters little how many times I declare myself to be a god and order people to listen to me. If I can't back up my claims with real rock-solid irrefutable evidence that I am real, then most people won't believe in me and won't care what I have to say. My book would be light on the bragging and storytelling, very heavy on scientifically verifiable proof. This way I could avoid leaving my loyal followers to rely on circular reasoning. I do not want this: "My god is real. I know this because my holy book says he is real. I know that my holy book is true because it was inspired by my god. I know that he inspired it because it says so in my holy book. And because my holy book is inspired, my god must be real."

Here is the table of contents of my holy book. The entire book would be no longer than fifty pages. If I were a god who wanted to reach across time with a book to inspire and save as many people as possible from missing out on my heaven, this is how I would do it:

Chapter 1: I am real and here is the proof
Chapter 2: Practical advice for making life as pleasant as possible
Chapter 3: Practical advice for making everyone else's life pleasant
Chapter 4: More proof to make sure you are convinced that I am real

Being fully aware of how petty, stupid, and corruptible mortals can sometimes be, I would avoid making it too easy to use my book for mischief and personal gain. Short, declarative sentences would communicate my message faithfully down through the centuries. The meaning of my words would survive multiple translations and even the twisted interpretations of those who have the nerve to say they speak on my behalf. In short, my book would work. On the other hand, if my intent was to confuse, leave lots of room for interpretation, and help corrupt people do bad things, then I might supernaturally guide the production of a book that is not even a single book with a clear theme but a collection of books with disparate stories and messages. I would wash away memories of who the actual human authors were and include numerous claims of supernatural events with no attempt to prove that they really happened. To top it off, I would drop in a few lines to say that faith, trusting, and believing without evidence are far superior to thinking and knowing. Add it all up, and I would have a surefire recipe for confusion, abuse, disagreement, and disharmony that would endure for centuries, just like the Bible.

I'm not trying to be mean or unfair here; I'm showing respect to Christians by being honest. From the skeptic's perspective, the Bible is an illogical mess. For all the hype and praise, one has only to look at its track record. Setting aside its failure to win over most people, the Bible can't even communicate clearly to the people who *already* cherish it deeply and believe in it with all their heart. Anyone who doubts this has only to review European history and note the many rivers of blood spilled between Christians who could not agree on what the Bible was trying to say to them. Tens of thousands of versions of Christianity exist today, and most of them trace their break to disagreements about what the Bible means.

People may blame human nature for the shattered state of Christian unity, but the fault for most of it rests with the Bible. It's too dense, too convoluted, and too confusing. There is no way millions and then billions could remain united for long with the Bible as their ultimate source for what God wants of them. One could hardly come up with a more perfect blueprint for fracturing a religion. The Bible fails because it doesn't communicate a clear message or intent. This is why one man can read the Bible and be inspired to campaign for human rights and fairness for all, while another man reads it and rushes to picket the funerals of gay men with a sign that reads "God Hates Fags!"

I remember the public debate leading up to the Iraq War in 2003. Some Christians on both sides of the issue confidently stated what Jesus would want and then backed it up with the Bible. How can a divinely inspired message demand peace and war simultaneously? How can it justify extravagant wealth while also demanding poverty? How can it unite and divide those who believe it? Skeptics, observing all this from the sidelines, can only think that when a book says everything to everyone, perhaps it's not really saying much at all.

EVOLUTION TABOO. Will large numbers of Christians forever be at odds with evolution or will all Christians one day accept modern biology, as many millions already have? *Photo by the author.*

ARE ANGELS REAL?

I have had many discussions with many Christians about angels. Skeptical or not, I can't imagine how anyone can resist being intrigued by this very common belief that magical, winged beings routinely visit the Earth and interact with us. The stories of angel believers have always fascinated me. Most of them involve an angel helping out or saving the day in some moment of crisis. Sometimes the angel does little more than offer timely wisdom or advice on how to handle a tough situation a person is stuck in. But usually the stories people tell me involve a guardian angel swooping in, almost always unseen, to guide the person out of harm's way. One of the most dramatic stories I have been told, however, was from an elderly lady who was with her husband when he died. She said that he suddenly called out to her: "Do you see? Do you see the angel here in the room?" And then her husband was gone. She believed he was taken away by an angel only he could see.

We often hear about angels, but what do they look like, who are they supposed to be, and what do they do? In the context of mainstream Christianity, angels are supernatural beings who travel back and forth between heaven and Earth. They obviously would have magical powers and are thought to be God's messengers and sometimes our protectors. However, they might be our executioners as well. Consider this prophecy from the Bible: "So the four angels who were ready for that hour, day, month, and year were released to kill one-third of humanity" (Revelation 9:18).

Although angels are widely admired, at least one of them, Satan, is cast as the ultimate villain. We don't really know what angels are supposed to look like. If real, they might be humanoids with giant wings, just like they are depicted in all those Renaissance paintings. But this is not clear, based on what the Bible says about them. Some angels blended in and mingled with regular humans, for example, so they probably didn't have wings. Other angels, however, clearly stood out in a crowd. Consider this remarkable description of an angel found in Daniel 10:

> I looked up and there before me was a man dressed in linen, with a belt of fine gold from Uphaz around his waist. His body was like topaz, his face like lightning, his eyes like flaming torches, his arms and legs like the gleam of burnished bronze, and his voice like the sound of a multitude.

Whatever angels are, it appears most Christians in the twenty-first century are firmly convinced that they exist. In the United States, 75 percent of all adults surveyed say angels are real, and 11 percent aren't sure. Just 14 percent of Americans say they don't believe in them.[1] Angel belief is even higher among young people: 83 percent of American teenagers think they exist.[2] In Canada, 56 percent of adults believe; and in Great Britain, 36 percent do.[3]

I lived in the Caribbean for more than fifteen years, and I would estimate the angel belief there to easily be above 90 percent. I constantly heard Caribbean believers talk about angels intervening and helping people. In the United States, 55 percent of Americans say they have been "protected from harm by a guardian angel."[4]

ANGELS, A GATEWAY BELIEF?

No one should be surprised that angel belief is so common. After all, angels are included in the package not just with Christianity but with Islam and Judaism too. These three religions may not agree on much, but they are in sync on angels. What is somewhat unusual is how angels have managed to transcend the bounds of mainstream religion. For example, angels are a big presence these days in the catchall world of New Age belief and that boundless arena of "spirituality." There seems to be something about angels that appeals to people who have little or no interest in organized religion but who still like the idea of a supernatural being close by and ready to help when needed. It's not surprising that angels would be popular; they are, after all, angelic, at least as popular culture prefers to imagine them. Some researchers think that angels may be a "gateway belief" that leads people to paranormal beliefs outside of their religion. For example, people who say a guardian angel has intervened on their behalf believe in ghosts at double the rate of people who do not make that claim.[5]

The fact that so many people think angels are intensely active among us—frequently saving us from car crashes and other mishaps—makes belief in Bigfoot and the Loch Ness Monster seem quaint and trivial by comparison. Bigfoot never guided a child out of a burning building or caused someone to miss a doomed flight. Unlike those elusive mythical beasts, angels are thought to be within arm's reach of us at any given moment. But as is the case with Bigfoot and Nessie, angel belief is unproven. There is no evidence, only eyewitness accounts and dubious interpretations of events. As a skeptic, I approach the angel claim the same way I would any other claim about an unusual invisible being that doesn't leave a trail. If people say such beings are real, then let's try to prove it. But if we can't, then we will have to admit that we just don't know, right?

Many Christians place a significant amount of trust in the eyewitness accounts of others—too much trust, in my opinion. For example, Lorna Byrne is a bestselling author with many fans who says that she sees angels "all the time." During an interview with CNN, she claimed to see them virtually everywhere she goes. According to her, everyone has a guardian angel regardless of their religious status. "I just see angels, physically, every single day and it's normal and natural," she said.[6]

When it comes to beings and creatures that always seem to find a way to escape confirmation, we have to consider other reasons for claims of their existence. Much of my research about belief in UFOs, ghosts, and other unproven things that are often seen but never captured began in disparate, faraway places, but the trail always leads back to the same spot—the human brain. It turns out we are all predisposed to see, hear, feel, and remember things that were never there. It matters little if you are smart, dim, young, old, rich, poor, uneducated, educated. If you carry a human brain around in your skull, then, sorry, you are vulnerable to experiencing phenomena that are not as they appear.

One thing that can have a big impact on what you see, experience, and remember are the beliefs you bring to the party. If, for example, you strongly believe in Bigfoot and then happen to see something dark and ominous moving in the shadows of the tree line at dusk, you might "see" Bigfoot, clear as day. But your friend standing next to you, the one who doesn't believe in Bigfoot, might see a bear and nothing more. In your head, however, you really did see Bigfoot, and nobody will be able to tell you any different. This suggestive influence of beliefs on what we see is only part of the problem. We don't actually "see" anything. Consider that and the following items of interest when thinking about claims of angel sightings and encounters.

Vision. Most people are surprised to learn that our brains are not faithful to reality when it comes to the scenery our eyes take in. But it's true. We don't see a perfect reflection of what we look at. The images race from the eyes to the brain via the optic nerves, but once the brain gets hold of those images, funny things happen. It focuses in on what it judges to be important—usually without your conscious consent. The rest fades out of sight, even if there happen to be details that are very important to us. So our brains are constantly editing what we take in from the world. Images thought to be unnecessary are trimmed away at the expense of an accurate and complete scene. It's efficient and necessary because we would be overwhelmed with data if we saw everything we looked at. Our brains would be overloaded with unnecessary details, and we wouldn't be able to get anything done.

But with this efficiency come obvious implications for all claims about seeing unusual or important things. For this reason, we can't even trust the most sensible and honest people who say they saw a ghost, Bigfoot—or an angel. Human vision is quirky, surprisingly creative, and definitely unreliable. This is the reason that eyewitness testimonies are likely to one day soon have a minimal role or no role in important court cases. In 2011, the New Jersey State Supreme Court moved in that direction by ruling that eyewitness testimonies alone aren't enough for convictions in that state's capital crime cases.[7] Human vision and the memory of what we saw are just not good enough when the stakes are high.

Patterns everywhere. Another function that comes standard with the human brain we were issued in the womb is the ability to recognize patterns. But sometimes we see patterns even when they are not really there or do not represent what we think they do. Look up at some passing clouds, and you probably won't have to wait long for your brain to find patterns that enable the shapes of people and animals to appear. This is your pattern-seeking and pattern-making brain at work.

We have an innate obsession to hunt for patterns without even realizing that we are doing so. We can't help ourselves. It's who we are; it's what we do. It's a skill that served us well for the 99.99 percent of our existence that was spent in the wild looking for food and trying to spot predators before they spotted us. Again, this is just part of being a normal, everyday human, and it is also a very likely explanation for why some people see angels.

Things to remember about memory. If you thought the reality of human vision is strange, wait until you hear about memory. As with vision, there is a vast difference between how people think memory works and how it really does work. Most people assume that human memory is something like a DVR system that records sights, sounds, and experiences for later playback. Sorry, that's not even close. The brain *constructs* our memories. There is no reliable and accurate playback when we want to recall something. It might feel that way. It might seem 100 percent accurate. But it's not. Similar to vision, the brain edits. It tosses out data that is deemed unimportant to our immediate needs. It emphasizes this, downplays that. In short, it *tells us a story* about our past. Our memories are more like little Hollywood film productions. They might be useful to us, maybe even mostly accurate, but they are not faithful replays of past experiences. Even memories of the most dramatic events of our lives can't be trusted.

Here is a short explanation I often give when I lecture on skepticism: You have a little old man who lives in your head. If you want to remember something from your past, the way it works is that you have to tap him on the shoulder and request that he tell you about it. Like any good storyteller, he caters to his audience. If he thinks you really need to know a certain detail, he'll be sure to include it. But he is just as likely to toss out things he thinks are unnecessary as if they never happened. Now comes the scary part. The old man is sloppy. Sometimes he shuffles the time sequences and says one thing happened before another thing happened to construct a total reversal of the real past. He also might tell the memory fairly true to reality but then drop it into the wrong year or set it in the wrong location. Perhaps worst of all, he might get confused and accidently insert a scene or two that never happened to you. Maybe it was something that happened to a friend, or maybe you read it in a book or saw it in a movie. And now it's part of your past. The most bizarre thing of all is that all this memory madness can exist in your mind in a way that feels totally accurate. You can "see" past events happening in your head and have total confidence that they happened exactly that way—even though they didn't.

Given all that science has revealed about the way our brains work, why would we want to accept eyewitness accounts of angel encounters without supporting evidence? It makes no sense. People say they see all kinds of things. Where do we draw the line? If I see an angel tonight before I go to bed, I might suddenly believe in angels, but once I calmed down and thought about it, I would have to second-guess my own brain and consider a more likely possibility. Maybe my brain misinterpreted something else that I had seen, or maybe it simply fed me a hallucination. It happens to people all the time. Why not me? Or maybe I'm just inaccurately remembering what happened. I have read and listened to hundreds of angel claims. Some saw an angel and some were sure an unseen angel helped them. In my view, these are all likely creations of human brain activity or misinterpretations of natural events. An unusual event alone, even one that can't be readily explained, is not proof of a supernatural occurrence. Weird things happen. People have close calls in traffic all the time. Somebody somewhere wins a lottery every day. No angels required.

Good skeptics do not deny the possibility that angels exist. After all, just as it is with gods, it's a tall order to absolutely rule out the existence of supernatural beings that can fly, make themselves invisible, and live in heaven. I would never tell a Christian that I know for certain that their angels are imaginary. All I can do is point out that after all these centuries of people claiming angels exist, no one has ever produced scientifically verifiable proof that they do. Instead, all we have are fallible eyewitness testimonies and illogical assumptions about random events deemed unusual. This is nowhere near enough evidence to conclude that angels are real.

Christians who believe in angels might consider giving some thought to the *jinn* (genies), believed by millions of Muslims to be real. Mentioned in the Koran, mischievous *jinn* are supposed to be very active in human affairs today. One can find videos on YouTube® of stern lectures from Islamic holy men about dangerous genies and even "real" *jinn* exorcisms. Christians I ask about this never hesitate to dismiss them as imaginary. But really, what is the difference? Why is it so easy to believe in angels and so difficult to believe in genies?

IS CHRISTMAS UNDER ATTACK?

**Don't expect a truce anytime soon—and if you love
America's favorite holiday too, don't give in. There's far too
much at stake!**
—War on Christmas website[1]

Aren't there enough real problems and genuine disagreements
between Christians and non-Christians without manufac-
turing fake ones or pretending that minor skirmishes are a full-blown
global conflict with the fate of civilization in the balance? At a time
when we all should be trying to improve communication and cooperation between believers and nonbelievers, some people on both sides
of Christmas insist on shamelessly exploiting Santa Claus and baby
Jesus to stir up trouble.

Is Christmas under attack? Is there actually a "War on Christmas,"
as many Christians claim? Absolutely not. Is Christmas exactly the way
it was in 1850? 1950? Of course not, because things change. They always
do. Christmas in America is different now than it was in the past—
but not because it's under an all-out assault from hordes of heathens
who hate Jesus. It has changed primarily because American Christians
have changed and American society has changed. First, there is the
ever-increasing commercialization of the holiday. Frenzied Christian
shoppers with credit cards and the mostly Christian-owned businesses
that market to them have put the biggest dent of all in Christmas as a
purely religious event. You can't blame atheists for that. America has
also been busy becoming simultaneously more diverse and more aware
of its diversity. Christmas does not exist in a vacuum. It had to change.

Wiping out Christmas is just not the high priority for non-Christians
that some people claim it is. It may surprise some, but many non-
Christians, including atheists, love Christmas. I know Hindu people,
for example, who adore the holiday. I know many atheists who cele-

brate Christmas in one way or another with as much enthusiasm as any Christian. Some non-Christians really do hate it, of course, but many embrace it or simply don't care about it one way or the other. I also know many, many Christians who celebrate Christmas every year but do so in a way that places much greater emphasis on Santa Claus and gift giving than on Jesus and eternal salvation. If there really is a War on Christmas, then the battle lines are very confusing.

For me, Christmas is a lot like Halloween. I never believed in ghosts and goblins, but I still went trick-or-treating when I was a kid. As an adult I usually put up something appropriately creepy on my front porch to mark the holiday each year. I certainly don't think handing out treats to neighborhood kids amounts to an endorsement of irrational belief in the paranormal. It's just a special day, a bit of fun, and a way to mark the passing of another year. No big deal. And notice that even the most passionate Halloween lovers are rarely if ever seen protesting the lack of government involvement in promoting the celebration of witches and ghouls during October. They seem to think it's up to them to make the holiday whatever they feel it should be. Imagine that.

For me, Christmas is the time to wind down from another year. It's about spending special time with family, enjoying the smell of a new Christmas tree. It's an excuse to be extraordinarily nice to strangers without having to worry that you are giving off that scary serial-killer vibe. It's the joy of giving to others, and, of course, getting neat stuff from others. Out of habit, I usually say "Merry Christmas" instead of "Happy holidays." I'm pretty sure that I'm not breaking the skeptic's secret code by doing that. As far as the religious elements of the holiday, I understand what it is supposed to represent, but I am not convinced that Jesus is a god, so I don't participate in any form of specific worship or ceremony to honor his birth. But I love many traditional Christmas songs, including some that mention Jesus. I don't see anything hypocritical or inappropriate about all this. It's part of my culture, part of who I am. I feel no need to deny Christmas. I grew up with it, and I'm keeping it. The way I look at it, Christians borrowed much of this winter celebration from pagans more than a thousand years ago, so they can't complain if I borrow some of it from them. Besides, the Christmas purists who are so eager to police the rest of us might want to check their own Christian history. Some of the most committed Christians of all time— the Puritans—banned Christmas!

"HAPPY HOLIDAYS" AS A TWENTY-FIRST-CENTURY INSULT

The issue of businesses replacing "Christmas sales" in favor of "holiday sales" or having their employees say "Happy holidays" instead of "Merry Christmas" is a popular flashpoint in the War on Christmas. Some Christians find this practice to be outrageous, not being satisfied by the fact that Christmas is the most intensely celebrated holiday in America. Companies that promote this deserve condemnation and boycotts, they say. Really? I don't know for sure, but I doubt there is an anti-Jesus agenda at work here. More likely these businesses are trying to be more inclusive for no other reason than to make more money. Shouldn't businesses be able to market themselves any way they want to? Companies tend to care about profit most of all, so I sincerely doubt that this is all part of some secret mission to wipe Christmas from the face of the Earth. To the contrary, many businesses love this holiday and depend on it. I'm sure that virtually every CEO of an American retail business looks at the month of December and sees dollar signs, not an opportunity to strike a blow for secularism. They aren't trying to make America forget the birth of baby Jesus; they want to cash in on him. If a company makes the decision to call that time of year "the holidays" rather than "Christmas," it's probably because it hopes to maximize the number of customers it can reel in. It's nothing personal; it's just doing business in a changing America.

CHRISTMAS VS. EVIL

Fox network's Bill O'Reilly is one of the more prominent generals in the War on Christmas. I'm not sure how much time he spends fighting in the trenches, but he definitely does his part to fire up the troops on his TV show. For example, he claims to be "convinced that the USA cannot defeat terrorism and any other evil without a strong, traditional foundation that clearly defines right from wrong. The struggle today is not about Christmas, but about the spirit of our country."[2] So there you have it, al-Qaeda wins if the US government does not officially and financially promote the celebration of Jesus's birthday. Evil triumphs if we don't celebrate Christmas in precisely the way Bill O'Reilly did when he was ten years old.

Sensible Christians should not be falling for this stuff. It's silly and is a distraction from the things that do matter. Believers and nonbelievers need to come together, in America and worldwide, to support one another, to solve problems, and to figure out ways to make the future better for all. Following the lead of professional rabble-rousers like O'Reilly is probably not the best use of our time and energy. In fairness, no one should go too far in the other direction either. If any secular activists have made it their life's mission to rid the world of all things Christmas, then they are living over in that parallel world with O'Reilly. Christmas is deeply entrenched in the culture of many societies. Whatever form it assumes, society won't be letting go of it any time soon, especially if there is money to be made from it. It's mostly harmless anyway. And it's not even a religious holiday for many of the people who enjoy it, so why not just ignore, hijack, or accept it?

Where the more vocal and active opponents of Christmas do have a point is when government can be said to be unfairly promoting a Christian belief over the beliefs of other religions or even of other Christians. (Not all Christians celebrate Christmas. Jehovah's Witnesses do not, for example.) A typical clash might involve an overtly religious Christmas display on government property. The reason this could be a problem is because government is not supposed to play favorites when it comes to religion. If a cross or a twenty-foot statue of Jesus is erected by government officials on government grounds, for example, then on what basis could government reject an application from Hindus to erect and display a twenty-foot statue of Ganesha, the elephant-headed god? What if a Satanist group fills out the proper paperwork and insists on erecting a monument to Satan to celebrate the start of summer? What if an atheist club demands the right to have a large display of nothing placed in the lobby of the local courthouse?

Seriously, I don't think many Christians would be happy about prominent displays of rival religions on government property, especially if it were done in a way that seemed to imply that the government endorsed them. How about government-funded Ramadan events? How would Christians feel about their tax dollars and government facilities being used to boost up Day of Ashura celebrations—the festival where some Muslims whip and cut themselves with knives and become drenched in blood to commemorate the death of one of Mohammed's grandsons?

America is a diverse nation, and, according to the Constitution, government is supposed to be fair to all its citizens. Government is also specifically prohibited by the First Amendment from promoting one religion over others. But this is not a tough spot for concerned Christians who want to publicly celebrate and share their religious holiday with others, because they can do that. Christians are free to publicly celebrate and share their holiday with others—they just shouldn't rely on government to do it for them. If it's important to you, then get out and do it yourself. What is stopping you? Remember, no one is filing lawsuits to ban manger scenes on church grounds and private yards or publicly demanding that Christmas be outlawed across the land. Christmas is fine. It's safe. The only thing that might be in jeopardy is government involvement in religious ceremonies and religious endorsements—things government has no business doing anyway. Remember, this is coming from a skeptic of religion, yes, but one who loves Christmas. I don't want Christmas to go away. I would miss it. But I don't feel my appreciation for this holiday is dependent on government assistance.

Isn't it strange that it is conservative Christians who tend to be the ones who are outraged about the War on Christmas? One would think that conservative Christians would support the "other side" on this issue. After all, aren't they supposed to be opposed to big government doing everything for us? Are those who support government endorsements and funding of Christmas displays and events suggesting that private citizens are incapable of celebrating Christmas and keeping it alive without government's help? Why would many of the people who want to privatize everything from schools to prisons insist on government being in the plastic manger scene and Christmas tree business? Seems like a colossal contradiction to me.

An even bigger problem for people who are fired up about the War on Christmas is that it was Christians who attacked this holiday first. It wasn't the ACLU (American Civil Liberties Union) or some atheist organization that imposed the overwhelmingly nonreligious theme that has come to define Christmas for most people today. A long time ago, it was Christians who embraced Santa Claus, elves, reindeer, that pagan tree, and blinking lights at the expense of a purely religious observance. Could it be that some Christians signed up to fight in this war, motivated by their own concerns about what they had made Christmas into? Maybe they feel bad because they had already pushed baby Jesus into the background long before Bill O'Reilly and others started accusing liberals and atheists of destroying "their" holiday. Just a thought.

I hope all Christians who love Christmas can recognize it for the popular and beloved cultural event that it has become. Sure it's probably excessive and way, way too commercial and materialistic. But it's still a sweet holiday, too. Maybe Christians have to accept that it is not an exclusive day or season for people of one specific belief system. It's bigger than that. This holiday offers many millions of people, Christian and non-Christian, an opportunity to come together and be a bit nicer to one another and show a little goodwill to all. If Jesus really is a god and really is filled with love for the world in the way many Christians describe, then wouldn't he like to see just that?

WILL THE END TIMES EVER END?

Truly, I say to you, there are some standing here who will not taste death until they see the Son of Man coming in his kingdom.

—Jesus, Matthew 16:28

I'm not completely sure why, but I've always been attracted to stories with an apocalyptic theme. Movies, books, and TV shows that dealt with this subject always left me with a warm and fuzzy feeling. My all-time favorite *Twilight Zone* episode is "Time Enough at Last," the story of a bookworm who finally gets a chance to catch up on his reading thanks to World War III. I love the 1940s end-of-the-world novel *Earth Abides* by George R. Stewart, and, more recently, *The Road* by Cormac McCarthy. Throughout my childhood, I loved watching planetary snuff films such as *The Last Man on Earth, Fail Safe, Planet of the Apes, The Omega Man, Soylent Green, The Andromeda Strain*, and so on.

But a funny thing happened on the way to adulthood: I never outgrew doomsday. Today I'm as fond of the subject as ever. I'm especially drawn to scenarios that are supported at least in some small degree by reasonable arguments and credible evidence. I can't resist the lure, for example, of an asteroid strike, global viral outbreak, supervolcano eruption, robot rebellion, deep-sea methane burp, or all-out nuclear exchange. I'm rational and realize that these events, while possible, are exceedingly unlikely to occur in our time. I should add that I'm not sadistic or masochistic. Movies are one thing, reality another. I don't actually want billions of people, including me, to die in a spectacular flash of pain and chaos. To the contrary, I'm optimistic about most things, including the long-term future of our species. My sincere hope is that we will find ways to survive ourselves and whatever nature throws at us for many millennia to come. Nonetheless, there's just something about civilization's final chapter that warms my heart.

And I'm not alone. In 2012 I was one of the speakers at "Doomsday Live," a show about the end of the world from a scientific perspective. It was hosted by the SETI (Search for Extraterrestrial Intelligence) Institute and turned out to be way more fun than the topic should have allowed. While sitting on the stage, I was struck by how energized and bubbly the live audience was. "It's not just me," I remember thinking. "Everybody loves doomsday!"

Christians certainly seem to share my fascination with human-kind's final hour. As with everything else in Christianity, there is great variation on this issue. Some Christians rarely ever think about the apocalypse, even though it is central to the religion, while others can't stop talking about it. I am very familiar with the Christian doomsday scenario, having heard about it early and often in life. One can scarcely avoid it in some parts of America. I heard all about the urgent need to "get right with God" because "no one knows the hour." I was told that I might get run over by a bus tomorrow and have to face my own personal Judgment Day, or that I might walk out the front door one morning to find the Four Horsemen of the Apocalypse on my lawn. "Get saved and be ready" was the message. It never came up at home, as I recall, but other people made sure I knew about it.

I was shown the book of Revelation. I heard how the world will shatter in a maelstrom of wars and natural disasters until Jesus finally returns to smash nations and establish the Kingdom of God. Such an ending will be wonderful for the minority of Christians who were smart enough or lucky enough to get their theology correct, but it will be one hell followed by another for most of us. The book of Revelation is an amazing story/prediction. Many Christians have never read it, of course. I highly recommend they do. Not only does it describe global death and destruction in general, but it also includes very specific descriptions of a red seven-headed dragon wearing crowns, a giant sea monster, and human-faced locusts with long hair and lion teeth. I could never get worked up over this scary story, however, because I recognized that it didn't come packaged with evidence or compelling reasons to believe any of it.

This book is not directed only at fundamentalist or evangelical Christians, and this chapter is not intended to hash out specific problems with the claim that Jesus will return "very soon" because of "signs" such as frequent earthquakes, slipping morality, and the use of scanners in grocery stores ("mark of the beast"). Many Christians have little interest in dragons, lion-toothed locusts, and the rapture. They view these subjects as uniquely fundamentalist/evangelical obsessions. So let's explore instead the bigger apocalypse question, the one relevant to all Christians. Specifically, why do most Christians give Jesus a pass on what appears to be a failed prediction and broken promise about his most important message? The lack of interest or concern about Jesus's words regarding the apocalypse seems to reveal either a general lack of biblical knowledge or perhaps an unspoken acceptance that Jesus and the Bible can't be trusted, even on very important matters. After all, it seems clear that Jesus was a first-century Jew who preached that the end of the world was imminent. According to him, a cataclysmic upheaval was going to take place *two thousand years ago*. It was to be so dramatic that no one could possibly miss it. God would judge the world, punish the wicked, and set up a new kingdom of divine rule on Earth.[1] But it never happened.

This is that profoundly important prediction and promise made by Jesus as it appears in Mark 13:24–30. Pay particular attention to the last line:

> But in those days, after that tribulation, the sun shall be darkened, and the moon shall not give her light, and the stars of heaven shall fall, and the powers that are in heaven shall be shaken. And then shall they see the Son of Man coming in the clouds with great power and glory. And then shall he send his angels, and shall gather together his elect from the four winds, from the uttermost part of the earth to the uttermost part of heaven. . . . Verily I say unto you, that this generation shall not pass, till all these things be done.

The following line is found in Matthew 16:28: "Truly, I say to you, there are some standing here who will not taste death until they see the Son of Man coming in his kingdom."

What happened? Obviously *all* who were standing there *did* taste death without ever seeing the Son of Man coming in his kingdom. I am familiar, of course, with several common explanations offered by some Christians today. Probably the best defense is that they did see Jesus "coming in his kingdom" when he rose from the dead and went to heaven. However, the claim that Jesus got it right gets it wrong regarding his primary message. According to the Bible, he clearly said that Judgment Day was upon the world. It was supposed to happen very soon, he said, and it certainly would not be as relatively subtle and silent as some now claim.

Bart D. Ehrman, a New Testament scholar and professor of religious studies at the University of North Carolina–Chapel Hill, concludes that over the centuries Christians have reacted to this problem by distancing themselves from who Jesus really was and what his primary message actually was about. In Ehrman's words:

> Why would Jesus be portrayed as an apocalypticist in our earliest sources but as a nonapocalyptic or even antiapocalyptic in our later sources? Evidently Jesus came to be deapocalypticized with the passing of time. And it is not hard to understand why. In our earliest sources Jesus is said to have proclaimed that the end of the age would come suddenly, within his own generation, before the disciples themselves died. But over the course of time, the disciples did die and Jesus's own generation came and went. And there was no cataclysmic break in history, no arrival of the Son of Man, no resurrection of the dead. What were Christians to do with the fact that Jesus predicted that "all these things" would take place in his hearers' lifetimes when in fact the predictions did not come true? They took the obvious next step and changed the tenor and content of Jesus's preaching so that he no longer predicted an imminent end of the age. Over time, Jesus became less and less an apocalyptic preacher.[2]

THE END IS ALWAYS NEAR, NEVER HERE

One can't present a single appropriate response to contemporary Christian beliefs about the end of the world because the beliefs vary so widely. Those Christians who are certain that the world is on the verge of divinely engineered collapse and rebirth—and there are many who think this—might reconsider their position for a few simple reasons. First, many generations of Christians have been confidently declaring this "certainty" for two thousand years. I have had long conversations with Christians who assured me that they knew the apocalypse would happen during their lifetimes. I have heard preachers promise their congregations that we are the generation that will see the return of Jesus. Some of these people are now dead. They were not raptured, they never saw the return of Jesus, and they never heard the seventh angel blow the seventh trumpet. They were wrong, just like every other Christian who said the same thing over the last two millennia. In 1993, I interviewed the late Guyanese lawyer and evangelist Sir

Lionel Luckhoo, who said, "I am sure of one thing. We [Christians] will not see December 31, 1999, because we will be in heaven. The return of the master is imminent. Jesus is at the door!"[3] Luckhoo died in 1997. Contrary to his confident declaration, the world's living Christians did see December 31, 1999, because Jesus failed to return, again.

In the spring of 2011, I interviewed a woman who was walking up and down a San Diego sidewalk with a sandwich board sign that read "End of the World—May 21, 2011." She was a follower of Rev. Harold Camping, the man who promised that the Christian apocalypse would kick off on that date—no doubt about it. Camping came up with his prediction by counting down from the Great Flood that occurred seven thousand years ago. Of course, as any credible geologist, biologist, archaeologist, anthropologist, historian, or marine scientist will tell you, there was no global flood seven thousand years ago, so Camping's date was a mistake based on a mistake. The woman was kind and seemed completely sincere about her mission. She wasn't asking for donations or trying to recruit people to Camping's church. She only wanted to warn people that the end was near. She explained that about 97 percent of the population wouldn't escape God's wrath and would be in for a terrible ordeal. She spoke of earthquakes, tsunamis, famine, the usual. I found myself liking her and caring about her well-being as we talked. I worried about what her reaction would be when Camping's prophecy failed, and I bluntly asked her if she would be okay. I told her that I hoped she wouldn't consider suicide or anything like that if she were disappointed. "No, that's not a concern at all," she replied. "I don't even think about the rapture not happening on May 21 because I know that it will. You will see."

How many more years will the "End Times" last? At what point will everyone admit that the evidence and reasoning behind this claim is hopelessly flawed and that no sensible case has been made for the "imminent" supernatural upheaval of Earth and the return of Jesus? It seems reasonable that "very soon" ought to carry an expiration date. If it did, that date would have passed long ago.

Confident declarations that everything from terrorism and teen pregnancy to earthquakes and economic turmoil prove that we are moments away from Judgment Day do not mean much in light of the fact that our world has always been a challenging and imperfect place. As if nature's indifferent destruction is not enough, we continually create our own problems to add to the mix. It's just the way it is and always has been. The end is always near but never here.

Scientists now believe that a supervolcano erupted some seventy thousand years ago, sending so much smoke and debris into the atmosphere that the entire world darkened, plant and animal life suffered, and the small number of humans living at that time almost slipped away into extinction. Had there been prehistoric churches with prehistoric preachers back then, I'm sure they would have delivered great sermons about how the end of the world was near. But it wasn't. Earthquakes and other natural disasters are not unique to our time. We live on a violent planet and have always been vulnerable to natural forces. Anyone who senses signs of divine doom in today's crime rates or in the behavior of rude high schoolers ought to read up on daily life during the Dark Ages. Do that, and you'll feel much better about our chances. We have had to endure the black death, mass slavery, and now reality TV. No matter how dim things get, tomorrow always comes.

Here is another simple question: Why should anyone fear (or eagerly anticipate) the Christian apocalypse specifically when it is just one of many doomsday predictions? Numerous religions have claimed or currently claim that a god is coming to shake up the world and set things right "very soon." By the measure of evidence, none of these apocalyptic claims is superior to the others. None of them have scientific verification of any kind. They all rest on a foundation of faith and tradition—anything but proof. So why would Muslims be concerned about the magical catastrophe promised in the book of Revelation when Christians couldn't care less about the imminent appearance of the Mahdi, redeemer of Islam? Most Christians probably haven't even bothered to learn about the Mahdi and the Muslim apocalypse. Few, if any, Christians seem motivated to build arks in anticipation of the great flood promised by Norse religion either. Why not?

There is also, of course, significant inconsistency within Christianity regarding the end of days. There is little agreement on how Christians can ensure that they are in good standing with the Lord. Have you been baptized? Are you gay? Born again? Loyal to the pope? Tithe? Shave your beard? Wear a scarf? Do you have a tattoo? According to which Christian you ask, some or all of these things matter. I once interviewed a group of Rastafarians about their beliefs, and the subject of the apocalypse came up. For them it was all about the scattered black people of the world returning to Africa. I'm pretty sure most Southern

Baptists disagree with that as the central theme of the apocalypse. Ultimately, it is for the same reasons Christians dismiss all other judgment day accounts that they should reconsider their own.

As for the many Christians who are not Bible literalists and who do not take the book of Revelation seriously, there is still much to ponder here. If the words of Jesus as reported in the Bible cannot be trusted on a matter as important to Christianity as this, what can be trusted? The fact is that Jesus incorrectly preached that the end of the world was going to take place during his generation. If Jesus and the Bible were wrong about this, then maybe they were wrong about other things too.

BLOOD SACRIFICE. Why was the torture and execution of Jesus necessary? Crucifixes like this one in a church in Ecuador remind us of Christianity's violent roots. *Photo by the author.*

DOES CHRISTIANITY MAKE INDIVIDUALS BETTER?

The fool says in his heart, "There is no God." They are corrupt, their deeds are vile; there is no one who does good.

—Psalm 14:1

One of the most frustrating charges that nonbelievers repeatedly hear from Christians is that people can be good only with God. These few words carry a lot of weight. They bluntly suggest that non-Christians are bad people or, at the least, are very suspect. Some Christians are a bit more charitable and allow all religious people up onto the higher moral plane they have staked out. "So long as you believe in something," they say. While I understand the source of this sentiment, I find it difficult to excuse because it's so insulting and so far out of line with reality.

The world we see right before our eyes simply does not support this idea. Just as we saw in a previous chapter about the claim that Christianity or other religions are necessary moralizing forces that make societies better, this claim is not supported by the facts either. The world's prisons certainly do not appear to be disproportionally filled with atheists. No one has shown a positive correlation between the level of Christian belief in the world's countries and low crime rates. No one has shown that higher rates of atheism make countries more violent and more prone to crime.

But moral behavior is not just about doing bad; it's also about doing good. As was seen with previous examples, less religion seems to have no damaging effect on behavior. Here are the top six foreign-aid donors, ranked by the percentage of their GNI (gross national income) that they give:

1. Sweden
2. Norway
3. Luxembourg
4. Denmark
5. Netherlands
6. Belgium.[1]

The rates of nonbelief in all the above countries are among the highest in the world. As far as individual motivations are concerned—something that gets closer to the roots of morality—a 2012 study published in the journal *Social Psychological and Personality Science* found that atheists are more driven to help others out of compassion than are religious people, who tend to "ground their generosity less in emotion and more in other factors such as doctrine, a communal identity, or reputational concerns."[2] The researchers noted that this goes against a common assumption in America. "Although less religious people tend to be less trusted in the U.S., when feeling compassionate, they may actually be more inclined to help their fellow citizens than more religious people," says social psychologist Robb Willer, one of the study's authors.

If it is true that Christianity is necessary for high moral behavior, then shouldn't Sweden and Norway be high among the worst nations on Earth? But they are among the most peaceful and generous of all societies. I wouldn't go so far as to suggest that being nonreligious makes you better, because there are obviously far too many examples of extraordinarily good people who are religious. But religious belief does not seem to be a prerequisite to what most people would identify as high moral behavior. Warren Buffett and Bill Gates are two of the richest individuals in all of history. They also happen to be atheists. But their lack of belief in a god or gods has not stopped them from finding the moral instinct or reasoning to spend billions of their dollars on people in need around the world.

Consider some of the most atheist-dense gathering places in all the world: the offices, labs, and classrooms of scientists. A 2009 Pew study found that 41 percent of American scientists do not believe in a god, universal spirit, or higher power, compared with 4 percent of the general public who say the same. Thirty-three percent of the scientists asked said they believe in God, compared with 83 percent of the public. Seven percent said they don't know or chose not to answer. Eighteen percent said they believe in a "higher spirit" or "higher power" but not a god.[3]

So what are we to make of this? The United States is the most intensely religious of the developed nations, but its scientists have relatively high rates of nonbelief in Jesus. Based on the idea that Christianity is a necessary influence or control agent for good, shouldn't we see American scientists in trouble more often than most other people? But we don't. Sure, individual scientists get in trouble here and there. But we do not see horrific and far-reaching scandals in the community of American scientists, certainly nothing like what has been revealed with the Catholic Church and its pedophilia problem with priests, for example. Why not? I don't know what they get up to behind closed doors, but biologists, astronomers, and the rest of the science community seem pretty tame and safe to me. One rarely hears about a geologist and an archaeologist teaming up to knock over liquor stores. But the daily news is never short of Christians in trouble. Think about all those Christian politicians, business owners, and everyday thugs who break laws and take falls. There might be a case to be made here, if Christians rarely if ever showed up in prisons and if societies with the highest ratios of Christians in their populations were the safest and fairest of all. But neither of these things is true.

WHERE DOES MORALITY COME FROM?

Many times in my life, I have come upon something of value that I could easily have stolen and probably avoided being caught. But I didn't. Why not? I've thought about it, and only two reasons come to mind: (1) I wouldn't want to make someone sad or angry, nor would I want to complicate their lives by taking their property. I know how I have felt when people stole things from me. It's not a nice feeling, and it's not one I would want to inflict on someone else. (2) If I steal, there is always a chance that I could get caught by the owner or an authority figure, and that could bring all sorts of problems into my life that I do not want.

That's it in a nutshell, my entire moral foundation described in a few words. It feels bad to make others feel bad, so I try to avoid it. Also, doing bad things to others can lead others to do bad things to me, so I try to avoid it. I'm human like the next guy, and there have been rare moments in my life when someone upset me or seemed to be enough of a threat to me that I considered applying an ample helping of elbows to their cranium, finished up perhaps with a nice rear naked choke hold. But even as the reptilian brain deep within screamed, "Do it!" higher thoughts whispered. They reminded me whom I have chosen to be and why I do not rely on violence if it is avoidable. I don't hurt people because I understand that it doesn't feel good when someone hurts you. I don't shoot people I'm angry at because anger fades, while death is permanent. I can imagine the broken-hearted family members of someone I had killed, the parents and the children. These are the motivations for good or moral behavior that keep me out of prison. Emotionally, I am able to sense pain and discomfort in others, and I do not want to be the cause of it. Intellectually, I can reason out how events may unfold if I engage in immoral behavior. It's almost always safer and more efficient to be nice and play by the rules.

How can anyone think that nonbelievers have no reason to be good to others? How can they suggest that nonbelievers are incapable of knowing right from wrong? Some people acknowledge that nonbelievers are capable of being moral, but they add that this behavior must come from their god, whether or not they are aware of it. Again, we have an extraordinary claim with no proof. Why would these feelings have to come from a supernatural source? This is pretty simple stuff. No gods required. No threats of a fiery lake, no promise of an eternal paradise needed. It's just basic social programming. And there is no evidence that a god did the programming because, as we shall soon see, moral behavior shows up in some of the most interesting and unexpected places.

One thing skeptics of religion often wonder about is who has the more admirable and respectable motivation to do good, believers or nonbelievers? Everyone is motivated by self-interest, of course, but that aside, let's compare the likely reasons why a typical Christian and a typical atheist might do a good deed. The Christian is likely to say that he does it because Jesus would want him to, the Bible commands it, or it's just what Christians are "supposed to do." Of course there is the lure of heaven and fear of hell to consider as well. But what about the atheist? What does she draw on to motivate her to do good? She might have millions of years of evolution to thank for her positive impulses. But she does not have a god looming over her.

It's not difficult to imagine how being nice to others and looking out for family, friends, neighbors, and sometimes strangers could have been beneficial to early humans and other primates. A group, tribe, or clan made up of selfish individuals who constantly bickered, fought, and stole from one another would probably be at a distinct disadvantage compared with groups that cooperated and cared about each other. How could such traits not be favored and passed on?

Primatologist Frans de Waal sees the roots of modern human moral behavior in the apes he studies. "Modern religions are only a few thousand years old. It's hard to imagine that human psychology was radically different before religions arose," he writes.[4] "It's not that religion and culture don't have a role to play, but the building blocks of morality clearly predate humanity. We recognize them in our primate relatives, with empathy being most conspicuous in the bonobo and reciprocity in the chimpanzee. Moral rules tell us when and how to apply these tendencies, but the tendencies themselves have been in the works since time immemorial."

There is still much to learn, of course, but thanks to numerous studies conducted on many kinds of animals—from mice to elephants—we can confidently say that more than one species on Earth displays moral behavior. So where does this urge come from? Monkeys are not Christian, Jewish, or Muslim. They do not read holy books, attend worship services, or—so far as we know—ponder the afterlife. When a monkey makes the decision to go hungry so that another monkey may eat, are we supposed to believe that this is because God placed that instinct in it? Isn't the more likely answer that the instinct developed by natural selection over millions of years?

ON THE RECORD

One late December afternoon when I was around seventeen or eighteen years old, a disheveled man with a camera slung around his neck approached me in a shopping mall. He was a reporter doing one of those "man on the street" public opinion features for the local newspaper. I agreed to participate, and he asked me the question of the day: "What is your New Year's resolution going to be?" Given my age at the time, my first thought was probably something like "Step up my game with the ladies." But I swallowed that thought because I knew I had to aim higher and try to impress the newspaper hack. So I paused and thought for a moment, and then the comment came: "I want to become a better Christian and be a better person." Yes, I said that. It's on record somewhere forever. Looking back, I'm embarrassed by what I said. Not because I was a Christian or aspired to be a better Christian. No, I regret my response because it was shallow and dishonest. It was shallow because I had bought into the cultural sales pitch that Christianity is necessary for high moral behavior. It was dishonest because I wasn't really a Christian! I may have wanted to be or thought I needed to be in order to be a "good person," but the truth was I was not convinced that Jesus was a god or that any gods existed. My thoughts about religious claims were much less sophisticated back then, but my doubts were very real, nonetheless, and they kept me from believing in Jesus. I'm pretty sure most people would agree that believing in Jesus is a prerequisite to being a Christian. If so, I didn't qualify. So why did I say what I said?

In defense of my teenage self, the comment I made to the reporter was sincere even if it wasn't completely sensible or accurate. I genuinely thought, as many people do, that "being good" and being a Christian are synonymous. I also probably had the concern, like many, that not being a Christian makes being a good person difficult, if not impossible. This, after all, is the warning that preachers and lay Christians have been repeating for centuries. Of course, if I had been born and raised in Egypt or Jordan, my answer to the man would have been "I want to become a better Muslim and be a better person." I wonder if my public attempt to attach myself to Christianity was that unusual. It would not surprise me if many others rush to embrace Christianity not because they are fully convinced that Jesus is a real god as described by the Bible but because they perceive Christianity to be the only route to a good and decent life. But is it?

A GOOD LIFE WITHOUT JESUS

What I learned in the years after making my New Year's resolution is that one does not have to be a Christian (fake or real) in order to be good and do good in life. Reading helped a little bit; traveling the world helped a lot. I met and observed many people who were not Christians but not monsters either. Of course, one can't judge another's life based on a glance, but I saw enough to sense that they were nothing more and nothing less than well-meaning people trying to make it through life as best they could. I have seen families laughing and playing together in Syria. While walking on a long, dusty road in Fiji, I was given a ride by an old Muslim man in a rusty truck. I offered him gas money, but he wanted nothing from our chance encounter other than the opportunity to be kind to a stranger. In Thailand I watched a "homeless" woman, probably Buddhist, sweep the front area of the large box she lived in under a bridge. She paused from her chore to play with a toddler who stumbled by. The woman glowed with dignity and love. In China a little boy who spoke no English grabbed my hand on the Great Wall and smiled. His mother looked on approvingly. It was a moment of pure human kindness breaching impure borders. I doubt that the goodness I saw in their eyes depended on whether or not they worshipped Jesus. For readers who are unimpressed by one person's subjective observations, there are other ways to assess this issue.

Anyone tempted to point to the moral failings of non-Christians as some kind of proof that we all need Christianity to lead positive and productive lives should resist the temptation because it won't work. First of all, no one is perfect. Of course non-Christians do bad things. The key question is whether people who believe in Jesus are better and safer human beings to be around than non-Christians. And the answer to that is clearly no. History overflows with examples of Christians behaving badly. It's not even worth describing in detail because the horrible crimes of so many Christians are well known to all. From the near-constant carnage that makes up much of European history and the wholesale slaughter and exploitation of people in the New World to the corruption and greed that is present in societies that are mostly Christian today. The fact is, Christianity has never been a guarantee of high moral conduct. Too often it has been used as the motivation and excuse to rob, abuse, and kill. Muslims, Hindus, nonbelievers, Sikhs, Buddhists, Jews, animists, pagans, and so on have often treated their fellow humans badly, but not significantly worse than Christians have.

Today, Muslim terrorists and the occasional Muslim outrage over what they perceive to be insults to their religion dominate perceptions of Islam in many societies. But Christianity has not outgrown or developed immunity to such madness either. Many people in Western countries may not be aware of this thanks to uneven news reporting. For example, I found it interesting that even after the much-hyped "Kony 2012" viral video campaign, few Americans seemed to know much about the Ugandan warlord's past and his stated motivations. Infamous for torturing and killing thousands and enslaving child soldiers, Kony is a former Catholic altar boy who wants to overthrow the Ugandan government in order to implement Christian rule based primarily on the Ten Commandments. Kony claims to be guided by the Holy Spirit and requires his soldiers to draw crosses in holy oil on the weapons. Anyone who fails to make the sign of the cross on their chest before battle can be shot per Kony's orders.[5] Osama bin Laden had nothing on this guy. We have seen Christians commit everything from murder to child rape. Belief in, or the guidance of, Jesus has not prevented countless crimes. Many Christians already know this, of course. Consider the popular saying "Christians aren't perfect, just forgiven."

Like everyone else, Christians are vulnerable to greed, poor judgment, and negative impulses. The only reasonable response to this idea of Christianity being the sole or best route to exemplary individual behavior is to point out that many people in many situations are capable of doing bad things—regardless of their religious beliefs. Based on what we have seen in the past and what we see today, it appears no gods are able to keep humankind safe from itself. For that we must take responsibility.

WHY DOES A GOOD GOD ALLOW SO MUCH SUFFERING IN THE WORLD?

More than ten million children die because of extreme poverty every year.

—UNICEF[1]

O ne of the most enduring and difficult challenges to Christianity has been the simple question of why so much evil and suffering exists in the world. Christianity promises that there is a just and loving god watching over us. If so, why have so many people been slaughtered in an endless series of wars? Why hasn't God done something to prevent all the rapes and murders that have occurred throughout history? The evil that we do to one another can be explained by free will, counter Christians. Many believe that God allows us to choose our way in the world, for better or worse. So if we decide to behead a foe or drop napalm on a village, then that's our choice. This could be true, but then why do so many people die agonizing deaths from injuries and disease every day? Why are so many people cut down by natural disasters? An all-knowing god would hear the cries and know the pain of every victim. An all-powerful god could do something to stop the suffering. A good god with these attributes would not just stand idly by, right? But it seems he chooses to let it go on, century after century and millennium after millennium. Does this absence of action mean the Christian god does not exist? Not necessarily; there could there be a rational explanation for all of this.

The three most common responses from Christians to this question are "God's ways are mysterious to us," "It's all part of God's plan," and "We deserve it." The first one seems more like a way of avoiding the question than attempting to answer it. It's a cop-out to claim that God's willingness to let so many people suffer is mysterious and beyond our comprehension. It effectively ends the discussion because all one can really say to that is, yes, any good and loving god who sat idly by while many billions of people suffered horribly over the last several thousand years or so would be mysterious, to say the least. But this issue is too important to simply give up and declare it unsolvable. If, as Christians say, God is the source of all morality, then this problem of evil needs to be confronted.

The second response claims that all the pain and death we see is okay. It's necessary because it's part of God's perfect plan for us. We may not understand the plan in full, but we can stop worrying and simply trust that the relentless horror of disease, poverty, war, violent crime, floods, and earthquakes is a good thing. I suppose this explanation could possibly be true, but my brain and my heart tell me otherwise. The amount of pain and suffering that has occurred and continues to occur every moment of every day is immeasurable. It's staggering and only acceptable by not truly accepting it. Right this moment, millions of people are in agony. Things are much better for some now, but for most of our existence life has been extraordinarily harsh. I would estimate that more than half of all humans ever born died before reaching adulthood—and probably with great pain. For this reason, Christians might want to reconsider the "divine plan" explanation. What plan designed by a good and compassionate god would include such astonishing levels of terror and torment for his creations? And keep in mind that this is a god who is supposed to know the future. That would mean he knew that the world and the human species he created would end up wading in so much misery. But he went through with the plan anyway? Couldn't he have at least left the malaria parasite off his creation list? It alone kills more than one million people each year, most of them very young children.[2]

The claim that mass suffering and early painful deaths must somehow be acceptable or necessary to a goal-oriented god with the big picture in mind doesn't hold up very well. The suggestion that God cares and would help but just can't because his hands are tied seems like a bit of a lame excuse for the omnipotent creator of the universe. The contradiction is too much. It is beyond all reason that a god who is good and loves people would initiate and maintain a course of action that includes so much unjust harm to so many people. Besides, if we were to accept this claim, why stop there? Can we also assume that bank robberies, rapes, and kidnappings are a necessary part of God's plan too? After all, bank robberies, rapes, and kidnappings occur without divine intervention stopping them, so they must be part of God's plan too, otherwise he would stop them, right? But if this is true, then why should anyone strive to be a good and decent member of society? If something as horrible as mass starvation or a million people killed by an earthquake can be explained away, then go ahead: rape, pillage, and plunder all you want. Just make sure to remind your victims—and the police—that God didn't stop you and therefore your crimes must be part of his divine plan.

WE DESERVE IT

The third common response to the problem of evil is even more difficult to digest than the first two: "We deserve it" explains all the misery, suffering, and death in the world, say many Christians. According to this explanation, humankind is getting precisely what it deserves because of our inherent sinful nature. "We" disobeyed God in the Garden of Eden long ago, and so "we" have to suffer the punishment. Who is this "we"? Why are people today sharing guilt with Eve and Adam? I never bit any forbidden fruit. Neither did any of the children and babies who will be diagnosed with cancer this year.

Today, all humans inhabit a "fallen" world, say many Christians, one in which disease, poverty, crime, war, famine, genocide, child rape, natural disasters, and so on are the consequences of Adam having made the decision to bite into a piece of forbidden fruit. We had it made in a perfect paradise, but we blew it by rebelling against God. Now we have to toil in this cesspool of a world that we brought on ourselves. From dictators to tornadoes to dysentery, it's "our" fault because "we" didn't follow God's rules in the Garden of Eden. While this may be a charming and credible story to some, it doesn't line up well at all with the popular image of that loving, compassionate, and fair god we keep hearing about.

There are multiple problems with the "we deserve it" explanation for all the disaster and misery that keeps happening on God's watch. First, how can it possibly be moral and just to hold all humanity, generation after generation, accountable for one rule infraction by a couple of prehistoric ancestors? That makes no sense by any basic concept of fairness. Even most lowly mortal humans in the twenty-first century understand that a criminal-justice system would be wrong to punish the twenty-first-century descendant of some ancient Greek criminal. If most of us can figure out that no sentence given to a convicted criminal by a judge or jury should carry on past the grave to the criminal's family, then wouldn't a god know that too?

Another problem with "we deserve it" is that the severity of the punishment is far beyond anything reasonable. No people or justice systems that are even remotely fair would hang a man for stealing a tube of toothpaste from a convenience store. So how can a good and fair god condemn the world to relentless agony? Given the duration and scope of the punishment, it cannot be justified.

Not all Christians are Bible literalists, of course. Many say that the Garden of Eden story is not to be taken as factually accurate. They believe we are in a state of sin and suffer simply because we turned away from God. "We" turned away? Again, how is this "we" determined? Why does "we" include some ten million babies and very young children who die horrible deaths in poverty every year due to disease and malnutrition? By what bizarre moral reasoning does a one-year-old infant deserve to be cooked to death by fever, consumed from within by parasites, or feel his vital organs slowly surrender as hunger devours them? The God who created the universe and all life would have the power to stop such agony. It is difficult, if not impossible, to imagine why any god who is filled with love and compassion for humans would not, could not stop it.

"THE HOLOCAUST OF THE CHILDREN"

An insightful article by Gregory Paul in the academic journal *Philosophy & Theology* provides a fascinating analysis of the issue of God and the suffering of children. Paul points out that this topic has largely been overlooked by both religious thinkers and nonreligious thinkers.[3] People generally just don't realize how much miserable, dangerous, and unfair the world is for many children. As one who often writes about child poverty and who founded a charity that raised funds for impoverished children in the developing world, I have firsthand experience about the public's ignorance on this issue. Sadly, when it comes to the scope of child deaths in the present and the past, most people are clueless. Most people know, for example, that the Holocaust during World War II left some six million Jewish people dead. But few are aware that nearly double that number of children die every year in the developing world. *Every year.*

Paul says that the "Holocaust of the Children" is more than a powerful argument against the claim that a good and loving god exists; he asserts that this argument actually falsifies the claim. Paul states that "natural evil," such as naturally aborted conceptions, death by disease, and natural disasters have been far more destructive to young human life than our "moral evil." Although more prominent in our thoughts, war, murder, induced abortions, and other causes of death that come directly from our actions account for only a small fraction of the young dead. This number is "only" perhaps ten or twenty billion, according to Paul. He estimates young deaths from natural causes, however, to be as high as a few hundred billion. Paul writes: "If a creator exists, then it has chosen to fashion a habitat that has maximized the level of suffering and death among young humans that are due to factors that are beyond the control of humans over most of their history. As a consequence, only a small fraction of conceptions have reached the age of majority. The number of unborn and children who died due to natural causes is literally thousands of times larger than those killed by the actions of dictators."[4]

What are we to make of all this suffering and dying? Can so many billions of cruel and painful child deaths from microbial diseases be a good thing? Can billions of horrific child deaths from natural disasters and accidental injuries be part of a good and moral divine plan? Maybe, but it's difficult to understand why a god couldn't have come up with a better way.

Popular Christian philosopher William Lane Craig presents a rebuttal to the claim that there is no contradiction between God and all the evil and suffering we see. "The problem with this argument is that there's no reason to think that God and evil are logically incompatible. There's no explicit contradiction between them."[5] Don't miss the sleight of hand here. Lane describes the skeptic's challenge as simply having to do with "God." But that's not quite right. Most people who bring up the problem of evil are careful to specify that all this suffering and death makes no sense in a world created and operated by a *loving and morally just god* who cares about our well-being. This is key. Of course, the existence of a god or gods is not necessarily contradicted by horrific levels of evil, violence, and suffering. There is plenty of that in the Old Testament! Many gods, as described by those who believe in them, are mean and capable of not only failing to stop human misery and death but also of gleefully causing it.

Jesus, however, is not supposed to be one of those gods, according to most Christians. Despite the Holy Trinity concept, which says Jesus is also the same God of the Old Testament who has much blood on his hands, Jesus is supposed to be filled with love for us. This is the specific kind of a god that does not match the reality we live in. Sure, we may inflict tremendous harm upon ourselves by robbing and exploiting one another, waging war against our neighbors, and spoiling the natural environment. Maybe God does let us run amok for reasons of "free will," but that is difficult to reconcile with the fact that "free will" too often leads to the torture, rape, and murder of children. Even more of a problem is the fact that all our self-inflicted evil is minimal compared to the destruction of life we have always faced from microbes, floods, earthquakes, and other things that most Christians claim God is in control of.

A WORLD THAT MAKES SENSE

This question of evil falls short of proving that anyone's god doesn't exist. I would never point to crime rates in Detroit or the death toll left behind by the latest flood in Bangladesh as proof that no gods exist. That's overreaching. However, the harsh realities of our past and our world today can create significant doubt in the minds of those who are willing to think honestly and deeply about the Christian god. If he is indeed real, then his moral compass seems vastly inferior to ours based on the world he made and his subsequent inaction. I have walked the back roads of Africa and Asia where I saw the dull eyes of struggling and dying children. Some things I encountered haunt me still. Perhaps that good and loving Christian god I hear of does exist; I don't know. But if he does not exist, then the world we actually see in motion around us, the one in which nature is indifferent to our suffering and the one in which we alone carry the responsibility of ignoring, helping, or harming our neighbors, makes perfect sense.

WOULD YOU TAKE JESUS'S PLACE ON THE CROSS?

The subject of Jesus's blood sacrifice is often inescapable in discussions with Christians. For most non-Christians, especially atheists, this is the most difficult aspect of Christianity to understand. And it comes up so often that many people no longer notice how strange and disturbing it is to constantly talk about nailing a man, divine or otherwise, to a cross and being "cleansed" by his blood.

During a live call-in radio show in 2012, I thought I was going to spend the hour talking about my new book *50 Popular Beliefs That People Think Are True*. I was eager to talk about aliens, psychics, Bigfoot, the Bermuda Triangle, the end of the world—all the fun stuff. But the audience wasn't having it. My opening statements were about the wisdom of being skeptical, the importance of asking questions and demanding evidence before accepting an unusual claim. I thought I was giving basic good advice and nothing more. But somehow my words triggered alarms in the minds of several Christian listeners who lit up the switchboard. A few tried to debate the existence of God with me. "Which one?" I asked. A couple asked me how I had the nerve to doubt religion. I asked if they had the nerve to doubt Islam and Hinduism. One caller skipped the small talk and declared, "I don't know who this man is, but he needs to be bathed in the blood of Jesus!"

Overall, the show was fun. I sensed that the callers meant well, and I was polite and respectful throughout. Later, however, I thought about how ghoulish and strange that one comment about my need to take a bath in blood was. Thanks to two thousand years of Christianity, it is widely accepted today as normal, reasonable, and not creepy in the slightest to talk about blood in this manner. Bathe in blood? In what other context but religion and low-budget slasher films can such an idea be spoken of in public without drawing ridicule or causing concern for one's mental health? "The blood of Jesus" is such a common concept and phrase in so many cultures that people are numb to it.

Holy Communion has to be mentioned as well. Eating the flesh of Jesus and drinking his blood do not sound like activities one should find in a religion that is described by its followers as peaceful and centered on the "God is love" concept. It sounds more like something that would be associated with a bloodthirsty war god. None of this carries any shock value today, except, perhaps, for people like me who are outsiders and actually pause to think about it.

Most people are probably unaware of how deep the blood flows through humankind's long obsession with religion. I knew a young woman in the Caribbean who suffered from mental-health problems, and her family's frustration with the inability of doctors to cure her led them to take her to see an obeah man (witch doctor). I wasn't there, but I heard all about it. The magic man performed an elaborate ritual that climaxed when he slashed the throat of a chicken and poured its blood over the woman. Somehow, this animal sacrifice and ritual blood shower was supposed to rid her of the demons or bad magic that had been tormenting her. She was not cured, of course, and continued to struggle with mental-health problems for years after.

While at Petra, the spectacular deserted stone city in Jordan, I climbed up to the "High Place," where I found an altar carved out of rock. The people who lived there used it for the ritual killing of animals— and possibly humans—in an attempt to keep their gods happy. I saw in the remains of the altar a groove that supposedly drained blood away from the killing surface.

I have seen the death of Jesus many times and in many places. From priceless paintings hanging in New York City's Metropolitan Museum of Art to terribly tacky Jesus souvenirs in Jerusalem gift shops to a small silver charm dangling from an old family Bible owned by a friend's mother, I've seen the image of Jesus on the cross, dead or dying, in many different forms. Crucifixes make the strongest impression on me. It's not hard to see why. Some of these three-dimensional pieces are large, stunningly realistic, and feature a life-sized Jesus. Protestants rarely carry or display crucifixes, preferring plain crosses. Crucifixes (any cross with Jesus on it) are favored by Catholics, Orthodox Christians, Lutherans, and Anglicans.

I'm not sure why, but the crucifix that made perhaps the biggest impression on me was a large wooden carving in Peru's Cathedral of Lima. The church was dramatic enough, but the pale, tortured body of Jesus was stunning. Just walking through the tall doors of the church

was like tumbling back in time five centuries. Before I came to the crucifix, I paused at Francisco Pizarro's tomb and thought about what an
unlikely life he had led. A broken man with every reason to give up and
return to Europe, he instead challenged a handful of men to follow him
for one last grasp at fame and wealth. They went on to conquer one of
history's largest empires. Unfortunately, the remarkable courage and
ambition of those conquistadores is overshadowed by the murder and
destruction they unleashed in the New World. Many years later, fame
and wealth failed to protect Pizarro when twenty assassins attacked
him in his home. In his sixties but still a warrior, Pizarro fought back,
killing at least two. Legend has it that after they cut him down he drew
a bloody Christian cross on the floor before dying.

Staring at the crucifix in front of me inside the Cathedral of Lima,
I can't help but wonder how this image of a man nailed to two planks
of wood became so popular. If Christians take a step back and think
about it, I'm sure they will understand why many nonbelievers and
non-Christian religious people find it disturbing. The crucifix shows a
suffering human being with spikes through his hands and feet, a blood
streak from where a Roman spear punctured his body, and a crown of
thorns jammed on his head. It's not the kind of image one would think
young children ought to be exposed to. Yet the figure appears in open
view in thousands of churches around the world. I understand what
it represents to Catholics and other Christians—the positive result of
sacrifice and salvation—but it's still remarkably negative and grim on
the surface.

Given my perspective on the crucifix, it would probably surprise
people to know my answer to a common question asked by Christians.
"Would you take his place?" Christians ask this as a challenge for me
to grasp how much Jesus suffered "for me" when he was beaten, tor-
mented, and finally executed. He did it for us, says the Christian, but
how many of us would take those nails in our palms and die slowly on
the cross for him? Very few, is the presumed answer. But I would.

If I was presented with the same scenario Jesus had, I wouldn't
hesitate. Don't be impressed. It's not that I'm extraordinarily brave; I
just understand the cost-benefit ratio, so to me, it's a no-brainer. Let's
assume that I'm placed in the situation Jesus was in moments before
he was arrested. I am given a choice, I can either escape to safety and
live a normal, long life or I can go willingly to be tortured and then
brutally killed by crucifixion. I'm not God or any other kind of god;

I'm just a human being with the opportunity to be the "blood sacrifice" for humankind. "Yes" is the only logical answer, and here's why. If I'm given this choice by God, then I would know that heaven and God are real. I would also know that the promise of salvation and eternal life in heaven are real promises that God will fulfill. Bowing out means I live to be seventy but I don't get to go to heaven after I die. Not only that, all seven billion people on Earth don't go to heaven either. They all go to hell because I didn't take the deal. If that weren't enough, add on the billions and trillions of people to be born over the coming decades, centuries, and millennia. That's a lot of people I could save. A few hours of torture would be tough, no doubt, but that's a lot of people. I don't care how selfish and self-centered I am when nobody is looking; I can't imagine turning my back on potentially trillions of people. But even then, if I'm still not feeling heroic enough to do it, there is my wife, two daughters, and son to consider. I would wrestle a shark, eat glass, anything for them. I cannot imagine myself shrinking from the opportunity to both save them from permanent death and send them to a permanent place of safety and contentment. A few sadistic Roman guards wouldn't be enough to extinguish the loyalty I feel for them. Not even the incredible horror of crucifixion would overwhelm the love. And I am sure that many, if not most, parents feel the same way.

I stress that none of this is intended as an argument or insult to Christians. I am only sharing honestly some of the things I and many other skeptics genuinely think about regarding the crucifixion of Jesus. Many Christians struggle to understand why some people are unimpressed when they bring up God sacrificing his only begotten son. This is why.

SHOULD CHRISTIANS TRY TO BE GOOD SKEPTICS?

W e are all skeptics. No one accepts *every* claim. No one believes *everything*. Belief is a matter of how many and to what degree. It comes down to how vigorous and consistent we choose to be about our skepticism. I have dedicated much of my writing career to promoting constructive skepticism and critical-thinking skills because I'm bothered that the common tendency to believe before thinking causes so much harm worldwide. For me, it's a moral issue. I know of too many cases of good people wasting their time or squandering their money or health simply because they failed to think for themselves and to demand proof when the wrong extraordinary claim came their way. There is an urgent need to spread skepticism and to encourage critical-thinking skills. Weak skepticism is the global crisis no one talks about. One can hardly turn on the TV these days without being exposed to an infomercial that promises to get rid of your fat, make you a better lover, or turn you into a real-estate tycoon in thirty days or less. We claim to live in the age of science, yet medical quackery is more profitable today than ever before. Astrology books outnumber astronomy books in many bookstores. Parents refuse to have their children vaccinated because a celebrity or talk-show host told them vaccines cause autism.

People who are good skeptics tend to be safer in our often crazy and dangerous world because they are less likely to fall victim to lies and bad ideas. I don't expect people to agree with me on everything, of course, and I certainly don't think I have all the answers. But I do know that skepticism is a good thing. The scientific process works. Asking questions matters. Requesting proof before accepting an important and unusual claim is wise. It is the best force field available to protect anyone—Christians too—from that mixed horde of crooked barbarians and deluded maniacs who are always there, clawing at the gate and ready to attack the gullible. Given the chance, they would rob us of everything. Skepticism literally saves lives every day. The lack of it costs lives every day. Everyone needs it, and Christians are certainly no exception. Christians are exploited and wounded by lies and crazy claims every day just like non-Christians. That's one reason why I don't stop promoting skepticism when I wander into religious territory. It's not something that should be toned down or switched off in polite company. There is nothing bad or offensive about skeptical thinking. It's nothing more than a mix of attitude and skills that prevent one from easily falling into the waiting arms of false claims. Who in their right mind wouldn't want that working for them twenty-four hours a day, seven days a week?

There is no good reason why Christians should not want to be good skeptics, just like any other person who decides they don't want be a victim. With so much fraud and crackpot nonsense flying around these days, Christians need protection like anyone else. Unfortunately, however, some Christians may fear or resist adopting a skeptical outlook because they view it as a threat to their religious beliefs. In all honesty, it might be a threat, but only to the elements within Christianity that are not true. Skepticism does not necessarily equal atheism. Being a skeptic does not imply a specific position on anything. Skepticism is not antireligion or anti-Jesus. It is anti-lie and anti-delusion. All Christians who do not want to be deluded or fooled by lies should embrace skepticism.

Skepticism has no agenda for or against any religion. If a religion's claims don't collapse under the weight of skeptical scrutiny, then so be it. Good skeptics don't pretend to know things they don't know regardless of a claim's positive or negative aspects. My skepticism and strong leanings toward science and reason prevent me from believing in the existence of Bigfoot, for example, but this same mind-set also leads me to admit that it's possible a giant primate is living undetected in the Pacific Northwest (although I wouldn't bet two cents on it). I also don't think the Loch Ness Monster is real, but only because the evidence is weak. I'm not committed to believing in a world that does not include the Loch Ness Monster. If someone nets Nessie tomorrow, then I'll adjust my thinking accordingly without skipping a beat.

A good skeptic wants to be aligned with reality, whatever reality may be. A good skeptic just wants to know. If Jesus is a real god, then I hope my honest inquiry and desire to learn as much as I can about everything, including religions, will lead me to that discovery one day. Conservative/liberal, atheist/religious, poor/rich, educated/uneducated—none of that stuff matters—or shouldn't. Skepticism is about trying to get to the truth while keeping one's feet firmly planted in the real world. Why would that be a problem for reasonable Christians? Surely most Christians are sensible people who wouldn't cling to lies, mistakes, and delusions if they knew better. Skepticism is for Christians too.

THE HIGH PRICE OF A LOW PROFILE

People waste time, money, and, too often, their lives on claims that a good skeptic could have defused and dismantled with ease. Despite the serious toll of diminished and lost lives linked to weak skepticism, however, this issue scarcely shows up on the world's radar. Why is this? Why don't we hear presidents and prime ministers bemoaning the high cost of credulity and promising to fix the problem if elected? Why aren't skeptical-thinking skills included on high-school exams? Why don't we teach our children to be critical thinkers?

A primary reason that skepticism is not universally recognized as a crucial life skill is because asking the hard questions, demanding evidence, and challenging any and all extraordinary claims have traditionally been portrayed as rude at best and threatening at worst by those in positions of power, from parents to priests to presidents. Skepticism is the force that exposes lies and reveals mistakes. It can be a game changer, and people who hold strong hands rarely want new cards dealt for fear of altering a game they are winning. Even when fair and necessary questions are asked in the most respectful and gentle language possible, some people will view them as attacks. I know this firsthand. I have upset people by asking the simplest question of all: "How do you know this is true?" But we can't be silent. The stakes are too high.

Human lives are too important for us to gamble on the anti-intellectual hands-off rule and simply trust that no parent, teacher, salesperson, celebrity, or politician would ever lead us astray. Have no doubt, we live in a world teeming with dangerous nonsense and unproven claims that do harm. For example, a 2008 Harvard University study found that more than 365,000 HIV-positive people in South Africa died prematurely because the government there promoted alternative medicine over scientific evidence-based treatments.[1] Weak skepticism kills.

A 2003 study of women in Pakistan diagnosed with breast cancer found that 34 percent of them delayed seeking evidence-based medical treatment in favor of unproven alternative medicine, mostly in the form of homeopathy or "spiritual" treatment. According to the researchers, the delay caused "significant worsening of the disease process."[2] It cannot be stressed enough: people suffer unnecessarily every moment because the world is short of good skeptics. Never forget, there is someone waiting around every corner who wants to give you an irrational belief in exchange for your time, money, good health, or dignity. A weak skeptic goes in harm's way every time she or he walks out the front door. So, too, does a good skeptic, of course. But the good skeptic has a better chance of returning home unscathed by the madness.

Skepticism may not guarantee a mistake-free life, but it certainly improves the odds of avoiding many problems. For example, it's difficult to imagine a scenario in which a good skeptic would join and remain with a club that asked him to commit suicide in order to catch a ride on a passing comet. A good skeptic who is seriously ill probably wouldn't rely on an unproven potion that has not been scientifically tested. A good skeptic is also unlikely to send her hard-earned money to a self-professed holy man who lives in a mansion and owns a fleet of luxury cars. Skepticism is a force for good. It keeps you safe, or at least safer than you would be without it. Anyone who is determined not to spend their life being a sucker and follow one dead-end path after another has to embrace the skeptical outlook. There is no other way. Despite the popular but inaccurate image of the skeptic as bitter and negative, skepticism is actually positive and constructive. It's the best way to lead an efficient and productive life, one with much less time squandered on irrational beliefs. This leaves more time for friends, family, romance, fun, creative work, physical activity, and rest. Everyone should want in on this.

HOW TO BE A GOOD SKEPTIC

So what exactly what does it mean to be a good skeptic, anyway? And how does one become a good skeptic? It's not as difficult as most people seem to think. After writing and talking about skepticism for many years, I have learned that people often assume that it is some sort of lofty status or state of being that can only be attained by "very smart people" who spend all their time reading thick science books and harassing hapless UFO enthusiasts and psychics in public debates. I assure you that this is not the case. Sure, intelligence and education can help one see the world more realistically, but skepticism is about so much more than having an impressive reading list or a university diploma. I have known many bright and highly educated people who were weak and inconsistent skeptics. I have also known many less accomplished people who exhibited skills and instincts worthy of world-class skeptics. One can go very far on a little bit of the right information. For example, it is very useful for the good skeptic to know how the scientific process works to reveal real things about the universe, the Earth, and ourselves. One who understands this is more likely to recognize a claim that is on shaky ground or entirely made up. One certainly does not have to be an expert on Newtonian orbital mechanics to figure out that astrology doesn't work as advertised, for example. You have only to ask the astrologers to prove their extraordinary claims. When they fail or refuse to try, the way forward is clear.

Knowing a little about how the human brain works can also help a great deal. While promoting my book about skepticism, *50 Popular Beliefs That People Think Are True*, I observed that most people have no clue about how our brains construct the world that we "see" in our heads, nor do they realize that our memories are little more than highly fictionalized docudramas. Most people think we see an accurate, mirror-like reflection of the world in front of us—wrong. Most people think our brains store memories like a computer hard drive for later retrieval— wrong. Simply learning what it means to think, hear, see, remember, and dream like a normal, healthy human being can give one a new perspective on extraordinary claims and unusual beliefs. Again, don't think this stuff is for elites only. It doesn't take a degree in neuroscience to be aware of how easy it is for people to believe in things that are not there.

Two questions can determine if you are ready and able to be a good skeptic: (1) Are you willing to ask questions when confronted by an important idea? and (2) Are you brave enough to accept the answer— or recognize the absence of an answer—no matter how unsettling it may be to the emotional investment in your current worldview? A good skeptic is someone who is unwilling to go down without a fight when weird claims attack. Good skeptics are people who make the decision to use their brains, to be honest, and to try their best to live in the real world—whatever world that may turn out to be. More than anything, being a good skeptic is about courage and commitment.

SKEPTICISM 101

The following is a brief look at some of the tricks, traps, and critical-thinking fundamentals that good skeptics know to keep in mind. All Christians, like everyone else, should be aware of them so they can navigate the world more safely and avoid tripping up on false claims and bad ideas.

Stories are not evidence. We are storytelling machines. We love them and can't get enough of them. I learned long ago while teaching science to children and giving lectures to adults that stories are irresistible to the human mind. I can go on and on for hours about very important statistics and scientific studies. I can wave my hands, modulate my voice, and flash visual aids all day. But nothing works as well as a story to reel in the audience. It only makes sense: we have spent more than 99 percent of human existence relying on stories to bond, to share important information and warnings, and to predict the future. "Storyteller" should be high on the list of things that define humans.

Being a skeptic does not mean that I'm anti-story. To the contrary, I love good stories, probably more than most people do. In December 2012, I was the subject of a full-page profile in *Geek* magazine in which I shared my undying love and devotion to science fiction and fantasy. But although I love wild and imaginative stories, I am keenly aware of the dangers they can pose. A good skeptic knows that stories can be seductive and can easily derail our thinking. They can send us staggering blind into the arms of quack medical cures, bogus business deals, and a million other places we don't want to go. Always remember that a great story is not great evidence. It's not even good evidence. It's just a story. Always ask for evidence, demand proof, keep thinking, and live happily ever after.

The evidence must balance the claim. One of the most basic concepts is also the most powerful. Your demand for evidence should rise in proportion with the weirdness and/or importance of a particular claim. For example, if my neighbor tells me that he is going to fly to Phoenix tomorrow, pick up a new puppy, and then eat a hamburger for lunch, I'd probably believe him and leave it that. However, if that same person told me that he was going to go time traveling tomorrow, pick up a juvenile triceratops in the Jurassic period, and then eat a saber-toothed-cat sandwich for lunch, I'm going to need a lot of very, very good evidence before I buy into the claim. The mantra popularized by the late astronomer and skeptic Carl Sagan puts it succinctly: "Extraordinary claims demand extraordinary evidence." Remember that one; it will serve you well.

Ignorance proves nothing. Irrational believers of all kinds love to point to unanswered questions and then assert that they are positive proof of their claim. Nice try. This sleight of mind serves as the entire foundation of the intelligent-design concept. But the simple truth is that not knowing means "not knowing" and nothing more. When the world's scientists cannot provide a complete, satisfying, natural, and evidence-based explanation for something, it only means they don't know. It does not somehow prove that there can only be a supernatural explanation. Perhaps one day scientists will figure out the answer. Or maybe they won't. In the meantime, we have to learn to live with some nagging mysteries hanging over us. If we see a strange light in the sky and can't figure out what it is, our inability to identify it is not proof that it must be an alien spaceship. Unanswered questions are not proof. Don't let anyone trick you into believing they are.

Whose burden? Keep in mind that your default position should be nonbelief rather than belief. Don't accept a claim or adopt a belief until the people trying to convince you of it have done their job and made a convincing case. Think first, believe later. If someone says they have a miracle weight-loss pill that makes unwanted fat vanish instantly, for example, a good skeptic is not going to accept this extraordinary claim until somebody proves it's true. The burden lies with the person making the claim. But many people get this backward. They make the mistake of believing in the pill until somebody proves it doesn't work. Far too many people who make bogus claims and promote irrational beliefs employ the slick trick of implying that the burden of proof is on the doubters and not on them. Don't fall for it. You don't have to prove that the miracle weight-loss pill does not work. The burden is on the snake-oil salesman to prove that it does work because he is the one who made the initial claim; it's his job to follow through.

Beware the comfort of the herd. When a large number of people around us believe something, it becomes easier to be persuaded or fooled into believing it too—even if the claim is very unlikely to be true. Never underestimate how strong a pull like this can be. We are social creatures, and it's instinctual for us to care about how we fit in with the group. It's easy to go along and do as the majority does. Swimming against the current, however, can be hard and sometimes scary. Trust me, I know. But groups or societies can't always be trusted to be right. We know this from history, so we have no choice but to think independently and courageously about important and unusual ideas. Truth is not a popularity contest. Reality is not something we get to vote on.

Don't be afraid to change. Many people have the crazy notion that change is bad. They think that changing your mind when better information comes along is a sign of weakness or indecisiveness. Nonsense. A key attribute of highly intelligent and honest people is the willingness to correct course when shown to be off course. Change is one of the primary reasons that science works so well. Science changes all the time. When better data and new discoveries make it clear that an established scientific fact is wrong, good scientists don't cover their ears and refuse to listen. They embrace it and celebrate progress toward a better understanding. We all should be bold enough to do the same.

WILL CHRISTIANITY ENDURE?

C hristianity has enjoyed a remarkable run. For twenty centuries, it has been faithfully transferred from parent to child, followers of rival religions have converted, and nonbelievers have seen the light. But will it all be gone one day? Will Christianity fade and drift into extinction? It may seem impossible now, as it is the world's most popular religion, with some 32 percent of the population calling itself Christian. But many powerful and popular religions have come and gone. It could happen. But Christianity's resilience to date is impressive. After all, it has been hit with persecution, scandals, and doubt and has still thrived. The future is uncertain, but, for reasons I'll share shortly, I think it will endure for a long time to come. However, that is not necessarily good news for today's more devout and traditional Christians because the Christianity of the future is unlikely to be the Christianity they know today.

The continuing rise of Islam threatens to topple Christianity from the top spot among world religions. Some predict that Islam may become the most numerically popular religion by the middle of this century. But religion is not a car race. Slipping one notch would mean very little to Christianity's long-term survival. It has a long, long slide to oblivion from its impressive 2.2 billion followers today.

One specific problem that future generations of Christians will have to face is the failure of Jesus to return "soon," as so many long-dead Christians were sure would happen. For two thousand years, the end has been near. One wonders how long this can go on. Will there come a day when Christianity revises this claim, or will it simply let it go? Is it really possible that in the year 3000, a significant portion of Christians will be speaking enthusiastically about the imminent return of the Messiah? If so, what about five thousand years from now? Ten thousand years? I admit, I don't know of any Christians today giving up due to rapture-ready fatigue, but the promise of the end of days must ring hollow at some point. Would that kill off Christianity? I doubt it.

Will the relentless march of science end Christianity's run by pushing it into obsolescence? Will science's consistent ability to answer questions and make new discoveries eventually overshadow Christianity? Will Christians become too envious of science's ability to actually solve problems and get things done? Will humankind abandon all traditional religions and become a species of spiritual Spocks? I doubt it. Science works like nothing else, no doubt, but it is not another religion. It's more of a tool or a process than anything. It cannot scratch the itch that religions have been servicing all these past millennia. No, for all its problems, I suspect that Christianity will endure a while longer.

I think Christianity will last because it has proven itself willing and able to accommodate virtually any human taste or need. If you want to hate, Christianity can support that desire. Just look at how well the Bible served conquerors and slaveholders. Hatemongers from the Ku Klux Klan to the Nazis and on down to the Phelps family of Kansas have found plenty of reassurance in Christianity for their despicable worldviews. Likewise, those who want to show extraordinary love for their fellow humans and help those in need can find all the inspiration they may require in Christianity and the Bible. Today there are tens of thousands of versions of Christianity, many of which are so different from other versions that it is logically impossible for all of them to be valid. But where many see this diversity as a weakness of Christianity, I see one of its greatest strengths. It is everything to everyone and anything to anyone. Christianity may well turn out to be extinction-proof.

Let's not kid ourselves, religions are infinitely flexible. And why is this? They are able to evolve, twist, bend, and contort into virtually anything a particular believer needs or desires because they are not based on reason, evidence, observation, or logic. There is no solid foundation, no collection of facts and truths that anyone, anywhere, at any time can verify. They are based on always-questionable claims of divine revelations by fallible humans and sacred books that are open to different interpretations, and they promote believing over thinking and loyal faith over vigilant skepticism. Given all this, it is inevitable that religions change, splinter, mutate, modify, and invent. For example, mainstream Mormonism, under pressure from the changing society around it, went from polygamy to monogamy and from racist to inclusive without skipping a beat. It didn't matter that in each case the earlier positions had been God's will, according to church prophets.

Pastors, popes, and preachers love to stress how unchanging their religion is. But this is untrue. Christianity today is far different from what it was in the past. In many churches and in many families, Christianity has moved on from the prehistoric view of how women should be treated and valued. Hopefully all Christians and churches will one day share this view. Many Christians embrace science and support the work of scientists. Some Christians *are* scientists. Many Christians do not adhere to the impossible claims of creationism or fall for the hollow philosophy of intelligent design. Some Christians expect no miracles and no apocalypse.

Many atheists and skeptics make the mistake of imagining that the future is not big enough for Christianity. But the future certainly can accommodate Christianity, at least it can if Christianity continues to evolve. No one should overlook the many Christians today who adhere to a Christianity that presents no problems for the world and does no harm to humans. I know many people who call themselves Christians, who apparently believe in Jesus, who probably pray, and who presumably hope they will go to heaven one day. But for all intents and purposes, that is the extent of it. They have no malice toward other kinds of believers or nonbelievers. They not only accept social and scientific progress, they want more of it. And they believe there is a future for humankind worth dreaming of and working toward. They see a better world on the horizon, not doomsday. I certainly have no problem sharing the planet with these Christians.

If I had a time machine, I would love to check in on Christianity a few centuries from now. I would not be at all surprised to find that no more Christians are breathlessly awaiting the return of their god or seeing angels everywhere. Perhaps they will be fully engaged in a deeply computerized global culture that has created lasting peace, solved poverty, ended the war on nature, and finally expanded permanently beyond the cage of Earth's gravity. This is a very optimistic view of our possible future, and I see no reason why something called Christianity can't be a part of it. The version of Christianity that would fit into that kind of a future would be very different, of course. But it would require a transformation no greater than the one this religion has already experienced over the last several centuries. Some in the future might say that the new Christianity is nothing more than a feel-good philosophy that provides a social network and an excuse to meditate and sing together. Christians, however, will say it is more than that, and it's their right to think so. This is only one of many possible scenarios for Christianity, of course. But there is at least one path that is very likely to kill off Christianity forever.

If the majority of the world's Christians drift toward the worst that we see in this religion today rather than the best, then the future is not likely to be so bright for it or, perhaps, for the entire world. If it must, humanity will pass Christianity by and never look back. Or, Christianity's dark side of division and intolerance might drag the rest of us down with it. But the vast majority of Christians probably won't let this happen. Much is made, and should be, of the disturbing number of Christians who believe in things like a six-thousand-year-old Earth and the inferiority of non-Christians. But we can't overlook the encouraging numbers of Christians who do *not* believe such things. They will change Christianity from within because they must. If they do not, and Christianity were to become dominated everywhere by regressive, intolerant people, then it has no future. Worse, if Christianity and Islam do not mature at a faster rate, then we might all burn up in one big fireball fueled by runaway irrational belief, tribalism, and fear. Atheists might have the satisfaction of saying, "I told you so," but it won't be much of a victory. If Christianity is here to stay for the foreseeable future, and it likely is, let's hope that it endures in a form that is good for all and compatible with the best that our world can be. On that, I trust most Christians and non-Christians can agree.

NOTES

CHAPTER 2. WHAT IS A GOD?

1. Ashley Fantz, "18 Years after Waco, Davidians Believe Koresh Was God," CNN, April 14, 2011, http://articles.cnn.com/2011-04-14/us/waco.koresh .believers_1_waco-sheila-martin-david-koresh?_s=PM:US (accessed August 19, 2012).

CHAPTER 3. IS IT RUDE TO ASK?

1. "God Has a Sense of Humor," *Malia Litman*, http://malialitman.word press.com/2012/01/12/god-has-a-sense-of-humor-2/ (accessed December 16, 2012).

CHAPTER 4. DOES JESUS ANSWER PRAYERS?

1. Christine Soares, "No Prayer Prescription," *Scientific American*, June 19, 2006, http://www.scientificamerican.com/article.cfm?id=no-prayer-prescription (accessed December 15, 2012).

2. "The Mothers' Index," Save the Children, 2012, http://www.savethe children.org/atf/cf/%7B9def2ebe-10ae-432c-9bd0-df91d2eba74a%7D/2012 _MOTHER%E2%80%99S_INDEX_AND_COUNTRY_RANKINGS.PDF (accessed September 8, 2012).

CHAPTER 5. WHO IS A CHRISTIAN?

1. "Global Christianity," Pew Forum on Religion & Public Life, December 19, 2011, http://www.pewforum.org/Christian/Global-Christianity-exec.aspx (accessed September 21, 2012).

2. "The Global Religious Landscape," Pew Forum on Religion & Public

Life, December 18, 2012, http://www.pewforum.org/global-religious-landscape
-exec.aspx (accessed January 10, 2013).

CHAPTER 6. DOES CHRISTIANITY MAKE SOCIETIES BETTER?

1. "International Human Development Indicators," Human Development
Reports, United Nations, http://hdr.undp.org/en/statistics/ (accessed September
1, 2012).
2. Phil Zuckerman, "Atheism—Contemporary Numbers and Practices," in
The Cambridge Companion to Atheism, edited by Michael Martin (New York:
Cambridge University Press, 2006), p. 56.
3. Phil Zuckerman, interview with the author, September 6, 2012.
4. Frank Newport, "Mississippi Is Most Religious U.S. State," Gallup®,
March 27, 2012, http://www.gallup.com/poll/153479/Mississippi-Religious-State
.aspx?utm_source=alert&utm_medium=email&utm_campaign=syndication
&utm_content=morelink&utm_term=Politics%20-%20Religion%20-%20
Religion%20and%20Social%20Trends%20-%20USA#1 (accessed July 23, 2012).
5. Ibid.
6. "Country Comparison: Infant Mortality Rate," *CIA World Factbook*,
https://www.cia.gov/library/publications/the-world-factbook/rankorder/2091
rank.html (accessed December 21, 2012).
7. "Infant Mortality Rate—2006," United States Census Bureau, http://
www.census.gov/compendia/statab/2012/ranks/rank17.html (accessed September 6, 2012).
8. Albert Bozzo, "Hot and Cold Rule Quality-of-Life Category in CNBC's
Top States Study," CNBC, July 10, 2012, http://www.cnbc.com/id/47818866/
Hot_and_Cold_Rule_QualityofLife_Category_in_CNBC039s_Top_States
_Study (accessed December 21, 2012).
9. "America's Most (and Least) Peaceful States," 24/7 Wall St., April 26,
2012, http://247wallst.com/2012/04/26/americas-most-and-least-peaceful-states/
(accessed June 7, 2012).

CHAPTER 7. WHAT IS ATHEISM?

1. Penny Edgell, Joseph Gerties, and Joseph Hartmann, "Atheists as
'Other,'" *American Sociological Review* 271 (April 2006); W. M. Gervais, Ara
Norenzayan, and Azim F. Shariff, "Do You Believe in Atheists? Distrust Is

Central to Anti-Atheist Prejudice," *Journal of Personality and Social Psychology* 101, no. 6 (2011): 1189–1206, http://www2.psych.ubc.ca/~will/Gervais%20et %20al-%20Atheist%20Distrust.pdf (accessed July 12, 2012).

CHAPTER 8. WHAT ARE MIRACLES?

1. "What People Do and Do Not Believe In," Harris Poll®, December 15, 2009, http://www.harrisinteractive.com/vault/Harris_Poll_2009_12_15.pdf (accessed March 22, 2012).
2. Ibid.

CHAPTER 9. DOES THE COMPLEXITY OF LIFE REVEAL AN INTELLIGENT DESIGNER?

1. Kathryn Lougheed, "There Are Fewer Microbes Out There Than You Think," *Nature*, August 27, 2012, http://www.nature.com/news/there-are-fewer -microbes-out-there-than-you-think-1.11275 (accessed September 23, 2012).

CHAPTER 10. HAVE YOU READ THE BIBLE?

1. "Barna Reviews Top Religious Trends of 2005," Barna Group, December 20, 2005, http://www.barna.org/barna-update/article/5-barna-update/166-barna -reviews-top-religious-trends-of-2005 (accessed August 30, 2012).
2. Alec Gallup and Wendy W. Simmons, "Six in Ten Americans Read Bible at Least Occasionally," Gallup®, October 20, 2000, http://www.gallup .com/poll/2416/six-ten-americans-read-bible-least-occasionally.aspx (accessed September 1, 2012).
3. David R. Carlin, "Why Catholics Don't Read the Bible," CatholiCity, February 9, 2009, http://www.catholicity.com/commentary/carlin/05386.html (accessed August 22, 2012).
4. Ibid.
5. Stephen Prothero, *Religious Literacy: What Every American Needs to Know—and Doesn't* (San Francisco: Harper, 2007), p. 1.

CHAPTER 11. WHY DO SOME CHRISTIANS DO BAD THINGS IN THE SIGHT OF JESUS?

1. Dana Garrett, "Can God's Love Be Enough? Inside Sandusky's Church," *Headline News*, February 8, 2010, http://www.hlntv.com/article/2011/11/23/penn-state-scandal-jerry-sandusky-church (accessed July 3, 2012).

CHAPTER 13. HOW DO WE KNOW THAT HEAVEN IS REAL?

1. Don Piper, *90 Minutes in Heaven* (Grand Rapids, MI: Revell, 2004), p. 201.

2. Guy P. Harrison, "God Is in This Place," *Caymanian Compass*, November 19, 1993.

3. Ibid.

4. Susan A. Clancy, *Abducted: How People Come to Believe They Were Kidnapped by Aliens* (Cambridge, MA: Harvard University Press, 2005), p. 35.

5. Michael Shermer, "Hope Springs Eternal: Science, the Afterlife and the Meaning of Life, *Skeptic*, http://www.skeptic.com/reading_room/the-great-afterlife-debate/ (accessed March 22, 2012).

6. Charles Q. Choi, "Peace of Mind: Near-Death Experiences Now Found to Have Scientific Explanations," *Scientific American*, September 12, 2011, http://www.scientificamerican.com/article.cfm?id=peace-of-mind-near-death&WT.mc_id=SA_WR_20110915 (accessed May 7, 2012).

7. Kevin Nelson, *The Spiritual Doorway in the Brain* (New York: Dutton, 2010), pp. 142–43.

8. Stephen Cave, *Immortality* (New York: Crown, 2012), p. 2.

CHAPTER 15. WHAT DO PROPHECIES PROVE?

1. Bart D. Ehrman, *Did Jesus Exist?* (New York: HarperOne, 2012), p. 310.

CHAPTER 16. HOW IMPORTANT ARE THE TEN COMMANDMENTS?

1. Billy Graham, "Billy Graham's My Answer," Billy Graham Evangelical Association, http://www.billygraham.org/articlepage.asp?articleid=3781 (accessed September 10, 2012).

2. Albert Winseman, "Americans: Thou Shalt Not Remove the Ten Commandments," Gallup®, April 12, 2005, http://www.gallup.com/poll/15817/americans-thou-shalt-remove-ten-commandments.aspx (accessed September 9, 2012).

3. "Ten Commandments No Match for Big Mac," World Net Daily, October 8, 2007, http://www.wnd.com/2007/10/43927/ (accessed September 4, 2012).

CHAPTER 18. IS CHRISTIANITY GOOD FOR WOMEN?

1. "The Thunder, Perfect Mind," in *Nag Hammadi Library*, trans. George W. MacRae, ed. James M. Robinson, rev. ed. (San Francisco: HarperCollins, 1990), Gnostic Society Library, http://gnosis.org/naghamm/thunder.html (accessed September 20, 2012).

2. Elizabeth Clark, "The Roles for Women," *Frontline*, PBS, http://www.pbs.org/wgbh/pages/frontline/shows/religion/first/roles.html (accessed September 2, 2012).

3. Ibid.

4. Karen L. King, "Women in Ancient Christianity: The New Discoveries," *Frontline*, PBS, http://www.pbs.org/wgbh/pages/frontline/shows/religion/first/women.html (accessed September 20, 2012).

5. Ruth Hurmence Green, *The Born Again Skeptic's Guide to the Bible* (Madison, WI: Freedom from Religion Foundation, 1999), p. 179.

6. *Wikiquote*, Steven Weinberg, from "Address at the Conference on Cosmic Design, American Association for the Advancement of Science," Washington, DC, April 1999, http://en.wikiquote.org/wiki/Steven_Weinberg (accessed July 24, 2012).

CHAPTER 19. IS IT SMARTER TO BELIEVE OR NOT BELIEVE?

1. Graeme Paton, "Intelligent People 'Less Likely to Believe in God,'" *Telegraph*, June 11, 2008, http://www.telegraph.co.uk/news/uknews/2111174/Intelligent-people-less-likely-to-believe-in-God.html (accessed July 19, 2012).

2. Ibid.

3. David DeWitt, quoted in "Unraveling the Origins Controversy," C-SPAN, March 23, 2012, http://www.c-spanvideo.org/program/305330-10 (accessed September 28, 2012).

4. Frank Newport, "More Than 9 in 10 Americans Continue to Believe in God," Gallup®, June 3, 2011, http://www.gallup.com/poll/147887/americans-continue-believe-god.aspx (accessed June 6, 2012).

5. Amitai Shenhav, David G. Rand, and Joshua D. Greene, "Divine Intuition: Cognitive Style Influences Belief in God," *Journal of Experimental Psychology*, American Psychological Association, 2011, http://www.anth.uconn .edu/degree_programs/ecolevo/divineintuition.pdf (accessed September 28, 2012).

6. Paton, "Intelligent People 'Less Likely to Believe in God.'"

CHAPTER 20. IS THE BORN-AGAIN EXPERIENCE IN CHRISTIANITY UNIQUE?

1. Albert L. Winseman, "Who Has Been Born Again?" Gallup®, January 18, 2005, http://www.gallup.com/poll/14632/who-has-been-born-again.aspx (accessed March 29, 2012).

2. "Barna Survey Reveals Significant Growth in Born Again Population," Barna Group, March 27, 2006, http://www.barna.org/barna-update/article/5 -barna-update/157-barna-survey-reveals-significant-growth-in-born-again -population (accessed March 21, 2012).

3. Barna Group, "American Piety in the 21st Century: Selected Findings from the Baylor Religion Survey," *New Insights to the Depth and Complexity of Religion in the US*, September 2006, p. 17, http://www.baylor .edu/content/services/document.php/33304.pdf (accessed December 17, 2012).

4. "What People Do and Do Not Believe In," Harris Poll®, December 15, 2009, http://www.harrisinteractive.com/vault/Harris_Poll_2009_12_15.pdf (accessed March 29, 2012).

CHAPTER 21. IS FAITH A GOOD THING?

1. "Søren Kierkegaard and Bertrand Russell," *Lapham's Quarterly*, http:// www.laphamsquarterly.org/conversations/sren-kierkegaard-bertrand-russell .php (accessed September 30, 2012).

2. "Faith," Mary Fairchild, About.com/Christianity, http://christianity .about.com/od/glossary/g/faith.htm (accessed, January 7, 2013).

3. Mark Twain, *Following the Equator* (Whitefish, MT: Kessinger, 2004), p. 70.

4. Peter Boghossian, interview with the author, July 15, 2012.

CHAPTER 24. HOW DO WE KNOW
THAT THE MAN JESUS EXISTED?

1. Bart D. Ehrman, *Did Jesus Exist?* (New York: HarperOne, 2012), p. 92.
2. Ibid.
3. Ibid., p. 93.

CHAPTER 25. WHAT ABOUT ALL THE OTHER GODS?

1. Carl Sagan, *Broca's Brain: Reflections on the Romance of Science* (New York: Ballantine, 1980), p. 240.

CHAPTER 26. ARE CHRISTIANS HAPPIER?

1. "Muslim Americans: Faith, Freedom, and the Future," Gallup®, August 11, 2011, http://www.gallup.com/strategicconsulting/154373/REPORT -BILINGUAL-Muslim-Americans-Faith-Freedom-Future.aspx (accessed December 14, 2012).
2. Ibid.
3. "Buddhists 'Really Are Happier,'" BBC, May 21, 2003, http://news.bbc .co.uk/2/hi/health/3047291.stm (accessed December 14, 2012).
4. Paul Ekman, quoted in ibid.
5. "Buddhists 'Really Are Happier.'"
6. "Psychologist Produces the First-Ever 'World Map of Happiness,'" *ScienceDaily*, November 14, 2006. Retrieved September 4, 2012, http://www.science daily.com /releases/2006/11/061113093726.htm (accessed September 4, 2012).
7. Michael Martin, *The Cambridge Companion to Atheism* (Cambridge: Cambridge University Press, 2007), pp. 56–57.
8. "Psychologist Produces the First-Ever 'World Map of Happiness.'"
9. Julie Ray, "Nearly One in Four Worldwide Thriving," Gallup®, April 10, 2012, http://www.gallup.com/poll/153818/Nearly-One-Four-Worldwide-Thriving .aspx (accessed September 4, 2012).
10. Martin, *Cambridge Companion to Atheism*, pp. 56–57.
11. Chaeyoon Lim and Robert D. Putnam, "Religion, Social Networks, and Life Satisfaction," *American Sociological Review*, American Sociological Association, 2010, http://www.asanet.org/images/journals/docs/pdf/asr/Dec10 ASRFeature.pdf (accessed September 4, 2012).

12. Chaeyoon Lim, quoted in Emily Sohn, "Why Are Religious People Happier?" Discovery News, December 7, 2012, http://news.discovery.com/human/religion-happiness-social-bonds.html (accessed June 4, 2012).

13. Chaeyoon Lim, quoted in "'Secret Ingredient' in Religion Makes People Happier," *ScienceDaily*, December 9, 2010, http://www.sciencedaily.com/releases/2010/12/101207091802.htm (accessed September 4, 2012).

14. Ibid.

CHAPTER 27. IS THE UNITED STATES OF AMERICA A CHRISTIAN NATION?

1. "Thomas Paine," About.com: Agnosticism/Atheism, http://atheism.about.com/library/quotes/bl_q_TPaine.htm (accessed January 14, 2013).

2. David Niose, *Nonbeliever Nation: The Rise of Secular Americans* (New York: Palgrave Macmillan, 2012), p. 60.

CHAPTER 28. HOW CAN WE BE SURE THAT JESUS PERFORMED MIRACLES?

1. "What People Do and Do Not Believe In," Harris Poll®, http://www.harrisinteractive.com/vault/Harris_Poll_2009_12_15.pdf (accessed August 9, 2012).

2. "When the Horse Came out, People Shouted and Ran," *Saturday Tribune*, September 15, 2012, http://tribune.com.ng/sat/index.php/features/8578-when-the-horse-came-out-people-shouted-and-ran-the-inside-story-of-a-woman-who-gave-birth-to-a-strange-creature-.html (accessed September 21, 2012).

CHAPTER 29. WHAT DO EVIL ATHEIST DICTATORS PROVE?

1. Richard L. Rubenstein and John K. Roth, *Approaches to Auschwitz: The Holocaust and Its Legacy* (Louisville, KY: Westminster John Knox Press, 2003), p. 122.

2. Jim Walker, "The Christianity of Hitler Revealed in His Speeches and Proclamations," http://www.nobeliefs.com/speeches.htm (accessed September 6, 2012).

CHAPTER 30. IS THE UNIVERSE FINE-TUNED FOR US?

1. Seth Shostak, interview with the author, September 21, 2012.

CHAPTER 31. COULD WE DESIGN A BETTER WORLD?

1. *Wikipedia*, s.v. "List of Natural Disasters by Death Toll," http://en
.wikipedia.org/wiki/List_of_natural_disasters_by_death_toll#cite_note-cbc
.ca-0 (accessed September 23, 2012).
2. *Action against Worms* 1 (March 2003): 2, http://www.dewormtheworld
.org/sites/default/files/pdf/WHO%20-%20Action%20Against%20Worms%201
.pdf (accessed January 10, 2013).
3. "Water Related Diseases," WHO, http://www.who.int/water_sanitation
_health/diseases/diarrhoea/en/ (accessed June 13, 2012).

CHAPTER 33. WHY ISN'T EVERYONE A CHRISTIAN?

1. John Zarrella and Patrick Oppmann, "Pastor with 666 Tattoo Claims
to be Divine," CNN, February 16, 2007, http://articles.cnn.com/2007-02-16/us/
miami.preacher_1_cult-leader-followers-tattoo?_s=PM:US (accessed September 30, 2012).

CHAPTER 34. WHAT IS THE PROBLEM WITH EVOLUTION?

1. "In U.S., 46% Hold Creationist View of Human Origins," Frank Newport,
Gallup®, June 1, 2012, http://www.gallup.com/poll/155003/Hold-Creationist
-View-Human-Origins.aspx (accessed January 14, 2013).

CHAPTER 37. DID GOD DROWN THE WORLD?

1. "Most Americans Take Bible Stories Literally," *Washington Times*,
February 16, 2004, http://www.washingtontimes.com/news/2004/feb/16/2004
0216-113955-2061r/ (accessed February 18, 2011).
2. "Six in 10 Take Bible Stories Literally, But Don't Blame Jews for Death

of Jesus," ABC News Primetime Poll, February 15, 2004, http://abcnews
.go.com/images/pdf/947a1ViewsoftheBible.pdf (accessed December 26, 2012).

CHAPTER 38. WHY DO BIRTH LOCATION AND FAMILY MATTER SO MUCH?

1. Stephen Prothero, *Religious Literacy: What Every American Needs to Know—and Doesn't* (San Francisco: Harper, 2007).

CHAPTER 40. WHY DO PEOPLE GO TO HELL?

1. "What People Do and Do Not Believe In," Harris Poll®, December 15, 2009, http://www.harrisinteractive.com/vault/Harris_Poll_2009_12_15.pdf (accessed March 22, 2012).

2. Bill Wiese, *23 Minutes in Hell: One Man's Story about What He Saw, Heard, and Felt in That Place of Torment*, 1st ed. (Lake Mary, FL: Charisma House, 2006), pp. 2–6.

3. "The Well to Hell," Snopes.com, http://www.snopes.com/religion/well hell.asp (accessed March 22, 2012).

CHAPTER 41. CAN ATHEISTS BE TRUSTED?

1. W. M. Gervais, Ara Norenzayan, and Azim F. Shariff, "Do You Believe in Atheists? Distrust Is Central to Anti-Atheist Prejudice," *Journal of Personality and Social Psychology* 101, no. 6 (2011): 1189–1206, http://www2.psych.ubc .ca/~will/Gervais%20et%20al-%20Atheist%20Distrust.pdf (accessed July 12, 2012).

2. Ibid.

3. Penny Edgell, Joseph Gerties, and Joseph Hartmann, "Atheists as 'Other,'" *American Sociological Review* 271 (April 2006): 230.

4. Ibid.

5. Ibid., p. 227.

6. Ibid., p. 230.

7. "For Goodness' Sake: Why So Many Want Religion to Play a Greater Role in American Life," Public Agenda, 2001, p. 12, http://www.publicagenda .org/files/pdf/for_goodness_sake.pdf (accessed September 7, 2012).

8. "America's Most (and Least) Peaceful States," 24/7 Wall St., April 26, 2012, http://247wallst.com/2012/04/26/americas-most-and-least-peaceful-states/ (accessed June 7, 2012).

9. "The Global Religious Landscape," Pew Forum on Religion & Public Life, December 8, 2012, http://www.pewforum.org/global-religious-landscape -unaffiliated.aspx (accessed December 23, 2012).

10. "Global Index of Religion and Atheism," Win-Gallup International, http://redcresearch.ie/wp-content/uploads/2012/08/RED-C-press-release -Religion-and-Atheism-25-7-12.pdf (accessed August 8, 2012).

CHAPTER 43. ARE ANGELS REAL?

1. Frank Newport, "Americans More Likely to Believe in God Than the Devil, Heaven More Than Hell," Gallup®, June 13, 2007, http://www.gallup .com/poll/27877/Americans-More-Likely-Believe-God-Than-Devil-Heaven -More-Than-Hell.aspx (accessed November 3, 2010).

2. David Kinnaman, quoted in "New Research Explores Teenage Views and Behavior Regarding the Supernatural," Barna Group, January 23, 2006, http://www.barna.org/barna-update/article/5-barna-update/164-new-research -explores-teenage-views-and-behavior-regarding-the-supernatural?q=angels (accessed February 23, 2010).

3. Ibid.

4. David Van Biema, "Guardian Angels Are Here, Say Most Americans," *Time*, September 18, 2012, http://www.time.com/time/nation/article/ 0,8599,1842179,00.html (accessed September 9, 2012).

5. Christopher D. Bader, F. Carson Mencken, and Joseph O. Baker, *Paranormal America* (New York: New York University Press, 2010), pp. 185–86.

6. Stephen Walsh, "Author Lorna Byrne: I See Angels," CNN, http:// religion.blogs.cnn.com/2012/12/24/author-lorna-byrne-i-see-angels/ (accessed January 2, 2013).

7. Benjamin Weiser, "In New Jersey, Rules Are Changed on Witness IDs," *New York Times*, August 24, 2011, http://www.nytimes.com/2011/08/25/ny region/in-new-jersey-rules-changed-on-witness-ids.html?_r=2& (accessed January 4, 2013).

CHAPTER 44. IS CHRISTMAS UNDER ATTACK?

1. "Atheists Launch Ad as Weapon in War on Christmas," War on Christmas, http://www.waronchristmas.com/atheists-publish-anti-christmas-ad/ (accessed September 17, 2012).

2. Bill O'Reilly, "Christmas under Siege: The Big Picture," FoxNews .com, December 24, 2004, http://www.foxnews.com/story/0,2933,140742,00.html #ixzz26k2eeyOV (accessed September 3, 2012).

CHAPTER 45. WILL THE END TIMES EVER END?

1. Bart D. Ehrman, *Did Jesus Exist?* (New York: HarperOne, 2012), p. 298.

2. Ibid., p. 301.

3. Guy P. Harrison, "God Is in This Place," *Caymanian Compass*, November 19, 1993.

CHAPTER 46. DOES CHRISTIANITY MAKE INDIVIDUALS BETTER?

1. *Wikipedia*, s.v. "Official Development Assistance," http://en.wikipedia.org/ wiki/Official_development_assistance#cite_note-OECD09-1 (accessed May 2, 2012).

2. "Atheists More Motivated by Compassion Than the Faithful," *LiveScience*, http://www.livescience.com/20005-atheists-motivated-compassion .html (accessed May 24, 2012).

3. "Scientists and Belief," Pew Forum on Religion and Public Life, November 5, 2009, http://www.pewforum.org/Science-and-Bioethics/Scientists -and-Belief.aspx (accessed August 4, 2012).

4. Frans de Waal, *Our Inner Ape* (New York: Berkley, 2005), pp. 225–26.

5. "Joseph Kony: Profile of the LRA Leader," BBC, March 8, 2012, http:// www.bbc.co.uk/news/world-africa-17299084 (accessed September 9, 2012).

CHAPTER 47. WHY DOES A GOOD GOD ALLOW SO MUCH SUFFERING IN THE WORLD?

1. "Millennium Development Goals," UNICEF, http://www.unicef.org/ mdg/childmortality.html (accessed January 11, 2013).

2. "Malaria Deaths Twice as High as Previously Reported," ABC News, February 2, 2012, http://abcnews.go.com/Health/malaria-deaths-high-thought/story?id=15499330 (accessed January 14, 2013).

3. Gregory Paul, "Theodicy's Problem: A Statistical Look at the Holocaust of the Children, and the Implications of Natural Evil for the Free Will and Best of All Worlds Hypotheses," *Philosophy & Theology* 19, nos. 1–2, http://gregspaul.webs.com/Philosophy&Theology.pdf (accessed September 1, 2012).

4. Ibid., p. 133.

5. William Lane Craig, "The Problem of Evil," *Reasonable Faith*, http://www.reasonablefaith.org/the-problem-of-evil (accessed March 22, 2012).

CHAPTER 49. SHOULD CHRISTIANS TRY TO BE GOOD SKEPTICS?

1. Pride Chigwedere, George R. Seage III, Sofia Gruskin, Tun-Hou Lee, and M. Essex, "Estimating the Lost Benefits of Antiretroviral Drug Use in South Africa," *Journal of Acquired Immune Deficiency Syndrome* (2008): 410, http://www.aids.harvard.edu/Lost_Benefits.pdf (accessed December 17, 2012). Page not active at time of publication.

2. I. A. Malik and S. Gopalan, "Use of CAM Results in Delay in Seeking Medical Advice for Breast Cancer," *European Journal of Epidemiology* 18, no. 8 (2003): 817–22, http://www.ncbi.nlm.nih.gov/pubmed?cmd=Retrieve&db=pubmed&dopt=AbstractPlus&list_uids=12974558 (accessed March 6, 2011).

BIBLIOGRAPHY AND RECOMMENDED READING

Aikin, Scott F., and Robert B. Talisse. *Reasonable Atheism.* Amherst, NY: Prometheus Books, 2011.

Bader, Christopher, F. Carson Mencken, and Joseph Baker. *Paranormal America.* New York: New York University Press, 2010.

Barker, Dan. *Godless.* Berkeley, CA: Ulysses, 2008.

———. *Maybe Yes, Maybe No: A Guide for Young Skeptics.* Amherst, NY: Prometheus Books, 1990.

Bellah, Robert N. *Religion in Human Evolution.* Cambridge, MA: Belknap, 2011.

Bering, Jesse. *The Belief Instinct.* New York: W. W. Norton, 2011.

Blackmore, Susan. *Dying to Live: Near-Death Experiences.* Amherst, New York: Prometheus Books, 1993.

———. *In Search of the Light: The Adventures of a Parapsychologist.* Amherst, NY: Prometheus Books, 1996.

Brockman, John, ed. *Intelligent Thought: Science versus the Intelligent Design Movement.* New York: Vintage Books, 2006.

Buonomano, Dean. *Brain Bugs: How the Brain's Flaws Shape Our Lives.* New York: W. W. Norton, 2011.

Burton, Robert A. *On Being Certain: Believing You Are Right Even When You're Not.* New York: St. Martin's Griffin, 2009.

Carroll, Robert Todd, ed. *The Skeptic's Dictionary.* Hoboken, NJ: John Wiley and Sons, 2003.

Chabris, Christopher, and Daniel Simons. *The Invisible Gorilla and Other Ways Our Invisible Gorilla Deceives Us.* New York: Crown, 2010.

Chaffe, John. *Thinking Critically.* Boston: Houghton Mifflin, 2000.

Chaline, Eric. *The Book of Gods and Goddesses: A Visual Dictionary of Ancient and Modern Deities.* New York: It Books, 2004.

Clancy, Susan A. *Abducted: How People Come to Believe They Were Kidnapped by Aliens.* Cambridge, MA: Harvard University Press, 2005.

Crumb, R. *The Book of Genesis.* New York: W. W. Norton, 2009.

Daniels, Kenneth. *Why I Believed: Reflections of a Former Missionary.* Duncanville, TX: Daniels, 2009.

Davis, Hank. *Caveman Logic: The Persistence of Primitive Thinking in a Modern World.* Amherst, NY: Prometheus Books, 2009.

Dawkins, Richard. *The Ancestor's Tale*. Boston: Houghton Mifflin, 2004.

———. *Climbing Mount Improbable*. New York: W. W. Norton, 1996.

———. *The God Delusion*. New York: Houghton Mifflin, 2006.

———. *The Greatest Show on Earth: The Evidence for Evolution*. New York: Free Press, 2009.

Dawkins, Richard, and Dave McKean. *The Magic of Reality: How We Know What's Really True*. New York: Free Press, 2011.

Dennett, Daniel. *Breaking the Spell: Religion as a Natural Phenomenon*. New York: Penguin, 2007.

De Waal, Frans. *The Age of Empathy: Nature's Lessons for a Kinder Society*. New York: Broadway, 2010.

———. *Our Inner Ape: A Leading Primatologist Explains Why We Are Who We Are*. New York: Riverhead Trade, 2006.

———. *Primates and Philosophers: How Morality Evolved*. Princeton, NJ: Princeton University Press, 2009.

Dunning, Brian. *Skeptoid: Critical Analysis of Pop Phenomena*. Thunderwood, 2007.

Ehrman, Bart. *Did Jesus Exist?* New York: Harper One, 2012.

———. *Misquoting Jesus*. New York: HarperSanFrancisco, 2005.

Epstein, Greg M. *Good without God*. New York: Harper, 2010.

Farr-Wharton, Jake. *Letters to Christian Leaders: Hollow Be Thy Claims*. Dangerous Little Books, 2011.

Feder, Kenneth L. *Encyclopedia of Dubious Archaeology: From Atlantis to the Walam Olum*. Santa Barbara, CA: Greenwood, 2010.

———. *Frauds, Myths, and Mysteries: Science and Pseudoscience in Archaeology*. New York: McGraw Hill, 2008.

Forrest, Barbara, and Paul R. Gross. *Creationism's Trojan Horse: The Wedge of Intelligent Design*. Oxford: Oxford University Press, 2004.

Green, Ruth Hurmence. *The Born Again Skeptic's Guide to the Bible*. Madison, WI: Freedom from Religion Foundation, 1999.

Gross, Mathew Barrett, and Mel Gilles. *The Last Myth*. Amherst, NY: Prometheus Books, 2012.

Guyatt, Nicholas. *Have a Nice Doomsday: Why Millions of Americans Are Looking Forward to the End of the World*. London: Ebury, 2007.

Harris, Sam. *The End of Faith: Religion, Terror, and the Future of Reason*. New York: W. W. Norton, 2005.

———. *Letter to a Christian Nation*. New York: Vintage, 2008.

Harrison, Guy P. *50 Reasons People Give for Believing in a God*. Amherst, NY: Prometheus Books, 2008.

Haught, James A. *Holy Hatred.* Amherst, NY: Prometheus Books, 1995.

———. *Honest Doubt.* Amherst, NY: Prometheus Books, 2007.

———. *2,000 Years of Disbelief.* Amherst, NY: Prometheus Books, 1996.

Hazen, Robert M. *Genesis: The Scientific Quest for Life's Origins.* Joseph Henry Press, 2007.

Head, Tom, ed. *Conversations with Carl Sagan.* Jackson: University Press of Mississippi, 2006.

Hines, Terrence. *Pseudoscience and the Paranormal.* Amherst, NY: Prometheus Books, 2003.

Hitchens, Christopher, ed. *The Portable Atheist: Essential Readings for the Nonbeliever.* New York: Da Capo, 2007.

Hood, Bruce. *The Science of Superstition: How the Developing Brain Creates Supernatural Beliefs.* New York: HarperCollins Paperback, 2010.

Hosler, Jay. *Evolution: The Story of Life on Earth.* New York: Hill and Wang, 2011.

Humes, Edward. *Monkey Girl: Evolution, Education, Religion, and the Battle for America's Soul.* New York: HarperCollins, 2007.

Jordan, Michael. *Encyclopedia of Gods.* London: Kyle Cathie, 2002.

Kelly, Lynne. *The Skeptic's Guide to the Paranormal.* New York: Avalon, 2004.

Kida, Thomas. *Don't Believe Everything You Think.* Amherst, NY: Prometheus Books, 2006.

Kurtz, Paul. *Affirmations: Joyful and Creative Exuberance.* Amherst, NY: Prometheus Books, 2004.

———, ed. *Skeptical Odysseys.* Amherst, NY: Prometheus Books, 2001.

———. *The Transcendental Temptation: A Critique of Religion and the Paranormal.* Amherst, NY: Prometheus Books, 1991.

Leeming, David. *A Dictionary of Creation Myths.* New York: Oxford University Press, 1994.

Lewis, James R. *Doomsday Prophecies: A Complete Guide to the End of the World.* Amherst, NY: Prometheus Books, 2000.

Loftus, John, ed. *The Christian Delusion.* Amherst, NY: Prometheus Books, 2010.

———. *The Outsider Test for Faith: How to Know Which Religion Is True.* Amherst, NY: Prometheus Books, 2013.

———. *Why I Became an Atheist: A Former Preacher Rejects Christianity.* Rev. ed. Amherst, NY: Prometheus Books, 2012.

Loxton, Daniel. *Evolution: How We and All Living Things Came to Be.* Tonawanda, NY: Kids Can Press, 2010.

Luhrmann, T. M. *When God Talks Back.* New York: Alfred A. Knopf, 2012.

Macknic, Stephen L., and Susana Martinez-Conde. *Sleights of Mind.* New York: Henry Holt, 2010.

Mark, Jeffery. *Christian No More.* Crescent Springs, KY: Reasonable Press, 2008.

Mayr, Ernst. *What Evolution Is.* London: Weidenfeld and Nicolson, 2002.

McAfee, David. *Disproving Christianity and Other Secular Writings.* Dangerous Little Books, 2011.

———. *Mom, Dad, I'm an Atheist.* Dangerous Little Books, 2012.

Medina, John. *Brain Rules.* Seattle, WA: Pear, 2008.

Miller, Kenneth R. *Only a Theory: Evolution and the Battle for America's Soul.* New York: Penguin, 2009.

Mills, David. *Atheist Universe: Why God Didn't Have a Thing to Do with It.* Philadelphia, PA: Xlibris, 2003.

National Academy of Sciences. *Science, Evolution, and Creationism.* Washington, DC: National Academies Press, 2008.

Nelson, Kevin. *The Spiritual Doorway in the Brain.* New York: Dutton, 2011.

Nickell, Joe. *Entities: Angels, Spirits, Demons, and Other Alien Beings.* Amherst, NY: Prometheus Books, 1995.

———. *Relics of the Christ.* Lexington: University Press of Kentucky, 2007.

Palmer, Douglas. *Origins: Human Evolution Revealed.* New York: Mitchell Beazley, 2010.

Pigliucci, Massimo. *Denying Evolution: Creationism, Scientism, and the Nature of Science.* Sunderland, MA: Sinauer, 2002.

———. *Nonsense on Stilts: How to Tell Science from Bunk.* Chicago: University of Chicago Press, 2010.

Potts, Richard, and Christopher Sloan. *What Does It Mean to Be Human?* Washington, DC: National Geographic, 2010.

Prothero, Donald R. *Evolution: What the Fossils Say and Why It Matters.* New York: Columbia University Press, 2007.

Prothero, Stephen. *God Is Not One: The Eight Rival Religions That Run the World.* New York: HarperOne, 2010.

———. *Religious Literacy: What Every American Needs to Know—and Doesn't.* San Francisco: Harper, 2007.

Putnam, Robert D., and David E. Campbell. *American Grace.* New York: Simon and Schuster, 2010.

Radford, Benjamin. *Scientific Paranormal Investigation: How to Solve the Unexplained Mysteries.* Corrales, NM: Rhombus, 2010.

Randi, James. *An Encyclopedia of Claims, Frauds, and Hoaxes of the Occult and Supernatural.* New York: St. Martin's, 1995.

———. *The Faith Healers*. Amherst, NY: Prometheus Books, 1989.

———. *Flim Flam! Psychics, ESP, Unicorns, and Other Delusions*. Amherst, NY: Prometheus Books, 1982.

Sagan, Carl. *The Demon-Haunted World: Science as a Candle in the Dark*. New York: Random House, 1995.

———. *The Varieties of Scientific Experience: A Personal View of the Search for God*. New York: Penguin, 2007.

Sawyer, G. J., and Viktor Deak. *The Last Human: A Guide to Twenty-Two Species of Extinct Humans*. New Haven, CT: Yale University Press, 2007.

Schick, Theodore, and Lewis Vaughn. *How to Think about Weird Things*. New York: McGraw-Hill, 2011.

Scott, Eugenie C. *Evolution vs. Creationism*. Berkeley: University of California Press, 2009.

Shermer, Michael. *The Believing Brain: From Ghosts and Gods to Politics and Conspiracies—How We Construct Beliefs and Reinforce Them as Truths*. New York: Times Books, 2011.

———. *Why Darwin Matters: The Case against Intelligent Design*. New York: Times Books, 2006.

———. *Why People Believe Weird Things*. New York: MJF Books, 1997.

Smith, Cameron M. *The Fact of Evolution*. Amherst, NY: Prometheus Books, 2011.

Smith, Cameron M., and Charles Sullivan. *The Top 10 Myths about Evolution*. Amherst, NY: Prometheus Books, 2006.

Smith, Jonathan C. *Pseudoscience and Extraordinary Claims of the Paranormal: A Critical Thinker's Toolkit*. West Sussex, UK: Wiley-Blackwell, 2010.

Stenger, Victor J. *The Fallacy of Fine-Tuning: Why the Universe Is Not Designed for Us*. Amherst, NY: Prometheus Books, 2011.

———. *God and the Folly of Faith*. Amherst, NY: Prometheus Books, 2012.

———. *The New Atheism: Taking a Stand for Science and Reason*. Amherst, NY: Prometheus Books, 2009.

Stringer, Chris. *Lone Survivors: How We Came to Be the Only Humans on Earth*. New York: Times Books, 2011.

Tattersall, Ian. *Extinct Humans*. New York: Basic Books, 2001.

Ward, Peter. *Future Evolution: An Illuminated History of Life to Come*. New York: W. H. Freeman, 2001.

Weinberg, Steven. *Facing Up: Science and Its Cultural Adversaries*. Cambridge, MA: Harvard University Press, 2003.

White, Nancy. *Archaeology for Dummies*. New York: For Dummies, 2008.

Young, Matt, and Taner Edis. *Why Intelligent Design Fails: A Scientific Critique of the New Creationism.* Piscataway, NJ: Rutgers University Press, 2006.

Zimmer, Carl. *Evolution: The Triumph of an Idea.* New York: Harper Perennial, 2006.

———. *The Tangled Bank: An Introduction to Evolution.* New York: Roberts, 2009.

Zuckerman, Phil. *Society without God.* New York: New York University Press, 2008.

INDEX

ABC News, 238

ACLU (American Civil Liberties Union), 285

Adam, 9, 97, 98, 123, 154, 305

Adams, John, 180

Africa/African, 30, 34, 46, 50, 59, 196, 201, 219, 308, 315

agnostics/agnosticism, 55-56, 262

Alaska, 48

Albania, 262

Aldrin, Buzz, 106

Alexander the Great, 22, 167

Alice in Wonderland, 144

Allah, 22, 23, 106, 145, 149, 169, 172, 230, 247

al-Qaeda, 51, 283

American Civil Liberties Union (ACLU), 285

American Humanist Association, 181

American Sociological Review (journal), 175

amygdala, 173

Andromeda Strain, The (film), 287

angels, 54, 57, 60, 89, 91, 100, 107, 137, 169, 211, 260, 275-280, 289, 323

animists, 64, 156, 166, 168, 169, 215, 301

Antarctica, 240

Antichrist, 43, 102

Anu (god), 263

Apollo Moon landings, 106

archaeology, 209-212

Aristotle, 62, 169

Arkansas, 47, 48

Armstrong, Neil, 106

Artificial Intelligence Lab at MIT, 128

Asia, 22, 308

astrobiologist, 144

astrology, 18, 31, 313, 317

atheists, and trust, 261-267

Athena, 212

Athens, 212

Atlantis, 162, 242

Australia, 35, 46, 174, 240, 241

Australopithecus afarensis, 53

Austria, 174

Aztecs, 241

Babylonians, 241

Bachman, Michele, 27

Bahamas, 174

Bahrain, 48

Bangladesh, 204, 308

Baptist, 41, 43, 180, 230, 293

Barna, George, 74

Barna Group, 131

BBC, 88

Belgium, 35, 296

Bellamy, Francis, 182

Bermuda Triangle, 209

Bhutan, 174

Bigfoot, 85, 92, 162, 242, 277, 278, 309 314

Blaine, David, 65

Blasingame, Loretta, 91, 92

blood of Jesus, 309

Boghossian, Peter, 144

Book of Kells, 269

Book of Mormon, 42, 211, 263

born-again experience, 131-139

Boston University's Religion Department, 76

Botswana, 48

Brady Bunch, The (television series), 110

Brazil, 82, 174

Brunei, 174

Buddha, 172, 274

Buddhism, 172-73

Buddhist monks, 173

Buddhists, 10, 64, 154, 172, 173, 208, 246, 308

Buffett, Warren, 296

Burkina Faso, 46

Burundi, 46, 174

Bush, George W., 27

Byrne, Lorna, 227

Caesar, Julius, 23, 167, 170

Cain, Herman, 27

California, 47, 173, 238, 256

Cambodian killing fields, 196

Cameron, Kirk, 222

Camping, Harold, 238

Canada, 46, 174, 276

Caribbean, 39, 41, 51, 156, 171, 172, 185, 192, 209, 276, 310

Carlin, David R., 75-76

Carter, Howard, 242

Case Western University, 127

Cathedral of Lima, 310

Catholic Church, 42, 75, 80, 109, 188, 190, 297

Catholic priests, 43, 80, 233

Catholics, 3, 44, 51, 52, 60, 75, 76, 120, 137, 172, 181, 238, 263, 310, 311

Cave, Stephen, 95

Cayman Islands, 45, 91

Central African Republic, 46

Central Intelligence Agency (CIA), 243

Chad, 46

China, 104, 204, 301

Christian nation, 177-182

Christian Scientist, 230

Christmas, 281-286

Church of Christ, 41, 230

Church of the Holy Sepulchre, 12, 40, 146

CIA (Central Intelligence Agency), 243

civil-rights movement, 47

Clark, Elizabeth, 121

CNBC, 48

CNN, 169

Cold War, 51, 182

Collins, Michael, 106

Colson, Chuck, 221

Compendium of the Catechism of the Catholic Church, 109

confirmation bias, 18, 37, 38, 63, 105, 107, 127, 165, 217

conquistadores, 311

Constitution (US), 30, 178-82, 284

Copperfield, David, 65

Cosmos (documentary), 260

Craig, William Lane, 307

Creation Studies at Liberty University, 126

C-SPAN, 126

Cuba, 48, 52

Daksha, 54

Dark Ages, 292

David and Goliath, 149

Dawkins, Richard, 30, 167

Day of Ashura, 284

Dead Sea Scrolls, 211, 212

Decline and Fall of the Catholic Church in America, The (Carlin), 75

Democratic Republic of the Congo, 46, 174

Denmark, 35, 46, 174, 251, 296

devil. *See* Satan

DeWitt, David, 126

doomsday, 101, 287, 288, 292, 323

"Doomsday Live" (radio program), 288

Dublin, 269

Duke University, 121
Dyson, Freeman, 126

Eagle Nebula, 201
Earth Abides (Stewart), 287
Eastern Orthodox Church, 42
Egypt, 23, 45, 94, 98, 168, 241, 300
Ehrman, Bart D., 108, 160-162, 290
Einstein, Albert, 259
Ekman, Paul, 173
El Salvador, 47
Episcopal churches, 41
evangelical, 131, 134, 153, 222, 238, 245, 261, 288, 289
Eve, 97, 98
evolution, 43, 53, 68, 69, 134, 137, 204, 219-225, 241, 251, 274, 298
extraterrestrials, 61, 92, 136, 263

Fail Safe (film), 287
faith, 141-145
faith healing, 153-157
feminists, 262
50 Popular Beliefs That People Think Are True (Harrison), 309, 317
50 Reasons People Give for Believing in a God (Harrison), 34
fine-tuned universe and Earth, 197-202
Finland, 35, 174
First Amendment, 178, 285
Florida, 41, 45, 167, 184, 218
forbidden fruit, 19, 98, 305
Four Horsemen of the Apocalypse, 288
Fox Network, 283
France, 35
Frank, Anne, 259
Franklin, Benjamin, 179
French Revolution, 150
Freud, 93

Gallup, 47, 127, 131, 172, 174, 220
Gandhi, 259
Ganesha (god), 30, 50, 64, 217, 284
Garden of Eden, 211, 305, 306
Gates, Bill, 296
Geek magazine, 318
Genesis, 76, 98, 122, 238, 241, 243
Germany, 46, 191, 213
Gibson, Mel, 14
Girl Scouts, 259
Global Wellbeing Index, 174
Gnostic Christianity, 42
"God is love," 260, 310
Gospels, 76, 160, 161
Graham, Billy, 109
graven image, 111
Great Britain, 105, 213, 276
Great Flood, 237-244
Greeks, 23, 215, 241, 246
Grisham, John, 74
Guinea, 46

Hades, 169, 258
Haiti, 155, 204
Halloween, 282
Harris Poll, 57, 184, 255
Harvard University, 122, 128, 315
Harvard University Divinity School, 122
heaven, 13, 14, 17, 20, 89-95, 137, 148, 154, 189, 190, 196, 211-214, 216, 217, 227, 228, 231-234, 256, 258, 259, 289, 291, 312
hell, 100, 132, 137, 150, 169, 190, 216, 217, 227, 228, 230, 255-260, 288, 312
Henry VIII, 42
Heston, Charlton, 110
Hindus/Hinduism, 10, 30, 37, 45, 64, 90, 104, 110, 156, 162, 167-169, 172, 215, 217, 246, 258, 284, 301

Hinn, Benny, 152, 157, 185

Hitchens, Christopher, 30

Hitler, Adolf, 187-191, 195, 223, 259

Holocaust, 306

"Holocaust of the Children," 306-307

Holy Communion, 310

Holy Spirit, 14, 57, 97, 179, 233, 302

Holy Trinity, 14, 76, 97, 98, 169, 233, 234, 308

homeopathy, 316

Homo erectus, 53

homosexuality/homosexuals, 28, 44, 74, 99, 264, 273, 292

Houdini, Harry, 65

Huckabee, Mike, 27

Human Development Index, 46

humanists, 93

Hundred Years' War, 193

Iceland, 174

Il Sung, Kim, 195

India, 34, 65, 147, 149, 167, 172

Indiana Jones, 242

Indian Ocean, 204, 244

infant mortality, 48

intelligent design, 67-71

Internal Revenue Service (IRS), 177

IQ, 128

Iraq War, 273

IRS (Internal Revenue Service), 177

Islam, 35, 45, 50, 84, 105, 106, 149, 168, 230, 246, 247, 255, 258, 263, 276, 280, 292, 301, 309, 321, 324

Israel, 99, 104-105, 118, 140, 174

Italy, 213

Iyamu, Silva Wealth, 184

Jamaica, 41, 82, 172

Japan, 47, 244

Japanese, 84

Jefferson, Thomas, 179, 180

Jehovah's Witnesses, 284

Jerusalem, 12, 85, 113, 161, 171, 310

"Jesus boat," 211

Jewish Americans, 172

Jewish people (Jews), 42, 60, 64, 96, 105-108, 112, 113, 117, 119, 120, 154, 163, 168, 170, 189, 191, 212, 251, 255, 262, 265, 301, 306

jinn (genies), 51, 136, 280

Jones, Jim, 196, 263

Jong-il, Kim, 196

Jordan, 45, 102, 300, 310

Josephus, 161

journalism, 87-88

Judgment Day, 42, 100, 288, 289, 291, 293

Jupiter (god), 212

Jupiter (planet), 200, 201

kamikaze pilots, 84

Kansas, 322

Kenya, 58, 219

Khepri (god), 94

King, Karen L., 122

Kingdom of God, 100, 107, 108, 288, 131

King James Version (Bible), 74, 75

King Tut, 23, 242

Kingu (god), 56

KKK (Ku Klux Klan), 259, 322

Knights Templar, 193

Kolob (alleged planet), 28

Kony, Joseph, 196, 301, 302

"Kony 2012," 301

Koran, 30, 50, 106, 148, 149, 151, 166, 217, 230, 246, 247, 250, 251, 263, 270, 280

Koresh, David, 23, 81, 84, 196, 263

Ku Klux Klan (KKK), 259, 322

Laden, Osama bin, 302

Last Man on Earth, The (film), 287

Left Behind novels, 74

Leonidas, 41

Liberia, 46

Liechtenstein, 46

Life Evaluation Index, 172

life expectancy, 46, 155

Lim, Chaeyoon, 175

literacy, 35, 46, 213, 269

Loch Ness Monster, 277, 314

Lord Xenu, 210

Louisiana, 47, 48, 266

Loving v. Virginia (Supreme Court case), 264

Luckhoo, Lionel, 291

Luther, Martin, 42

Lutherans, 310

Luxembourg, 296

Lynchburg, Virginia, 126

Madison, James, 179

Madrassa, 147-150, 250, 251

Magdalene, Mary, 121

Mahdi, 292

Maine, 48, 266

malaria, 34, 58, 205, 304

marijuana, 172

"mark of the beast," 288

Mars (planet), 198

Mary (mother of Jesus), 64

Massachusetts, 48

Massachusetts Institute of Technology (MIT), 128

Massai, 58-60

Maya, 241

McCarthy, Cormac, 287

Mein Kampf (Hitler), 188

Mendel, Gregor, 126

Methodist, 80, 230

Metropolitan Museum of Art, 310

Mexico, 82

Middle Earth, 215

Middle East, 105, 210-212

militant atheists, 30

Miranda, Jose Luis de Jesus, 167, 218

Mississippi, 47, 48

MIT (Massachusetts Institute of Technology), 128

Mohammed, 89, 90, 106, 246, 247, 284

Moon-landing hoax, 70

Mormon/Mormonism, 218, 230, 322

Mormons, 28, 44, 51, 144, 211

Moses, 99, 100, 109, 112, 117-119, 149

Mothers' Index, 35

Mount Ararat, 242

Mount Athos, 128

Mount Parnassus, 136

Mount Sinai, 109, 117, 149

Mozambique, 46

Mumbai, 45, 155, 245

Muslims, 10, 30, 37, 45, 51, 64, 84, 90, 104-106, 113, 144, 147, 301, 149, 156, 162, 168, 170, 172, 215, 246, 251, 258, 262, 264, 265, 280, 284, 292, 301

National Academy of Sciences, 125

National Geographic, 195

National Rifle Association (NRA), 52

Native Americans, 192

Nazis, 322

near-death experience, 89, 90, 94, 95

Nepal, 34, 130, 172

Netherlands, 35, 46, 174, 296

New Age, 64, 276

New Delhi, 45, 147

New Hampshire, 47, 48, 266

New Jersey State Supreme Court, 278

New Testament, 97, 99, 107, 119, 121, 160, 162, 183, 185, 290

Newton, Isaac, 126
New York Times (newspaper), 88, 257, 270
New Zealand, 35, 46, 174
Ngai (god), 50
Nickell, Joe, 26
Niger, 46
Nigeria, 184
90 Minutes in Heaven (Piper), 90
Niose, David, 181
Nixon, Richard, 221
Nobel Prize in Physics, 124
North America, 156
North Korea, 195
Norway, 35, 46, 296
Nostradamus, 103
NRA (National Rifle Association), 52

Obama, Barack, 28
Odin (god), 56
Oklahoma, 155
Old Testament, 74, 97, 99, 104, 109, 110, 119, 120, 155, 307, 308
Omega Man, The (film), 287
Oregon, 47
O'Reilly, Bill, 283-285
Oriental Orthodox, 230
out-of-body experiences, 89, 91, 94
Oz, 215

Pacific Northwest, 314
Paine, Thomas, 177
Pakistan, 246, 247, 315
Paley, William, 197
Palin, Sarah, 27
Passion of the Christ, The (film), 15
Pasteur, Louis, 126
Paul, Gregory, 306, 307
Paul (apostle), 41, 83, 85, 86, 173
Pauline Christianity, 42

Pennsylvania State University, 80
Pentecostal, 43, 230
Pericles, 41, 170
Perry, Rick, 27
Persian Empire, 22
Peru, 310
Petra, 102, 310
Pew Research Center, 266
Phelps family, 322
Philosophy & Theology (journal), 306
Phoenix, 318
Piper, Don, 90
Pitzer College, 47
Pizarro, Francisco, 311
Planck, Max, 126
Planet of the Apes (film), 287
Pledge of Allegiance, 181, 182
Pontius Pilate, 162
Pope John Paul II, 43
Pope Urban II, 192, 196
Portland State University, 144
Portugal, 213
Pot, Pol, 187, 188, 191, 194-196
Prometheus Books, 34
Protestant, 41-44, 51, 60, 73, 117, 120, 131, 134, 137, 172, 181, 231, 233, 238, 263, 310
Protestant Reformation, 42
Prothero, Stephen, 76
puja, 172
Pythia, 136

Qatar, 48

Radford, Ben, 26
Raël, 263
Raëlism/Raëlians, 263
Ramesses II, 167
Randi, James, 26, 65

rapture, 74, 102, 288, 290, 291, 321

Rastafarians, 172, 292

Religious Literacy: What Every American Needs to Know—and Doesn't (Prothero), 76

Road, The (McCarthy), 287

Roman Empire, 86

Romans, 161, 241, 246

Rome, 42, 212

Romney, Mitt, 28

Royal Society, 125

Russell, Bertrand, 141

Sabbath, 43, 99, 112, 113, 119

Sagan, Carl, 165, 319

St. Paul's Methodist Church, 80

San Diego, 291

Sandusky, Jerry, 80

Santa Claus, 281, 282, 285

Santorum, Rick, 27

Satan, 10, 16, 51, 169, 261, 75, 284

Saudi Arabia, 177, 247

Save the Children, 35

Scientologists, 168

Scientology, 28, 210, 216

Sea of Galilee, 211

Search for Extraterrestrial Intelligence (SETI), 198, 288

Sermon on the Mount, 28

SETI (Search for Extraterrestrial Intelligence), 198, 288

Seventh-Day Adventist, 43, 113, 230

Shermer, Michael, 26, 93

Shostak, Seth, 198-199

Shroud of Turin, 160, 210

Siberia, 258

Siddhartha Gautama, 172

Sierra Leone, 46

Sikhism, 255

Sikhs, 64, 154, 215, 301

Skeptic (magazine), 93

Skeptic's Annotated Bible (website), 270

Smith, Joseph, 42, 144, 90, 218, 263

Social Psychological and Personality Science (journal), 296

Socrates, 41

South America, 156, 240

South Carolina, 245, 246

Southern Baptists, 293-294

Soviet Union, 51

Soylent Green (film), 287

Spain, 213

Spock, 322

Sri Lanka, 48

Stalin, Joseph, 82, 187, 188, 191-196, 263

State College, Pennsylvania, 80

Stewart, George R., 287

Sudan, 155

Sweden, 35, 46, 47, 174, 251, 296

Syria, 45, 172, 301

Tacitus, 162

Taj Mahal, 34, 147

Tampa, Florida, 184

Thailand, 173, 301

Themistocles, 41

"Time Enough at Last" (*Twilight Zone* episode), 287

Today Show, The (television show), 56

Treaty of Tripoli, 179

Trinity College Library, 269

Truman, Harry, 269

tsunami, 204, 244, 291

Turkey, 242

Tut (Tutankhamen), 23, 242

Twain, Mark, 143, 259

23 Minutes in Hell (Wiese), 256

Twilight Zone (television show), 287

UFOs, 61, 85, 127, 138, 162, 277, 317

Uganda, 47, 301, 302

UNICEF (United Nations Children's Fund), 303

United Nations Children's Fund (UNICEF), 303

United Nations Development Program, 46

United States, 46-48, 57, 74, 75, 82, 105, 110, 122, 136, 177-182, 213, 264, 266, 276, 297

University of California–San Francisco Medical Center, 173

University of Leicester, 173

University of Minnesota, 264

University of North Carolina–Chapel Hill, 108

University of Wisconsin, 173

Utah, 48

Van Praagh, James, 70

Vatican, 171

Vermont, 47, 48, 266

Vishnu (god), 50

Waal, Frans de, 299

Waco, Texas, 23

Walls of Jericho, 212

Washington, George, 160, 179

waterboarding, 243

Watergate, 221

Weinberg, Steven, 124

White, Adrian, 173

Wiese, Bill, 256-257

Willer, Robb, 296

Willy Wonka, 203

women, and Christianity, 121-124

World Map of Happiness, 173

World War II, 84, 114, 150, 193, 223, 306

Xerxes, 59

Yomiuri Shimbun (newspaper), 88

YouTube, 280

Zambia, 47

Zedong, Mao, 187, 188, 191, 192, 194, 195, 263

Zeus (god), 17, 90, 212, 215

Zimbabwe, 174, 262

Zuckerman, Phil, 47